P9-DWX-379

LEARNING TO TEACH
PHYSICAL
EDUCATION
IN THE
SECONDARY SCHOOL

There are many teaching skills and issues covered in initial teacher education which student PE teachers must apply to their own subject. However, the complexity of teaching PE can make this difficult to do. This book focuses, therefore, on the requirements of student PE teachers in relation to teaching skills and issues covered in initial teacher education courses.

Throughout the book the theory underpinning those skills and issues is interlinked with tasks which can be undertaken alone, with another student teacher or with a tutor. The book is designed to help student PE teachers to develop teaching skills, knowledge and understanding of the wider context of PE, along with the ability to reflect critically and to develop professional judgement.

Susan Capel is Director of the Academic Standards Unit and a Principal Lecturer in the Department of Sport Science at Canterbury Christ Church College.

Learning to Teach Subjects in the Secondary School Series

Series Editors
Tony Turner, Institute of Education, University of London; Sue Capel, Canterbury Christ Church College; and Marilyn Leask, De Montfort University, Bedford.

Designed for all students learning to teach in secondary schools, and particularly those on school based initial teacher training courses, the books in this series complement *Learning to Teach in the Secondary School* and its companion, *Starting to Teach in the Secondary School*. Each book in the series applies underpinning theory and addresses practical issues to support students in school and in the training institution in learning how to teach a particular subject.

Learning to Teach English in the Secondary School
Jon Davison and Jane Dowson

Learning to Teach Modern Foreign Languages in the Secondary School
Norbert Pachler and Kit Field

Learning to Teach History in the Secondary School
Terry Haydn, Martin Hunt and James Arthur

Learning to Teach Physical Education in the Secondary School
Susan Capel

LEARNING TO TEACH
PHYSICAL EDUCATION
IN THE
SECONDARY SCHOOL

A companion to school experience

Susan Capel

London and New York

First published in 1997
by Routledge
11 New Fetter Lane, London EC4P 4EE

Simultaneously published in the USA and Canada
by Routledge
29 West 35th Street, New York, NY 10001

Typset in Ehrhardt by
J&L Composition Ltd, Filey, North Yorkshire

Printed and bound in Great Britain by
T.J. International Ltd, Padstow, Cornwall

British Library Cataloguing in Publication Data

A catalogue record for this book is available from the British Library

Library of Congress Cataloguing in Publication Data

A catalogue record for this book has been requested

ISBN 0–415–15301–8

Contents

Introduction to the series

This book, *Learning to Teach Physical Education in the Secondary School*, is one of a series of books entitled *Learning to Teach Subjects in the Secondary School: A Companion to School Experience*, covering most subjects in the secondary school curriculum. The books in this series support and complement *Learning to Teach in the Secondary School: A Companion to School Experience* (Capel, Leask and Turner, 1995), which addresses issues relevant to secondary teachers. These books are designed for student teachers learning to teach on different types of initial teacher education courses and in different places. However, it is hoped that they will be equally useful to tutors and mentors in their work with student teachers. In 1997 a complementary book was published entitled *Starting to Teach in the Secondary School: A Companion for the Newly Qualified Teacher* (Capel, Leask and Turner, 1997). That second book was designed to support newly qualified teachers in their first post and covered aspects of teaching which are likely to be of concern in the first year of teaching.

The information in the subject books does not repeat that in *Learning to Teach*, rather, the content of that book is adapted and extended to address the needs of student teachers learning to teach a specific subject. In each of the subject books, therefore, reference is made to *Learning to Teach*, where appropriate. It is recommended that you have both books so that you can cross-reference when needed.

The positive feedback on *Learning to Teach*, particularly the way it has supported the learning of student teachers in their development into effective, reflective teachers, has encouraged us to retain the main features of that book in the subject series. Thus, the subject books are designed so that elements of appropriate theory introduce each behaviour or issue. Recent research into teaching and learning is incorporated into this. This material is interwoven with tasks designed to help you identify key features of the behaviour or issue and apply these to your own practice.

Although the basic content of each subject book is similar, each book is designed to address the unique nature of the subject. In this book, for example, the unique contribution of PE to promoting physical development and physical competence and the specific consideration which needs to be given to safety, organisation and management in PE are highlighted.

We, as editors, have found this project to be exciting. We hope that, whatever the type of initial teacher education course you are following and wherever you may be following that course, you find that this book is useful and supports your development into an effective, reflective PE teacher.

Susan Capel, Marilyn Leask and Tony Turner
January 1997

Illustrations

FIGURES

TABLES

TASKS

Contributors

Jenny Bott is a Senior Lecturer and Head of Gymnastics at De Montfort University Bedford.

Peter Breckon is a Senior Lecturer in the Department of Sports Sciences at Brunel University (formerly West London Institute).

Susan Capel is Director of the Academic Standards Unit and a Principal Lecturer in Sport Science at Canterbury Christ Church College.

Tim Hewett is a Senior Lecturer in Outdoor Education at De Montfort University Bedford.

Liz Kelly is a Senior Lecturer at De Montfort University Bedford and tutor of coaches for All England Netball Association courses.

Jean Leah lectures at De Montfort University Bedford, where her major responsibility is as teaching practice co-ordinator for the Secondary B.Ed.PE degree.

Andrea Lockwood is the PE section leader in the School of PE, Sport and Leisure at De Montfort University Bedford.

Elizabeth Murdoch is Professor of PE and Head of Chelsea School of PE, Sport and Exercise Science, Dance and Leisure at the University of Brighton.

Helen Queen is a Senior Lecturer and Head of Games and Inset Co-ordinator at De Montfort University Bedford.

Patricia Shenton is Head of I.M. Marsh Centre for PE, Sport and Dance at Liverpool John Moores University.

Roger Strangwick is a Principal Lecturer at De Montfort University Bedford where he is Course Leader for the Secondary B.Ed.PE degree.

Philip Vickerman is a Senior Lecturer within the Centre for PE, Sport and Dance at Liverpool John Moores University.

Gill Watson was until recently a Senior Lecturer in Secondary Education at De Montfort University Bedford.

Margaret Whitehead is Associate Head of the School of PE, Sport and Leisure at De Montfort University Bedford.

Acknowledgements

Acknowledgement is gratefully expressed for material from the following sources. To Alan Ahlberg for his poem which appears in Chapter 6 (reproduced by permission of Penguin Books Ltd), and to Stangrounds Community College, Peterborough for use of the accident report form presented in Chapter 8. Also to the British Association of Advisers and Lecturers in Physical Education (BAALPE) for quotations and material from *Safe Practice in Physical Education* (available from Dudley LEA Publications, Saltwells EDC, Bowling Green Road, Netherton, Dudley, West Midlands, Telephone: (01394) 813807; Fax (01384) 813801, price £20), and to the European Education Consultants for material from *Whole School Management of Health and Safety: Risk Assessment Database* (available from European Education Consultants, Gatehouse Lodge, Station Road, Chapeltown, Bolton BL7 0HA, Telephone/Fax: (01204) 853554, e-mail: eeceurope.msn.com) both of which appear in Chapter 8. Finally, to the Open University for permission to use the archery diagram which appears in Chapter 11.

I would like to acknowledge the support of the Governing Body of Canterbury Christ Church College in granting study leave to enable me to work on this book.

I would also like to express appreciation to all those who have contributed to this book and to those who have influenced the thinking of the contributors, assisted in refining and editing material, helped in numerous ways to get a finished manuscript, and supported and encouraged me throughout. Thank you to you all.

Introduction

LEARNING TO TEACH

All top sports people and dancers spend hours learning and practising basic skills in order to be able to perform these effectively. Once learned, skills can be refined, adapted and combined in various ways appropriate for a performer's personality and a specific situation, in order to create a unique performance. Developing excellence in performance is informed by scientific understanding, including biomechanical, kinesiological, physiological, psychological and sociological knowledge. There is therefore art and science underpinning excellence in performance.

Likewise, there is an art and a science to teaching. There are basic teaching skills in which teachers require competence. Effective teaching also requires the development of professional judgement in order to be able to adapt the teaching skills to meet the demands of the specific situation, to take account of, for example, the needs and abilities of pupils, the space and the environment in which the lesson is being delivered. Teachers also require broader knowledge and understanding, for example, of the wider world of education. However, there is no one right way to teach. As we know, teachers have different personalities and characteristics. They therefore refine and adapt basic teaching skills and combine them in different ways to create their own unique teaching style. The process of development as a teacher is exciting and the ability to blend art and science should lead to a rewarding experience as a teacher.

In PE, skills are sometimes described on a continuum from open skills (those performed under variable conditions) to closed skills (those performed under consistent conditions). For open skills (for example, a dribble in hockey or basketball), it is important to have competence in the basic skill, but it is just as important to be able to use the skill appropriately in a game situation. For closed skills (for example, performing a forward roll or throwing a discus), it is most important to refine the technique and the ability to perform the skill under the pressure of competition. Some skills (for example, a putt in golf), fall along the continuum.

Different methods of practice are needed in order to learn and perform effectively skills at different points on the continuum. For an open skill practice is needed in the basic techniques of the skill, but practice is also needed in how to adapt the skill to respond to different situations which arise. On the other hand, for a closed skill it is most appropriate to practise to perfect the techniques of the skill.

Using the analogy of open and closed skills, teaching skills can be considered as open skills. You need to practise and become competent in basic teaching skills, but you also need to be able to use the right skill in the right way at the right time. On your initial teacher education (ITE) course you are likely to have a variety of opportunities and experiences to develop competence in basic teaching skills, starting in very controlled practice situations and moving onto teaching full classes. You are unlikely to become a fully effective teacher during your ITE course. Refinement and the ability to adapt teaching skills as appropriate to the situation are continued into your work as a newly qualified teacher and beyond, as part of your continuing professional development as you continue to develop your ability to reflect and your professional judgement.

There is a lot to learn to develop into an effective teacher. There are bound to be ups and downs. We cannot prepare you for a specific teaching situation, but we can help you to understand the complexities of teaching. We aim to help you to develop:

- competence in basic teaching skills (the craft of teaching), to enable you to cope in most teaching situations;
- knowledge and understanding of the wider context of PE;
- your ability to reflect critically on what you are doing and on your values, attitudes and beliefs; and
- your professional judgement.

In so doing, you should be able to adapt and refine your teaching skills to meet the needs of specific situations, respond to the changing environment of education and inform your continued professional development as a teacher.

ABOUT THIS BOOK

The book can be divided into three main sections. Section 1 (Chapters 1 and 2) provides an introduction and background information about teaching and about PE. Section 2 (Chapters 3 to 11) introduces some of the teaching skills in which you need to develop competence during your ITE course. Section 3 (Chapters 12 to 18) looks at how you can extend your expertise and at the wider context in which you are learning to teach PE.

In this book we look at general principles which can be applied to activities taught in PE. We do not consider subject content in detail although, throughout the book, there are references to activities taught in PE. You need to refer to other sources for subject content. There are many books which focus on specific activities taught in PE and Chapter 18 looks at ways in which you can gain subject knowledge and understanding. In addition, you need to draw on material you covered in your first degree course, including the disciplines of biomechanics, kinesiology, physiology, psychology and sociology. Your understanding of these disciplines should underpin your work as a PE teacher – for example, the use of biomechanical principles in identifying teaching points for a skill, of aspects of physiology in teaching health related fitness, or understanding the effects of competition or reasons for attrition from sport in considering an extra-curricular programme.

In this book and in *Learning to Teach in the Secondary School* (Capel, Leask and Turner, 1995), each chapter is organised as follows:

- **introduction** to the content of the chapter;
- **objectives** presented as what you should know, understand or be able to do having read the chapter and carried out the tasks in the chapter;
- the **content** interwoven with **tasks** to aid your knowledge, understanding and ability to do;
- **summary** of the main points of the chapter;
- **further reading** selected to enable you to find out more about the content of each chapter.

We try to emphasise links between theory and practice by including examples from relevant practical situations throughout each chapter and interweaving theory with tasks designed to help you identify key features of the behaviour or issue. A number of different inquiry methods are used to generate information – for example, reflecting on the reading, an observation, an activity you are asked to carry out, asking questions, gathering information, observing lessons, discussing issues with your tutor or another student teacher. Some of the tasks involve you in activities that impinge on other people – for example, observing a PE teacher teach or asking for information. If a task requires you to do this, **you must first of all seek the permission of the person concerned**.

Remember that you are a guest in school(s), you cannot walk into a teacher's lesson to observe. In addition, some information may be personal or sensitive, and you need to consider issues of confidentiality and professional behaviour in your inquiries and reporting.

The main text is supported by:

- a **glossary** of terms to help you interpret words and abbreviations used in this book. Many of these words are specific to PE. The glossary in *Learning to Teach in the Secondary School* should provide you with a wider range of educational definitions;
- **addresses** of PE and sport organisations;
- two **appendices**. **Appendix 1** provides examples of questions and observation schedules to help you gather information to inform your work in school. You can use these examples of observation schedules to help you devise your own for a specific purpose. **Appendix 2** provides two sample apparatus plans for gymnastics.

ABOUT YOU

We recognise that you, as a student PE teacher, have a wide range of needs in your development as a teacher. We therefore do not feel that there is one best way for you to use this book. The book is designed so that you can dip in and out rather than read it from cover to cover; however, we encourage you to use the book in ways appropriate to you.

We also recognise that you are studying in different places and on different types of ITE course. We have tried to address as many of your potential needs as possible, irrespective of where you are studying and what type of ITE course you are on. Throughout the book we ask you to refer to the competences you are working towards achieving during your ITE course, and to the PE curriculum being used in the school experience schools in which you work. However, where we have needed to link the theory to specific situations in schools or specific requirements of teachers in implementing the curriculum, we have linked it to the National Curriculum in England and Wales. We recognise that some of you are not on ITE courses which are preparing you to teach in state schools in England and Wales, therefore we suggest that you do two things whenever information and tasks specific to the National Curriculum in England and Wales are used in the book:

(i) substitute for the information and task given, the curriculum and requirements which apply to your situation;
(ii) reflect on the differences between the curriculum and requirements

which apply to your situation and those of the National Curriculum in England and Wales.

In so doing, not only are the information and tasks relevant to your own situation but, also, you can attain a greater understanding by comparing your situation with another situation: the National Curriculum in England and Wales.

Although it is expected that most student PE teachers using this book will be on ITE courses in which there is a partnership between a higher education institution (HEI) and schools, we recognise that some of you may be on courses which are not in partnership with an HEI, for example, school-centred initial teacher training (SCITT) courses. The book should be equally useful to you. Where we refer to work in your HEI, you should refer to the relevant person or centre in your school.

YOUR PROFESSIONAL PORTFOLIO

We strongly recommend that you keep a professional portfolio. As you read through the book and complete the tasks, we ask you to record information in your professional portfolio. You can use this information for a number of purposes – for example, to refer back to when completing other tasks in this book, to help you with assignments on your course, to help you reflect on your development and to provide evidence of your development, your strengths and areas for further development to use in your Career Entry Profile (CEP) (see Chapter 18). You should refer to Chapter 18 and the introduction to *Learning to Teach in the Secondary School* for guidance about keeping and using your professional portfolio.

TERMINOLOGY USED IN THE BOOK

We have tried to mix, and balance, the use of **gender terms** in order to avoid clumsy he/she terminology.

We use the word **PE** to cover activities taught in a PE curriculum. We have based this on the six Areas of Activity in the National Curriculum for PE in England and Wales: Athletic Activities; Dance; Games; Gymnastic Activities; Outdoor and Adventurous Activities; and Swimming. It therefore includes sport and dance.

We call school children **pupils** to avoid confusion with students, by which we mean people in further and higher education.

The important staff in your life are those in your school and HEI with a responsibility for supporting your development as a teacher; we have called all these people **tutors**. Your ITE course will have its own way of referring to staff.

Your ITE course may use terminology different to that used in this book; for example, where the word **evaluation** is used in this book, on some courses, the word appraisal is used. You should check terminology used on your ITE course.

1 Starting out as a PE teacher

INTRODUCTION

As a student PE teacher you are embarking on the long, but exciting, process of becoming an effective PE teacher; of translating your knowledge and love of PE into the ability to encourage pupils' learning. To develop into an effective teacher you need to understand yourself, your values, attitudes and beliefs and be able to reflect on how these influence what you are doing. You need also to understand your role as a teacher and as a PE teacher, as well as what you are trying to achieve in your lessons.

There are numerous teaching skills you need to develop, along with the ability to use the right teaching skill in the right way at the right time. An understanding of how teaching skills interact with each other in a lesson is also helpful. Your development into an effective teacher is challenging and not always smooth. At times you may be anxious or concerned about your development or your teaching performance, may lack confidence to try something out or may feel frustrated or despondent at not being able to cope with a situation or not knowing how to respond. Early in your development you may not have the teaching skills or experience to cope effectively with a specific situation. Part of the challenge of learning to teach is becoming able to adapt what you do to suit the unique needs of any situation. When you can adapt your teaching skills to the situation you are rewarded for your hard work as you are well on the way to a rewarding and exciting career as a teacher.

OBJECTIVES

By the end of this chapter you should:

- be able to recognise the variety of reasons as to why people choose to become PE teachers and the implications of this;
- have an overview of your role as a teacher and as a PE teacher;

- have an overview of the teaching activities and skills required to develop into an effective teacher.

WHY DID YOU BECOME A PE TEACHER?

TASK 1.1 WHY DO PEOPLE WANT TO BECOME PE TEACHERS?

List your reasons for wanting to become a PE teacher. Compare your reasons with those given by other student teachers and by experienced PE teachers you know. Are there any reasons common to all those to whom you spoke? Why do you think this is so?

You have been at school for 11 years or more and in all probability wanted to become a PE teacher because you enjoyed PE, were able and successful, wanted to pass on your knowledge, understanding and love of PE and wanted to work with young people. If you found also that these were the major reasons given by other people for becoming a PE teacher, your findings support results of research (for example, Evans and Williams (1989) and Mawer (1995)). Similar reasons for becoming a PE teacher suggest some homogeneity in values, attitudes and beliefs about PE and about PE teaching.

Your positive experiences of PE give you positive perceptions of PE teachers, their role, what they do and how they teach the subject. As you are likely to spend considerable time, professionally and socially, with other PE professionals, it is easy to forget that there are many pupils in schools and, indeed, people in society at large, who do not share your values, attitudes and beliefs about PE and hence about participation in physical activity and sport. You can, no doubt, think of friends who had less positive experiences of PE at school, who have more negative perceptions about PE lessons and PE teachers. Unfortunately, these negative perceptions seem to be all too common. An effective PE teacher is one who can help pupils who are not as successful in PE to value their experiences and to enjoy participation in PE and, hence, to be physically educated (see Chapters 2 and 17). How do you develop into such a teacher and enjoy the rewards that this brings?

HOW ARE YOU GOING TO DEVELOP INTO AN EFFECTIVE PE TEACHER?

Many changes occur as you develop your teaching skills and teaching style. Guillaume and Rudney (1993) found that in developing as teachers, student teachers not only think about different things but also think about the same things differently. Changes have been identified by a number of authors as stages or phases of development (for example, Capel, Leask and Turner (1995), Maynard and Furlong (1993) and Perrott (1982) who identified stages in the development of student teachers, and Siedentop (1991) who identified these specifically for student PE teachers).

If there are different stages in your development as teachers, it follows that you may need different opportunities and experiences at different stages. Opportunities and experiences include observing experienced teachers teach; role play; small group micro-teaching situations with peers or groups of pupils; team teaching with your tutor, either teaching a small group or the whole group for part of the lesson; teaching a full class. These opportunities and experiences allow you to practise and become competent in basic teaching skills and to spend time using your developing teaching skills in a variety of situations in order to refine them so that you can adapt them as appropriate to the situation and therefore use the right teaching skill in the right way at the right time.

Metzler (1990) indicated that tutoring should be a teaching process in itself. Your tutor should help you to make the most of the opportunities and experiences on your ITE course in order to study, observe and practise teaching skills in situations appropriate to your stage of development. You and your tutor may undertake different roles as you undertake different learning experiences in school, therefore you need to determine how best to work with your tutor at different stages in your development.

Getting started

In order to make the most of the opportunities and experiences in school you need to understand the context in which you are working. Gathering background information to inform your work in school is an essential part of this. On your preliminary visits prior to each school experience you collect information about the school and the PE department. This information comes from many sources. You observe the PE environment, including the facilities, displays and equipment. You ask questions. You talk to tutors about policies and procedures of the school and the PE department and observe them in practice. You read school and department documents such as schemes or units of work, policy statements, prospectuses, governors minutes. A document such as the school prospectus can provide valuable information about the school and its pupils. PE policy statements covering such issues as assessment, equal opportunities and extra-curricular activities are important in providing the context for your work in the department. Other documents give you essential guidance on how to conduct yourself (for example, the school dress code) and how to relate to pupils within the department. You will, no doubt, be given guidance about what information to collect and mechanisms to help you. To supplement guidance from your higher education institution (HEI), if needed, Appendix 1 includes examples of questions designed to help you gather information about the school, the PE department, the PE facilities and resources, by focusing your observations, the questions you ask and identifying some key documents to look at.

Appendix 1 also includes examples of observation schedules to help you to observe different teaching skills in action. You can use these to observe the teaching skills identified or to help you devise your own for a specific purpose. Chapter 13 addresses observation and other information gathering techniques to help you make the most of your opportunities and experiences in schools.

We now look at the role of teachers, specifically focusing on part of that role, teaching lessons, and the teaching skills required to undertake the teaching role effectively.

AN OVERVIEW OF TEACHING

First and foremost you are a teacher of pupils; a member of a profession with a responsibility to help pupils to learn by developing knowledge, practical skill and understanding. Second, you are a teacher of PE, with a specific responsibility for teaching the knowledge, practical skill and understanding specific to PE.

You therefore undertake a wider role as a teacher (see Chapter 15 and unit 8.3 in Capel, Leask and Turner, 1995) as well as a subject-specific role. As a PE teacher you provide pupils with a variety of experiences to promote their physical learning and their enjoyment of PE in order to physically educate them (see Chapters 2 and 17).

TASK 1.2 WHAT IS THE ROLE OF PE TEACHERS?

Record in your professional portfolio what you believe to be the role of PE teachers. You may want to use two lists for this task: one list which identifies how the role of all teachers applies specifically to PE teachers and one which identifies the role undertaken specifically by PE teachers. Compare your list with that of another student teacher, then discuss it with your tutor so that you understand what you are working towards, and therefore the knowledge, teaching skills and understanding required to enable you to get there. Store this information in your professional portfolio to refer back to at different times on your ITE course.

Here, we concentrate on helping you to develop your skills for teaching PE.

You cannot address at the same time all the teaching skills required to develop into an effective teacher. On your ITE course, and in books such as this, teaching skills are addressed separately. If your tutors on your ITE course, or we in this book, tried to address teaching skills in combination, we would be likely to give you too many things to think about and concentrate on at any one time, overwhelming you with information or even confusing you, rather than helping you to develop as a teacher. However, an approach in which you look at teaching skills separately only provides you with a partial picture of teaching which gradually builds up over time. You only recognise the complete picture when you suddenly realise that you see it. It is helpful to have an overview of teaching so that you know what you are aiming at and how the teaching skills in which you are developing competence fit together.

This overview should help you to think about what you are doing, its effectiveness in terms of pupils' learning and on which teaching skills you need to concentrate in order to develop further. This can be compared with planning lessons and units of work. You know what you want to achieve by the end of a lesson and series of lessons (your objectives) and therefore can plan how to achieve these objectives (see Chapter 3).

What is required for effective teaching of PE?

Teaching is a complex, multi-faceted activity. First and foremost it is an interaction between **what** is being taught (the content) and **how** it is being taught (the process).

What is taught in PE is guided by the aims of the curriculum used in the school experience schools in which you work. The content of PE is varied. See, for example, the introduction (p. 5) for the six Areas of Activity in the National Curriculum for PE in England and Wales. Within each area of activity there are many different activities, for example, different athletic events, different dance forms, different games. You need to be able to teach activities within each area of activity, fully appreciating the safety implications of each activity (see Chapter 8).

TASK 1.3 ACTIVITIES IN THE PE CURRICULUM

Familiarise yourself with the content included in the PE curriculum used in the school experience schools in which you are working (the National Curriculum for PE in England and Wales). Find out what activities are taught in your school experience school. Compare this with the activities identified by another student teacher working in another school. What are the similarities and differences and why? Are other activities frequently taught in schools which should be included on your list?

Obviously, every teacher needs good knowledge and understanding of the subject content. You are likely to have considerable expertise in one or more activities. You need to identify which activities are your strengths and in which you need to gain further knowledge and understanding in order to teach effectively. During your ITE course there is limited time available to learn about each activity, or even to address all activities in which you can identify weaknesses in knowledge or understanding. This book is not designed to cover the content of a PE curriculum. You therefore need to consider ways in which you can gain the required knowledge and understanding of activities in which you are weak. There are many ways in which you can do this, some of which are identified in Chapter 18. We advise you to start on this aspect of your teaching as soon as you can.

TASK 1.4 ADDRESSING YOUR SUBJECT CONTENT WEAKNESSES

Using the lists of activities taught in your school experience school (compiled for Task 1.3), identify whether each is a strength or a weakness in terms of your knowledge and understanding. Make sure you observe some lesson in activities in which you identify weakness.

Task 18.1 helps you to identify other ways of addressing your weaknesses. Do not try to address weaknesses in a number of activities at once, but consider how you can spread this over your ITE course and even into your first year of teaching.

How do you teach PE?

How the content of the PE curriculum is taught is left to the professional judgement of the individual teacher, department and school (see also unit 1.1 in Capel, Leask and Turner, 1995). How you teach relates to the aims of the school and the PE curriculum (see Chapter 2), as well as your own objectives for a unit of work and any particular lesson (see Chapter 3). In Chapter 9 aims and objectives are considered in relation to teaching strategies.

What you see happening in a lesson is only the tip of the iceberg (see Figure 1.1.1 in Capel, Leask and Turner, 1995). Prior to the lesson longer-term objectives for the unit of work have been established along with short-term objectives for the lesson, followed by general planning of the unit of work and detailed planning and preparation of the lesson. During the lesson the teacher needs to be flexible and to adapt the plan, if necessary. After the lesson the effectiveness or otherwise of parts of the lesson and the whole lesson should be evaluated to inform planning and preparation of the next lesson. Planning and evaluation are addressed in Chapter 3.

The tip of the iceberg, i.e. what happens in the lesson, is also important. This stems from unit of work and lesson objectives and detailed planning, but also forms the basis for evaluation.

TASK 1.5 WHAT HAPPENS IN A PE LESSON?

Observe a lesson taught by an experienced PE teacher and note the types of activity in which the teacher is involved, their sequence and the time spent on each one. You should aim to get an overview of what happens rather than great detail. You may want to organise your observation into what happens:

- before the teaching starts (for example, takes the register whilst pupils are changing, collects and reads excuse notes and talks to any pupils not doing the lesson, collects valuables, hurries along anyone slow to change, locks the changing room after the last pupil has left, etc.);

- during the teaching part of the lesson;
- after the teaching has finished.

Remember that the lesson starts as soon as pupils arrive at the changing rooms and finishes when they move to their next lesson or to a break in the day.

Rink (1985) and Siedentop (1991) (see Further Reading section at the end of the chapter) both provide an overview of teaching PE in which they categorise what the teacher does in the lesson into categories similar to those below, i.e.:

- **instructional activities** (activities associated with imparting subject content to pupils);
- **organising and managing activities** (activities associated with organising the learning environment and managing the lesson to maintain appropriate behaviour in order for subject content to be imparted effectively); and
- **other activities** (activities to develop and maintain an effective learning environment).

You can allocate what you identified the teacher does (from Task 1.5) into these three categories. Some teaching skills are important in all categories of lesson activities (for example, communication).

Along with planning and evaluating, the skills required in these three categories of activity are the **teaching skills** in which you need to develop competence.

A starting point for identifying teaching skills in which you need to develop your ability by the end of your ITE course could be the competences expected of newly qualified teachers (NQTs). By the end of your ITE course you will be assessed against the competences set out in *Circulars 9/92 and 35/92: Initial Teacher Training (Secondary Phase)* (Department for Education and the Welsh Office, 1992), (NB at the time of publication the Teacher Training Agency (TTA) is considering the introduction of standards rather than competences as the basis for assessment of student teachers in ITE in England and Wales), or *Teacher Competences: Guidelines for Teacher Training Courses* (Scottish Department for Education, 1993) or *Arrangements for Initial Teacher Education in Northern Ireland from 1 September 1996* (Department of Education Northern Ireland, 1996). The competences in each of these documents are included as Appendices 2, 3 and 4 in Capel, Leask and

Turner (1995). However, your HEI has probably produced its own set of competences based on those in the relevant document.

TASK 1.6 TEACHING SKILLS

Look at the competences identified for your ITE course and identify the teaching skills on which you particularly need to work in order to become competent. Discuss with your tutor which teaching skills you should work on immediately and which you should leave until later. As part of the regular reviews you undertake with your tutor during your ITE course you should consider which teaching skills you should work on at that particular time.

Being competent in basic teaching skills is not enough for your lessons to be effective. In order to develop into an effective teacher you need to be able to refine and adapt these teaching skills and combine them so that they are used in a way appropriate to the specific situation. You also need to consider how the skills interact in a lesson.

How do teaching activities and skills interact in any one lesson?

The situation and environment of any specific lesson is unique. What you aim to achieve is defined by your objectives for the lesson, which in turn are defined by your objectives for the unit of work (see Chapter 3).

There are a number of reasons why you do not always achieve your objectives. Sometimes this is due to lack of appropriate planning. We have seen some student teachers plan the content of their lessons thoroughly, but leave the organisation and management of the tasks, the equipment or the pupils to chance. On the other hand, we have seen some student teachers plan how they are going to control a class without considering the appropriateness, quality and progression of content. If a student teacher has not planned how to organise and manage the lesson, the pupils may not be clear about what they are to do and what is expected of them; therefore the teacher has to spend considerable time organising and managing and cannot deliver the lesson in the way intended. On the other hand, if the student teacher concentrates on organising and managing the class, pupils are likely to achieve little and what they do achieve is likely to be of low quality.

You must be aware that pupils 'test out' student (and new) teachers and try to negotiate an acceptable standard of performance, effort or behaviour. We have all seen situations where pupils try to negotiate a longer game if they do a practice effectively or where pupils promise to work hard if they can work with friends. Discuss with another student teacher other ways in which pupils may try to negotiate boundaries, so that you are aware of them as you start to teach a new class.

Make sure that you only accept performance, effort or behaviour of an acceptable standard right from the beginning, otherwise you will find it hard to get pupils to accept this later. Pupils may make less effort to complete a task appropriately in future if you accept initially a performance, effort or behaviour below that of which they are capable. You may, for example, set a task in gymnastics which requires pupils to develop a sequence comprising nine movements, with at least two each of three different types of movement – rolls, jumps and balances. Pupils are given the opportunity to develop and practise an appropriate sequence then show this to the class. How you respond to the way pupils complete the task is important. If, for example, a pupil uses the three required movements to complete a sequence but makes no effort to link them together or to perform them in an effective way and you accept this, you send a message to the class that they can complete the task in any way they want.

There are other reasons why pupils may not perform or make an effort or behave to the standard expected. The task may be, for example, too easy or too difficult or not interesting, therefore pupils are not motivated to do the task. You may not have presented the task clearly or you respond differently to the same performance, effort or behaviour on different occasions. Pupils may, therefore, be bored, unclear or confused about what is required of them, and therefore may modify the task to make it easier or more difficult, not try to accomplish the task or, on occasion, refuse to do the task altogether. Can you think of any other reasons?

As you develop as a teacher you become aware of how different teaching activities and skills interact to influence what happens in the lesson and hence the effectiveness of pupils' learning. You will need to develop the ability to use these interactions effectively.

SUMMARY

Your past experiences of PE have influenced your decision to become a PE teacher and have moulded your values, attitudes and beliefs about PE and about PE teaching. In order to become an effective PE teacher, you need to be aware of how your values, attitudes and beliefs influence you and to understand that not all pupils you teach, nor all parents, nor all other teachers, share your values, attitudes and beliefs. As you start out as a student PE teacher you are likely to find that teaching is more complex than you thought. Your previous experience, your enthusiasm and your wish to pass on your knowledge, understanding and love of PE are not enough. Your ITE course is designed to give you different opportunities and experiences to help you develop as a PE teacher.

You need also to be conversant with your role as a teacher and as a PE teacher, and with the teaching activities and skills you require for effective teaching. You need competence in basic teaching skills before you can refine and adapt these skills so that you can use them in the right way at the right time and can combine them effectively to enhance pupils' learning and achieve the objectives of a lesson and unit of work. In order to do this, you need also to understand the complex interactions between teaching activities and skills. Teaching skills tend to be introduced on your course, and written about in books such as this, in isolation from one another. This chapter has attempted to provide a picture of how they fit together and interact so that you know at what you are aiming. In this overview, some basic teaching skills have been identified. In the chapters that follow, these basic teaching skills are addressed in more detail. After you have read those chapters we suggest that you return to this chapter to help you reflect on how teaching skills fit together and interact.

FURTHER READING

Mawer, M. (1995) *The Effective Teaching of Physical Education*, London: Longmans.
Chapter 1 in this book considers why people become PE teachers, their socialisation into the PE profession and stages in their development as teachers. Chapter 2 focuses on being a student PE teacher and early lessons taken by student PE teachers.

Rink, J. (1985) *Teaching Physical Education for Learning*, St. Louis, Mo.: Times Mirror/Mosby College Publishing.
Chapter 1 provides an overview of the teaching process, including content and organising and managing activities and skills used in a lesson.

Siedentop, D. (1991) *Developing Teaching Skills in Physical Education*, Mountain View, Calif.: Mayfield Publishing.
Chapter 1 addresses a number of issues concerned with learning to teach PE effectively, including stages of teaching skill development of student PE teachers. Chapter 5 introduces three primary systems: the managerial task system, the instructional task system, and the student (pupil) social system and how they interact.

2 Aims of PE

INTRODUCTION

In Chapter 1 you were provided with a picture of a whole lesson so that you know where you are going and what you are aiming to achieve and can judge when you have got there. In this chapter you are provided with a larger picture of the subject through the educational purposes or intentions of the curriculum. These educational purposes clarify what you are aiming to achieve and, hence, serve to guide your planning of a series of lessons (units of work) and planning and delivery of individual lessons, including choice of content and teaching strategies. You will probably want to return to Chapters 1 and 2 regularly throughout your initial teacher education (ITE) course to remind you of what you are aiming to achieve in PE and in your development as a PE teacher.

OBJECTIVES

By the end of this chapter you should be able to:

- understand the terms aims and objectives;
- identify aims for the school curriculum and for PE;
- understand how aims influence your objectives and delivery of lessons.

DEFINITIONS

You will hear the words **aims** and **objectives** frequently in your ITE course and beyond. Aims and objectives serve a number of purposes:

- they identify where you are going;
- they guide how you will get there;
- they enable you to establish if you have arrived.

Aims and objectives are the basis for educational planning. **Aims** provide **overall purpose and direction**, and therefore relate to more general intentions. A school has long-term aims or purposes. You should be able to find these in the school documentation. There are aims for the curriculum (for example, the National Curriculum in England and Wales) and for the subject, PE. The aims or purposes of the subject form the starting point for devising units of work and lesson plans, each of which has specific objectives. **Objectives** are **more specific purposes and intentions**. Thus, objectives are building blocks or stepping stones which, when put together, result in the achievement of an aim(s).

Aims and objectives become more specific and precise the shorter the term and the closer to the point of delivery they become. Therefore, aims become more specific from education, to school, to curriculum, to subject. Aims of education offer general guidance about the purposes of, and outcomes from, education rather than defining any specific achievements, whereas the aims of PE, although still long-term aspirations, are more specific. They provide the justification for the subject as they articulate its value or significant place in the whole educational process. They specify what should be achieved over a period of time, for example, for the time pupils are required to be at school. The aims of PE in the National Curriculum in England and Wales are given on page 23 as an example.

Aims cannot be used directly to help you plan a particular unit of work or lesson. They need to be broken down into 'operational' segments, each with a more specific focus. These are the objectives for units of work and lessons. Objectives for a unit of work define the end products of the unit, whereas objectives for a lesson define the outcomes of the specific lesson. Objectives for lessons within a series of lessons should show progression in learning in order to meet unit objectives. Objectives become more specific from unit of work to lesson (refer to objectives in Chapter 3).

AIMS

Aims of the curriculum

Unit 7.1 in Capel, Leask and Turner (1995) considers aims of education. We suggest that you refer to that unit now for background information. In this chapter we consider the aims of the school curriculum and of the PE curriculum. At this point find out the aims of the curriculum in the school experience schools in which you work. In England and Wales, for example, the National Curriculum requires a broad and balanced curriculum in schools which:

- promotes the spiritual, moral, cultural, mental and physical development of pupils at the school and of society;
- prepares pupils for the opportunities, responsibilities and experiences of adult life.

(Education Reform Act, 1988, Chapter 40 1.(2))

These aims serve to guide the school curriculum but, by themselves, are not capable of informing specific teaching and learning situations.

Aims of PE

As a PE teacher you work with particular content. If you focus only on teaching content, pupils gain only knowledge, skill and understanding related to that content (for example, a lay-up shot in basketball). However, as a PE teacher you are expected to achieve more than pupils' knowledge, skills and understanding of content. Much is claimed in the name of PE as is shown by the 29 aims identified in Figure 2.1, drawn from various sources.

As you can see from the list of aims in Figure 2.1, there is an embarrassment of riches in relation to what you might be able to achieve in PE. It is clearly impossible to achieve all of the aims identified above, therefore a selection of the most important has to be made. A starting point for selecting aims is to consider the **common educational aims** to which PE contributes as one of many subjects and **the more focused aims** towards which it makes a primary contribution. Although social development, for example, is an aim for PE, it is also an aim for other subjects. As such, you have a cross-curricular role (see Chapter 15). On the other hand, PE makes a major contribution to physical development and developing physical competence, therefore as a PE teacher your primary aims should be promoting **physical development and physical competence**. Although other subjects contribute to promoting physical development and physical competence, most notably Art and Music, in these subjects promoting physical development and physical competence is not the major aim. Further, these subjects are largely concerned with fine motor skills, whereas PE is concerned with gross as well as fine motor skills, for example, developing motor competence needed for controlled, co-ordinated and **successful participation in physical activity**. Although emphasis in the development of physical competence in PE is on **performance** in an activity, pupils also need to be taught to be able to **plan** and **evaluate** their performance in order to learn and improve (see also Chapter 17).

- develop physical skills;
- develop self-esteem and self-confidence;
- introduce every pupil to a wide range of activities;
- ensure pupils continue with physical activity after leaving school;
- develop creativity and inventiveness;
- produce world-class athletes;
- provide activity to keep youngsters off the street and away from crime;
- teach pupils the role of physical activity in stress prevention;
- promote joint flexibility and muscle strength;
- teach respect for the environment;
- teach pupils to handle competition;
- develop social and moral skills;
- prepare pupils to be knowledgeable spectators;
- teach pupils the place of sport/dance in UK (English/Welsh/Scottish/ Northern Irish) culture;
- open up possibilities for employment post-school;
- promote health and freedom from illness – especially cardio-vascular health;
- promote physical growth and development;
- develop perseverance;
- promote emotional development;
- provide enjoyment;
- win inter-school matches and tournaments;
- ensure pupils are alert to safety at all times;
- provide an area of potential success for the less academic;
- ensure every pupil has sufficient time to become proficient at a particular sport;
- develop water confidence to promote personal survival;
- develop aesthetic sensitivity;
- enable pupils to express themselves through movement;
- promote cognitive development;
- develop good posture and approach a mesomorph build, neither over or under weight.

Figure 2.1 Possible aims of PE

It is important also that pupils are taught about the impact of gross muscular exercise on the body and its consequences for **health** as well as how they can participate in physical activity in leisure time enjoyably and constructively (see, for example, DES, 1985). Your major responsibility for promoting physical development and physical competence is sometimes referred to as the development of a **physically educated** person. But what do we mean by being physically educated?

TASK 2.1 WHAT IS A PHYSICALLY EDUCATED PERSON?

What is a physically educated person? Write a list of characteristics that you feel describe a physically educated person.

Discuss your list of characteristics with those identified by another student teacher who has undertaken the same task. How do your characteristics compare? What differences are there? Discuss with your tutor your characteristics and how they influence the aims for PE in the school and the development of objectives for units of work and lessons. Record this information in your professional portfolio and refer back to it at later stages in your ITE course as you are able to reflect better on what you are aiming to achieve in PE. This task may help you when you apply for your first teaching post and when you complete your Career Entry Profile (see Chapter 18).

Refer to Chapter 17 for further information about being physically educated.

TASK 2.2 RANKING AIMS OF PE

Select the top ten aims for PE in Figure 2.1 and rank them according to what you believe is the importance of each as an aim for PE. You may find it helpful to consider whether each aim for PE is a common educational aim to which PE contributes as one of many subjects, or a more focused aim towards which PE makes a primary contribution. Compare your ranking with that of another student teacher. Store this information in your professional portfolio for later reference.

For many of you the selection of aims for PE has been made in the PE curriculum used in the school experience schools in which you work (the National Curriculum for PE in England and Wales).

TASK 2.3 AIMS OF THE PE CURRICULUM USED IN THE SCHOOL EXPERIENCE SCHOOLS IN WHICH YOU WORK

Obtain a copy of the PE curriculum used in the school experience schools in which you work on your ITE course and look at the aims. An example is given below for the aims of PE in the National Curriculum in England and Wales. Compare these aims to those you identified as most important in Task 2.2. Discuss with another student teacher what differences there are and why you think there are differences.

Physical education should involve pupils in the continuous process of planning, performing and evaluating. This applies to all areas of activity. The greatest emphasis should be placed on the actual performance aspect of the subject. The following requirements apply to the teaching of physical education across all key stages.

1. To promote physical activity and healthy lifestyles, pupils should be taught:

    (a) to be physically active;
    (b) to adopt the best possible posture and the appropriate use of the body;
    (c) to engage in activities that develop cardiovascular health, flexibility, muscular strength and endurance;
    (d) the increasing need for personal hygiene in relation to vigorous physical activity.

2. To develop positive attitudes, pupils should be taught:

    (a) to observe the conventions of fair play, honest competition and good sporting behaviour as individual participants, team members and spectators;
    (b) how to cope with success and limitations in performance;
    (c) to try hard to consolidate their performances;
    (d) to be mindful of others and the environment.

3. To ensure safe practice, pupils should be taught:

    (a) to respond readily to instructions;
    (b) to recognise and follow relevant rules, laws, codes, etiquette and safety procedures for different activities or events, in practice and during competition;

(c) about the safety risks of wearing inappropriate clothing, footwear and jewellery, and why particular clothing, footwear and protection are worn for different activities;

(d) how to lift, carry, place and use equipment safely;

(e) to warm up for and recover from exercise.

(DFE, 1995, p. 2)

These aims clearly show that in England and Wales PE is not confined to promoting physical development and physical competence. Other aims include those related to mental development, such as knowledge or ability to think about information – for example, knowing about the benefits of participation in physical activity, problem-solving, making decisions, selecting, refining, judging and adapting movements. Can you identify the contribution of PE to other aims of the National Curriculum set out on page 20; for example, the spiritual, moral and cultural development of pupils? Refer to the aims of the PE curriculum used in the school experience schools in which you work to help you with this.

There have, in the past, been some claims for PE which have not always been met; for example, 'PE is character building'. However, does PE build character? How is this aim realised? To achieve an aim such as this does not just happen, it has to be planned for as an integral part of your unit of work and lesson. Appropriate objectives need to be identified, content selected and how that content will be delivered planned (i.e. teaching strategies selected in order to achieve the objective (refer to Chapter 9)).

TASK 2.4 TEACHING APPROACHES TO ENABLE OBJECTIVES TO BE MET

Identify one aim which is unique to PE and one that is shared by many subjects. Translate each of these aims into an objective for a unit of work. Identify teaching approaches you could use to achieve each of these objectives. Discuss your ideas with your tutor to check that your approach would be feasible, then try to implement this objective and approach in one of your lessons.

SUMMARY

The aims of education and schooling, and more specifically the aims of the school curriculum and PE curriculum used in the school experience schools in which you work (for example, the National Curriculum in

England and Wales), provide guidance about what you are aiming to achieve. In this chapter we have introduced you to a range of possible aims for PE and to one set of more specific aims: those of the National Curriculum for PE in England and Wales.

The aims of the PE curriculum used in the school experience schools in which you work should guide your decisions about objectives for units of work and lessons (see Chapter 3) and the selection of appropriate content and teaching approaches. Early in your development as a PE teacher the principal aims for you to include in your lessons should be those that are unique to PE (for example, promoting physical development and physical competence and developing a physically educated person). At this stage, aims that are focused on the physical activity you are teaching provide a focus for your early planning. They enable you to check that you understand the material you are teaching and form the criteria against which you judge the success of your lessons and against which you are judged by others. As you become able to plan Units of Work and lessons that enable your pupils to work towards achieving these aims, and as you gain experience and confidence, you can start to address some of the other aims of the PE curriculum used in the school experience schools in which you work.

In order to make the most of this chapter and to prepare you for the following chapters we suggest that you make sure you are familiar with the requirements of the PE curriculum used in the school experience schools in which you work, in addition to the aims which you were asked to look at in Task 2.2.

TASK 2.5 THE REQUIREMENTS OF THE PE CURRICULUM

Make sure you are familiar with the requirements of the PE curriculum used in the school experience schools in which you work (for example, the National Curriculum for PE, DFE, 1995). Discuss the Curriculum and its implementation in school with your tutor, especially how requirements inform the setting of objectives for units of work and lessons.

We suggest that you return to this chapter at different points in your ITE course, and consider its content in detail towards the end of your course when you have mastered the basic teaching skills and can reflect on the aims of PE and what it means to physically educate pupils (see also Chapter 17).

FURTHER READING

Capel, S., Leask, M. and Turner, T (1995) *Learning to Teach in the Secondary School: A Companion to School Experience*, London: Routledge. Aims and objectives, including aims of education, are introduced in a number of units in the book.

Cohen, L. and Manion, L. (1989) *A Guide to Teaching Practice* (3rd edn), London: Routledge.
In Part II, 'Preparation and planning', there is a discussion of aims and objectives.

3 Developing lessons and units of work

INTRODUCTION

If your lesson time is to be used effectively, and your pupils are to be provided with a positive and stimulating learning environment, then your planning of each lesson should follow a particular structure. This structure could vary according to the length of the lesson, the type of activity and the environment in which the lesson is taking place. Some lessons are short in comparison with others, some are indoors whilst others are outside, and some lessons require a lot of equipment whilst others do not. These are all variables which must be taken into account when you are planning a lesson and you must learn to plan according to the demands of each situation.

The need for continuity and flow in your teaching is most important, not only through one lesson, but also from one lesson to another and throughout a whole unit of work. Continuity and progression can be achieved if you have carefully thought out your objectives for the lesson and for the unit and if you constantly work towards these objectives, both in your planning and teaching. Before you can begin to set objectives for a particular class, you need some information about the class: their age, gender, abilities, capabilities and previous learning and teaching experience in the activity that you are teaching them. In England and Wales you also need to know which National Curriculum End of Key Stage Descriptions (EKSD) you are addressing.

In the National Curriculum for PE (DFE, 1995, pp. 3–10), each key stage has a Programme of Study (PoS). Definitions of terms are included in the Glossary, and Chapter 17 explains some of these terms in more detail. The National Curriculum document sets out the various units that pupils have to cover, for example, for key stage 3 (KS3), it says:

> Pupils should be taught **Games**, at least one other full area of activity (Units A + B), and at least two additional half areas of activity

(Unit A) taken from different areas of activity. At least one half area of activity (Unit A) must be either **Gymnastic Activities** or **Dance**. Games should be taught in each year of the key stage.

(DFE, 1995, p. 6)

The recommendations for activities to be covered in each key stage are set out in full or half units in the document. These units vary in length of time according to how each school organises its blocks of teaching, but they cover a specific number of weeks – for example, half a term, a whole term or perhaps just four weeks. The block of time given to a particular activity relates to a unit of work. If the schools in which you work on school experience are not working towards the National Curriculum for PE in England and Wales, find out if there are any requirements for units of work that pupils must cover.

This chapter is designed to help you plan your lessons and units of work and to help you think about continuity and progression in both your planning and teaching.

OBJECTIVES

By the end of this chapter you should be able to:

- appreciate the importance of setting objectives;
- develop a lesson plan through a logical structure;
- plan within the requirements of the National Curriculum for PE in England and Wales;
- appreciate the need for effective time management in lessons;
- understand the importance of the beginning and end of a lesson;
- evaluate your lessons;
- develop a framework for planning a unit of work.

THE STRUCTURE OF A PE LESSON

Base structure

Ideally, a PE lesson is divided into four parts. However, even though the lesson might be divided into four parts, it is very important that the lesson flows smoothly throughout, and that it is not too noticeable when you have completed one part and are moving on to the next.

When you are preparing a lesson plan you need to consider the different parts of the lesson, but you must also think carefully about progression.

Your selection of material should therefore be appropriate and logical in its development throughout the lesson.

The four parts of the lesson to consider in your planning are:

1   introduction and warm-up;
2   development of skill or topic;
3   climax;
4   conclusion.

Before considering these in detail, it is important to note that before you can begin to plan the content of a lesson you must decide what you hope to achieve in the lesson, i.e. your objectives (see page 37).

Although the first teaching part of the lesson is the introduction and warm-up task, the lesson actually begins at the moment the bell goes. It is important, therefore, that you think about what happens before you begin teaching. The beginning and end of lessons, especially in PE, can eat into a large amount of lesson time. You must get pupils changed and into the teaching space as quickly as possible so that you can begin your lesson promptly.

TASK 3.1 PRE-TEACHING TASKS

Observe the beginning of a PE lesson taken by an experienced PE teacher. Make a list of all the tasks the teacher is engaged in from the moment the school bell goes up until the moment that actual teaching begins. Also, time this part of the lesson and note how long it takes before the practical part of the lesson begins.

Some of the points you noted might be concerned with these questions:

- Are the pupils expected to line-up outside the changing rooms or can they go in?
- Can the pupils get into the changing rooms or are they locked?
- Do the pupils know what activity they are going to be doing and therefore what clothes/shoes to put on?
- Does the teacher have to take a register and, if so, when is this best done?
- How are valuables or jewellery collected and stored?
- What does the teacher do about those pupils who are not participating because of illness or injury?
- Do the pupils know where they are going for the lesson?
- Is any equipment needed and, if so, who collects and carries it?
- Does the changing room have to be locked once the last pupil is out?

- Are the pupils allowed into/onto the working space before the teacher arrives?
- Does the teacher set up a practice/warm-up task for the pupils to be getting on with?
- Are there certain rules or routines which are evident in relation to these?

These are all matters you have to cope with each and every lesson. You soon get to know the procedures in your school and must follow these whilst you are on school experience. You can begin to evaluate the procedures used and decide for yourself what procedures you consider are the most effective. When you start teaching, you can develop your own procedures, rules and standards within school and departmental aims. Pupils get to know what is expected of them so, provided you maintain a constant procedure, your lesson can begin promptly and with the minimum of fuss. Once your class is assembled in the teaching area you can start your planned warm-up task.

1   Introduction and warm-up

This part of the lesson might start with a brief **verbal introduction**. Perhaps you could remind pupils of work covered in the previous lesson, explain the topic for this lesson, or just set up the first task. In any case, keep your talk to a minimum at this stage in order that pupils can immediately be involved in activity, especially if it is a cold day. The initial warm-up task needs to be of an **aerobic nature** to increase the heart and lung rate and begin to warm the pupils. However, you need to **tune-in** the pupils to the topic or theme of the lesson as well. With this in mind, try to select material for this early part of the lesson which has a bearing on what is to follow. This not only emphasises what is being covered but it also helps you to give pupils the right sort of preparation and practice.

2   Development of skill or topic

This part of the lesson is probably the most important because it is the **development** and **practice** of a particular skill (or skills) associated with the activity. It therefore forms the major part of the lesson, both in time and work covered. It is the part of the lesson in which pupils are introduced to new skills, revise old skills and are given the opportunity to practise and improve their individual skill level. This part should also help to promote pupil understanding and prepare pupils to use the skills that they have acquired for the climax of the lesson – for example, the game, the sequence or dance.

3   Climax

Pupils probably enjoy this part of the lesson the most and you might have to remind them that an improvement in the earlier practices enables them to perform well in this part of the lesson. You must therefore allow time for pupils to put their skills into practice, as well as seeing your lesson build up to an appropriate climax. This would usually be some sort of **game situation** in a games lesson (though not necessarily a full game), a performance of a short **gymnastic sequence** or **dance**, or merely a **showing and sharing** of the work achieved during the lesson.

4   Conclusion

This is a very small part of the lesson in terms of time, perhaps only a couple of minutes, but an extremely important part for a number of reasons. You must allow for this part of the lesson in your overall plan, and give time for a **calm, orderly** and **purposeful** conclusion. Also, make sure that you finish your lesson on time, so that pupils are not late for their next lesson.

TASK 3.2 BEGINNING AND END OF LESSONS

Discuss with your tutor the importance of the beginning and end of lessons, remembering what you have read in this chapter. Then meet with another student teacher and between you make a list of:

1   the objectives of the warm-up, considering the physical, social and psychological values (see also Chapter 2);
2   four different and simple concluding tasks for a gymnastics lesson.

Keep the warm-up objectives in mind when planning your next lesson. Try out some of the concluding tasks when you next teach a gymnastics lesson.

Lesson plan

A sample lesson plan is included in Figure 3.1. It is a suggestion for a first gymnastics lesson with a year 7 group, based on the theme of locomotion. As such, it is an introductory lesson, so one of the objectives relates to pupil understanding of the theme of locomotion and awareness of some of the movements associated with it. The objective of improving footwork and agility and mobility is particularly important because you must always try to improve pupil performance and skill level. This is stated in the EKSD in the National Curriculum (DFE, 1995).

LESSON PLAN

GYMNASTICS

DATE: 10 September 1997

Topic:	Locomotion
Class:	7JB
Time:	10 am – 11 am
Number:	34 (Mixed set)
Lesson number:	1 of 6

LESSON OBJECTIVES

1   Pupils should understand the theme of LOCOMOTION and be aware of some of the movements associated with it;
2   pupils should have improved their footwork and general agility and mobility in floorwork and on low apparatus;
3   pupils should be able to show ability and potential in basic gymnastic skills.

RESOURCES

Lesson plan/Teaching notes
Mats and benches

Figure 3.1 Sample lesson plan for gymnastics

CONTENT/MATERIAL	ORGANISATION
1 Introduction and warm-up	
a) Rise, lower, stretch feet and ankles	Class well spaced, facing teacher
b) Jog on spot: knees high, slow/fast	
c) Jog around room, in and out, using space	Class well spaced (safety)
d) Jog fast, stop on command	
e) Jog, form groups on command	Finish in 2's
2 Development of skill or topic	MATS OUT – in 2's
a) Jump on mats – landings (1 to 2)	
b) Shape jumps (2 to 2)	
<u>Weight on Hands</u>	
a) Front support/back support	
b) Scramble round mat (chase partner on hands and feet)	Start opposite corners and ensure mats well spaced
c) Across mat using hands Across mat with a roll. Skills: catspring forward roll bunny jump/cartwheel	
<u>Bench Work</u>	BENCHES OUT
a) Jumps off: shapes, landings	In 4's – 1 bench + 2 mats
b) Jump, land and roll	
c) Across using hands – floor or bench	
3 Climax	
Sequence: LINK – jump, roll, use hands (cross bench any number of times)	Individual Show sequence (half class)
	APPARATUS AWAY
4 Conclusion	
Long sitting – straight back and legs Leg circle – to front lying, to long sit Stand – correct posture	Class well spaced All sitting

Figure 3.1 (cont.)

TEACHING POINTS   EVALUATION

High on toes, extend ankles
Jog on toes, use whole foot in action
Light footwork, on toes, aware of
space
Watch others, weave in and out
Be <u>still</u> on command, get low, feet
apart
Aware and quick to form groups

Land on toes, bend knees, ankles,
hips
Soft, controlled landings
Shape clear – extended or tucked etc.

Arms straight, body tight and
straight
Shoulders under hands, move feet
and hands quickly
Strong arms, control in movement
Push from legs, swing arms for cat-
spring
Reach forward, tuck head, legs push
for roll
Arms straight, good shape – bunny
jump/cartwheel

Bend knees, land safely on toes,
controlled
Jump high, good shape in air on
jump
Land and roll smoothly and
immediately
Arms strong/straight, push off feet

Skills to link smoothly, no walks in
between
Control landings, keep body tight,
show clear shapes, stretch and
extend
Good start and finish position

Legs tight and straight, toes pointed,
ankles extended
Swing legs straight, use arms to push
Stand head up, shoulders down, body
tight, tummy in, feet together . . .
stand tall

Figure 3.1 (cont.)

You can see in Figure 3.1 that the taught part of the lesson has been set out in **four** columns, under the headings of:

Content/Material;
Organisation;
Teaching Points;
Evaluation.

Writing down your plan in the four columns helps you to think through each aspect of the lesson and to prepare yourself carefully with regard to the content/material you plan to teach, the relevant teaching points and the various organisational points. The final column you leave blank and use for your evaluation of the lesson after it has taken place.

This four-column plan is a very useful method of providing thoughtful detail in planning and preparation. By reading **across** the inside two pages of the lesson plan, you can see a logical link between the organisation and the teaching points in columns two and three in relation to the content/material in the first column. However, it is just one way of writing lesson plans. Your higher education institution (HEI) may provide a different format, in which case you should use that, but it is quite likely that you will be required to think through and plan using similar headings to those listed in the four columns.

The front sheet of the lesson plan, when completed, provides not only vital factual information about the class, but, most importantly, the objectives that you set for your lesson prior to the detailed planning of the lesson content, teaching methods and organisation.

Allocating time

Most of your lesson time should be given to parts two and **three** of the four-part structure shown in Figure 3.1. as they form the main parts of the lesson. The introduction and warm-up can be shortened or extended according to the total length of time available. You can save a lot of time in the first part of the lesson by using tasks which serve as a warm-up but also involve the practice and development of skill. By doing this, the move from the first to the second part of the lesson should not be evident, thus promoting continuity and progression, as mentioned earlier. The conclusion need only take a couple of minutes, but needs to be built into the plan.

You could write down a time allocation at the side of each part of your lesson plan. Indeed, in some HEIs this is included in the lesson planning format. This might help you to keep within certain time limits, but you must allow for some deviation and be prepared, if necessary, to change the time allocated to each part as you go through the lesson.

An important consideration initially must be whether the 'teaching time' of the lesson (that is, the amount of time you actually have on the field or in the gymnasium) is sufficient for you to follow the four-part structure on page 29 effectively. If not, then you must adapt the overall structure, and vary the length of time given to each part.

Think about the following suggestions which also help you save time, but ensure that you still achieve quality in your teaching. Can you:

- simplify the game (for example, smaller numbers, fewer rules, less complex to set up)?;
- shorten the sequence (for example, fewer moves or skills required)?;
- show half a class at a time instead of many groups (and focus the observation)?;
- cut down on your instructions (keep explanations concise) (see also Chapter 5)?;
- keep up the **pace** of your teaching (be brisk and avoid any time-wasting) (see also Chapter 7)?

Also, always encourage pupils to change quickly at the beginning and end of the lesson, otherwise your teaching time is cut down. If the lesson is 35 minutes long, you could finish up with only 15–20 minutes of teaching, so it is essential that as little time as possible is wasted.

TASK 3.3 OVERALL LESSON STRUCTURE

Observe a full lesson taught by an experienced PE teacher. See if you are able to identify the different parts of the lesson (introduction and warm-up, development of skill or topic, climax, conclusion). Make a note of the amount of time given to each part. Discuss this with the teacher afterwards and see if you can agree an appropriate rough percentage allocation for each part of the lesson.

Changing the structure

Sometimes you might need to structure your lesson quite differently; for example, if you have a very short gymnastics lesson you might only be able to complete a floorwork session as there is not time to get apparatus out. Alternatively though, in another short lesson, perhaps the following one, you might spend all the time doing apparatus work. However, you could still work to the structure above and include all four parts, but in a different way.

TASK 3.4   MANAGING LESSON TIME

Plan a lesson for an activity and group of your choice, allowing for 40 minutes of teaching time. Work to the four-part structure and apportion the time as you think most appropriate. If you get an opportunity, try out the plan with a class and evaluate it in terms of time allocation.

TASK 3.5   STRUCTURING LESSONS

Write out two *different* but *consecutive* lesson plans for short lessons of gymnastics (maximum teaching time 25 minutes), one of which must include apparatus work. Discuss the plans with your tutor and evaluate the feasibility of each one. Some suggested plans for the lay-out of apparatus are included in Appendix 2.

PLANNING FOR PROGRESSION

Objective setting

Before any planning can occur, you need to set a target or a series of targets (an **objective or series of objectives**) for your class. These need to be realistic objectives for your pupils, in that they need to be attainable, but also appropriate and challenging. It is no good planning to play a full game of volleyball with a group who have never done volleyball before, for example. However, given the opportunity to introduce the skills and rules of the game and the chance to practise and put these into action over a series of lessons, the end target could well be to play a full game of volleyball. This would form an overall target, or **unit objective**; something that can be achieved over a series of lessons. You might have one or more than one unit objective.

Additionally, **each lesson** within a unit is planned around smaller mini-objectives, all of which go towards achieving the end of unit objectives.

Objectives are generally written in terms of what you expect pupils to have achieved (i.e., what pupils are expected to know, understand or be able to do) by the end of the lesson or unit of work. By writing objectives in this way you can assess whether pupils are making progress.

TASK 3.6   SETTING LESSON OBJECTIVES

Observe a PE lesson taught by an experienced PE teacher. Write down what you think the lesson objectives are. Afterwards discuss with the teacher:

- the objectives to see if you are in agreement;
- whether you think the objectives (both yours and the teacher's, if they were different) were achieved in the lesson; and
- how the lesson objectives relate to the overall unit objectives.

Progression in planning

By setting objectives, whether they are over a longer term (unit of work) or over a shorter term (lesson plan) you have begun planning the **end** of your work first. This is vital in keeping you on course and ensuring that you and your pupils can see a **purpose** to the task.

Now for the second stage of planning, which is to go to the **beginning**. Having decided on your objectives, you need next to look at how you can begin to achieve them. Where do you start? What would be the most appropriate way? What do you want to achieve initially? These are questions which you need to ask yourself in this stage. Having decided on these two stages, the **end** and the **beginning**, the stages in between are somewhat easier to fill in. However, you must not forget the overall objectives and always keep these to the forefront of your planning.

TASK 3.7   TAKING ACCOUNT OF EKSD IN THE NATIONAL CURRICULUM FOR PE

Refer to the EKSD in your National Curriculum for PE document (DFE, 1995, p. 11). Read through the descriptions for KS3, then write a list of three lesson objectives that you perhaps might be setting a class for their first lesson in: (a) netball; (b) football; (c) swimming, in order to meet *one* of the EKSD. If you can, try these out.

Setting challenges

Your pupils usually rise to a challenge. The setting of **appropriate, realistic** and **achievable** challenges helps you to motivate and interest your classes. A series of challenges or targets, perhaps increasing in difficulty, or perhaps building up in stages, can keep your pupils working and give them (and you!) a tremendous sense of satisfaction when they achieve something they have been working hard for. By giving out constant challenges, you are helping your pupils to make progress. Do think carefully about what you are asking your pupils to do though – a very difficult or unattainable task can seem not only daunting but demotivating or even dangerous and you could find that you have put someone off, rather than encouraging them. See also 'Motivation' in Chapter 7.

Get to know your pupils: this allows you to set a high level of expectation by selecting appropriate tasks. Your pupils have a tremendous appetite for knowledge and activity, so use this to your advantage and push your pupils to their maximum. You will be surprised at what they can achieve, but only if **you set a high standard**. Knowing your pupils is addressed in Chapter 7.

Developing material

You are the key person when it comes to your pupils' progress. In order to set the high level we have just talked about, you need to have the material to teach your pupils. That means that you need **knowledge** of your subject. PE is a vast area and you must learn as much as you can about **all** the activities. If you are asked to teach one of your weaker areas, perhaps rugby, badminton or dance for instance, you cannot refuse. Take every opportunity to learn as much as you can and get practice in teaching as many activities as possible on your school experiences or in other teaching situations (see 'Subject knowledge' in Chapter 18). Once you have the technical knowledge and a model of the end product, you begin to understand how to break down and build up skills, adapt and modify practices, and so improve pupils' performance. However, you can only make an impact on pupil progress if you have certain other skills. These follow the pattern of:

- **knowing** the appropriate teaching points;
- **observing** movement performance;
- **identifying** faults in performance;
- **deciding** how to effect an improvement;
- **acting** on your decision.

The process of knowing, observing, identifying, deciding and acting should be apparent in all good PE teaching, but takes time and experience to acquire. Chapter 4 addresses observation of pupils.

TASK 3.8   PLANNING PROGRESSIONS

Select one particular physical skill (for example, a cartwheel in gymnastics or a lay-up shot in basketball) and think out three stages of practice (progressions) which would help a beginner pupil to build up to the skill. Try these practices out yourself and ask another student teacher to observe. Decide between you whether the progressions are logical, but also how you could adapt the practices to make them easier or harder. Try these out in a teaching situation.

EVALUATING A LESSON

Once you have taught a lesson or part of a lesson, and before you can begin to think about planning the next one, you need to evaluate the effectiveness of the lesson in terms of what the pupils learnt and also what you as the teacher learnt from it. This is essential if pupils are to make progress. You have to consider not only whether the objectives of the lesson were achieved, but also whether the objectives were, in fact, realistic and appropriate. You will find it helpful to evaluate the lesson and write down comments about it as soon as possible after you have taught it. This makes it easier to clarify your thoughts whilst they are still fresh in your mind and allows you to reflect on what happened in that particular lesson (especially if you have to teach a similar lesson to a different class on another day).

If you structure your evaluation under the three headings shown in Figure 3.2, you can begin to be quite critical in your analysis of each part of the lesson. Ask yourself some of the following questions. Though you might not be able to find an easy answer, this helps you to question and debate the success or otherwise of the lesson.

The list of questions in Figure 3.2 is by no means exhaustive, but in asking yourself some of them you are beginning to analyse the effectiveness of the lesson and, consequently, the learning outcomes achieved by the pupils and how they matched up with the lesson objectives. In any evaluation all the questions are focused around one important factor: 'what did the pupils achieve?'.

There are many aspects of your lessons on which you can focus in evaluation. You cannot consider them all in each lesson, therefore you may want to focus some evaluations on selected aspects of the lesson. The aspects on which you focus may be the result of, for example, previous evaluations or observations. In answering the questions in Figure 3.2, or any other questions you may ask, you might identify follow-up questions

1. **The pupils:**
      What was their overall ability level?
      How did they respond to you/the tasks/the teaching?
      How hard did they work?
      What was their level of understanding?
      Were they of average or above average intelligence?
      Were they a well disciplined group?
      Were they a friendly group?

2. **The material:**
      Were the objectives appropriate and met?
      Was it an appropriate level/too easy/too difficult?
      Was it suitably challenging?
      Did it allow for differentiation?
      Was it interesting/motivating?
      Did it have purpose?
      Was some of it new to the pupils?

3. **The teacher (you):**
      Had you planned and prepared?
      Did you feel knowledgeable about the activity/material?
      Did you have good organisation?
      Were instructions clear, concise and appropriate?
      Did you give praise and encouragement?
      Did you allow opportunity for practice?
      Were you aware of individual differences?
      Did you manage the class well?
      Did you exercise good control and discipline?
      Did you establish a good rapport with the pupils?

Figure 3.2 Example of questions to be asked in evaluating lessons

– for example, why such an outcome resulted. You must also consider how you can address any issues or negative points in the evaluation and try to put this into practice in future lessons.

PLANNING A UNIT OF WORK

Unit objectives

Because unit objectives are worked towards over a period of time, they are directly linked to the EKSD which are laid out in your National

Curriculum for PE document for each key stage (see p. 11). These are the targets that you are working towards, the attainment targets, and it is vital that you plan and teach to achieve these throughout your individual units of work.

All your objectives lead towards the three-stranded approach that is laid down in the National Curriculum, that of:

PLANNING
PERFORMING
EVALUATING

Chapter 17 addresses this three-stranded approach in more detail. All three strands are important in PE, though the most important one is considered to be performing. As mentioned earlier in this chapter, you must always put the emphasis on improving your pupils' practical work. **Quality in performance** is a prime objective.

TASK 3.9   SETTING UNIT OBJECTIVES

By referring to your National Curriculum for PE document for KS3, select one EKSD which relates to pupil performance and which you consider relevant for a year 7 class doing either netball or football. Decide three appropriate unit objectives which cover the aspects of performing (i.e. practice and improvement).

Discuss these objectives with your tutor and decide whether they are realistic. Try to incorporate them into a unit of work if appropriate.

Planning structure

Initially, the thought of having to plan a whole unit of work seems a little daunting. However, if you work to a structure and plan step by step, you should find that it is not as difficult as it might at first seem.

Before you can begin to think out any ideas, glean as much information as you can about the class you are going to teach. Remember that it is the **pupils** you are teaching who are the most important and they must have first consideration. The activity or material that you are teaching comes second. A simple formula for planning might go in this order:

- **who** am I teaching?   (information about pupils);
- **what** am I teaching?   (activity and material);
- **how** can I teach it?   (unit and lesson plans).

Accepting that you have the information about the **pupils**, you know what the **activity** is and you have the **knowledge** about the activity, then you can begin planning by **setting your objectives**. To do this you think about what you could hope to achieve through a six-week unit of work and have a good idea what the end product should be. This product forms the basis for the **last** lesson in the unit of work.

The second stage is to decide where to **start**; in other words, what you might cover in the **first** lesson (i.e. the introduction to the topic, a brief assessment of pupil abilities and some improvement in pupil performance).

The third stage is the completion of a proposed structure for the lessons in between. In a unit plan this structure forms an outline, or a **framework**, for further planning. It refers only to a general procedure. The detailed planning occurs each week in the lesson plan. This system for planning a unit of work (i.e. starting at the end first) is the same as the one given earlier in this chapter for lesson planning (see p. 38).

TASK 3.10   UNDERSTANDING A UNIT PLAN

Look at the completed sample unit of work in Figure 3.3. You can see that the EKSD for KS3 are filled in and that the two which are being addressed are **underlined**. Go through each stage of the planning structure in the order given in this chapter.

Now, using the *same* two EKSD, plan a similar unit for hockey for the same pupils. Work with another student teacher and share your ideas in planning.

TASK 3.11   DEVELOPING A FULL UNIT OF WORK

A blank unit of work sheet is included in Figure 3.4 as a template. Using the blank sheet, plan a full unit of work for a class of which you have some knowledge and for an activity that you are likely to teach in the future.

Compare your final plan with the plan of another student teacher. Amend your own if necessary and put it into action if given the opportunity.

| PHYSICAL EDUCATION   – | Area of Activity: **GYMNASTICS** |
| | Activity: **GYMNASTICS** |

KS3	**END OF KEY STAGE DESCRIPTION** (DFE, 1995, p.11)
UNIT 1	Pupils devise strategies and tactics for appropriate activities, and plan or compose more complex sequences of movements;
	They adapt and refine existing skills and apply these to new situations;
	<u>Pupils show they can use skills with precision and perform sequences with greater clarity and fluency;</u>
	Pupils recognise the importance of rules and apply them;
	<u>They appreciate strengths and limitations in performance and use this information in co-operative team work</u> as well as to outwit the
YEAR 7	opposition in competition;
	They understand short-term and long-term effects of exercise on the body systems and demonstrate how to prepare for particular activities and how to recover after vigorous physical activity.

UNIT OBJECTIVES

1   pupils should have an understanding of **partnerwork**, and awareness of skills on the floor and apparatus;
2   pupils should show some skill in jumping, rolling and travelling skills using hands and feet, also body tension and control;
3   pupils should be able to co-operate through partnerwork;
4   pupils should be able to produce an interesting sequence in pairs on apparatus.

6 lessons   UNIT FRAMEWORK

1   Introduction to work in 2's on floor – travelling, jumping and rolling – including matching/mirroring.
2   Revision and continuation of matching/mirroring in 2's and over/under. Use of benches – jumping, rolling, weight on arms and travelling in 2's.
3   Introduction of large apparatus + benches.
    Exploration and practice in 2's – travel, jump, roll, weight on arms. Introduce unison/canon.
4   Continuation of work on apparatus – rotate groups to different apparatus. Select best 2 or 3 skills and link together.
5   Revise and continue to compose and develop sequence in 2's. Include travel, jump, roll, weight on hands, plus matching/mirroring and over/under and unison/canon.
6   Polish sequence and perform in groups to rest of class.

RESOURCES	**ASSESSMENT**
Apparatus Plan: Boxes, Bars, Ropes, Table, Benches	1 Performance of sequence in 2's
	2 Composition and evaluation of sequences.

Figure 3.3 Example of completed template for a unit of work

PHYSICAL EDUCATION –	Area of Activity: Activity:

KS3	**END OF KEY STAGE DESCRIPTION** (DFE, 1995, p.11)
	Pupils devise strategies and tactics for appropriate activities, and plan or compose more complex sequences of movements;
UNIT	They adapt and refine existing skills and apply these to new situations; Pupils show they can use skills with precision and perform sequences with greater clarity and fluency; Pupils recognise the importance of rules and apply them;
YEAR	They appreciate strengths and limitations in performance and use this information in co-operative team work as well as to outwit the opposition in competition; They understand short-term and long-term effects of exercise on the body systems and demonstrate how to prepare for particular activities and how to recover after vigorous physical activity.

UNIT OBJECTIVES

UNIT FRAMEWORK

RESOURCES

ASSESSMENT

Figure 3.4 Template for a unit of work

Two other issues are of vital importance and you must build these into your unit planning: the **resources** needed to assist you in your teaching of the unit and the **assessment** (whether in fact this unit of work is to be assessed, and if so, how and what is to be assessed). If the unit is to be assessed, then this should be an integral part of your planning and teaching throughout. For help in this, refer to Chapter 11 on assessment.

SUMMARY

The effectiveness of your teaching depends to a large extent on your planning and use of time. This includes how you use time in and out of lessons. You need to be organised in your approach and maximise the time which is at your disposal for teaching. In considering the structure of your lessons, remember that all schools and all situations are different, even to the extent that what works sometimes in some situations does not necessarily work at another time or in another situation. A structured plan, such as the four-part plan introduced here, goes a long way towards achieving the most effective learning situation for your pupils. At the same time it provides you with a framework within which to teach. This should give both continuity and purpose to your lessons.

Progression is going to be a feature in all stages of your teaching. Always consider your overall objectives first when you are planning. You then have a clear objective in mind and should be able to see the way forward. At first you will probably have too much material to teach in one lesson, but once you know your pupils and know what they can cope with you can begin to set tasks which are demanding of your pupils' abilities. **Always expect** a high standard of work, and settle for nothing less. You can achieve what you want, if you **persist**.

The one message that should come through in this chapter is how important planning is. If you organise yourself and your time sensibly and prepare well for your teaching, including considering the importance of safety aspects (see also Chapter 8) then you are much more likely to be a really effective teacher. Careful thought leads to purposeful teaching which provides an effective learning situation for pupils.

FURTHER READING

Kyriacou, C. (1991) *Essential Teaching Skills*, Oxford: Basil Blackwell. A small, easy to read book which deals with the basic skills required for teaching. Chapter 2, 'Preparation and Planning', and Chapter 4, 'Lesson Management', are very relevant to the topics in this chapter.

Williams, A. (1987) *Curriculum Gymnastics*, London: Hodder and Stoughton. This book is especially helpful if you are planning gymnastics lessons. 'Lesson Structure and Progression' (Chapter 6) and 'Teaching Styles and Techniques' (Chapter 5) are both helpful and can also be applied to activities other than gymnastics.

4 Observation of pupils in PE

INTRODUCTION

Central to your development as a teacher is your ability to observe and analyse what is happening in lessons. This chapter considers observation of pupils in PE. Your observation of the pupils' response to tasks set is the key to your improving their performance. The observations made will inform your teaching in the current lesson and also help you in the planning of future lessons and units of work. As a PE teacher, your role is to educate your pupils physically, to provide them with a variety of physical experiences and to promote their physical learning. To fulfil that role you need to draw on and develop your knowledge and understanding of movement. You need to become a skilled analyser and observer of movement to be able to evaluate pupil performance and provide feedback.

OBJECTIVES

At the end of this chapter you should:

- appreciate the role of observation in a movement environment and its use to you as a PE teacher;
- understand how you can observe movement;
- understand the use of criteria to extend your skills in observing movement.

MOVEMENT

When you observe a range of physical activities you can identify certain movement patterns, some of which are unique to a particular activity, some of which are common to two or more activities. A movement pattern is a series of movements organised in a particular sequence. A movement is a change of position in space and time, such as an arm swing, elbow bend, push with the foot. It may help you in your observations to think of a skill as being a movement pattern performed in a particular context with a specific outcome as an objective. A sports skill, or a skill specific to a particular physical activity, is then a modified version of a more general skill produced to meet the requirements of the particular sport or activity. Each activity can therefore be seen as requiring a combination of specific skills, selected and refined to meet the particular goals of the activity.

OBSERVING AND ANALYSING MOVEMENT

Movement in physical activity can be described in different ways, such as anatomically, biomechanically, aesthetically. You, as a PE teacher, are concerned in your observations with **what** the pupils are doing (**quantitative** analysis) and **how** they are doing it (**qualitative** analysis). Observations you make of a quantitative nature place movement into established compartments or categories (for example, knees bend, pointed toes, running, leaping). Qualitative descriptions refer to the quality of the movement (for example, suddenly, slowly, strongly). You also need to be able to analyse a wide range of movement skills or tasks, varying in complexity from relatively simple closed skills such as leaping, rolling or javelin throwing, to the highly complex open skills found in some sports and dance.

In developing skills in observing movement you need to:

- have knowledge and understanding of specific activities and the movements they demand;
- be able to make judgements of those movements based upon clear criteria;
- use this information in the planning of future progressions and developments in performance and/or participation.

These are summarised in Figure 4.1 and addressed in more detail below.

The observational skills you require as a PE teacher vary with the objectives of the task set. The majority of your feedback is directed towards improving pupil performance skills. If, however, the focus is on developing the pupils' planning and evaluating skills then the focus of your observation and the feedback you give is different. If, for example, you want to develop pupils' observational skills as an initial step in their learning to evaluate, then your focus of observation should be on the pupils' ability to observe. Similarly, if your intention is to develop pupils' planning skills in a particular context you may be looking for variety and originality of response rather than at the performance itself.

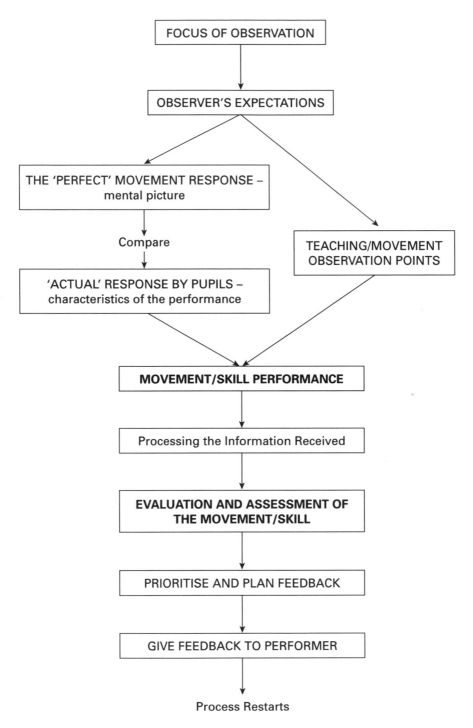

Figure 4.1 Observation of movement in PE

Process of observation

You may find it helpful to consider the process of observation and analysis in three stages: pre-observation, observation and post-observation.

Pre-observation

At this stage you need to collect together the relevant information by analysing the movement being observed. It may be necessary to break down a complex movement into smaller components. When looking at a skill such as a tennis serve or handspring, for example, preparation, action and follow through (or recovery) are appropriate. Other considerations at this stage are the purpose of the movement, the constraints of the environment and its characteristics and level of ability of the performer. Your expectations will differ with pupils of different ages, even if they are performing the same skill or task, for example. You must be sure to identify both quantitative and qualitative elements in your analysis. You should draw from this pre-observation stage the most important or critical features: a mental check list of **teaching points**. Teaching points are essential for you to be able to carry out meaningful observation of your pupils. See also Chapter 3.

Observation

At this stage you make direct subjective assessment with reference to the teaching points you have previously identified.

Post-observation

Here you compare what you expected to happen with what actually happened. You should give feedback to pupils using the teaching points in order of importance. Do not overload the pupils by giving too much information at one time. Your expectations need to be realistic, taking into account the stage of development of the pupils and their characteristics: physical ability, experience, level of understanding, motivation and readiness to learn (see Chapter 7).

Knowledge and understanding of activities

Good knowledge and understanding of activities enables you to be sure of the pre-requisites of movement, the characteristics of performance and any critical features pertaining to any activity you are teaching. The more you know, understand and observe movement the better the information you can eventually pass on to the pupils (see 'Subject knowledge' in Chapter 18).

Observation is vital to assessment of the effectiveness of pupils' learning. Chapter 11 identifies this link as part of the assessment of pupils. Progression and improvement of pupil performance in activities depend on your ability to identify appropriate teaching points by using your skills in observing movement. To establish clear and meaningful teaching points you need sound technical knowledge and understanding to inform your observations. Your knowledge and understanding, together with your personal participation experiences, define your expectations for your pupils and their performances in the activity. The more you are involved in an activity as a participant, a spectator and as an official, the more effective you will be.

TASK 4.1 CHECKING YOUR KNOWLEDGE OF MOVEMENT IN DIFFERENT ACTIVITIES

Select an activity you know and understand well. Choose one movement or skill from the activity, for example, a swimming stroke, a push pass in hockey, a forward roll in gymnastics. Make a comprehensive and detailed list of the associated teaching points for that skill.

Now take an activity where your knowledge and understanding are suspect. Choose one movement or skill from this activity. Again, compile a comprehensive and detailed list of the associated teaching points.

Compare the two lists and answer the following questions:

- Are the details of the movements/skills comparable in detail?
- Do the lists demonstrate similar depth of knowledge and understanding of those movements/skills and therefore similar specificity?
- Is the first list based upon a clear 'picture' of what the skill/sequence of movement may look like in isolation and in a game/sequence situation?
- What is the second list based upon?
- Have you got a clear 'picture' of this movement/skill in isolation and in a game/sequence situation?

In completing Task 4.1 you will have found that your depth of knowledge and understanding of an activity influenced your ability to select appropriate teaching points. Effective observation of pupil movement in your lessons is dependent on these points being clearly identified. You need to know what you are looking for in order to see it. Identify ways you can gain this knowledge and understanding of subject content (see also Chapter 18).

Judgements of movement

With experience you build up a fund of relevant teaching points. Your observations increase your knowledge and help you update and refine these teaching points. However, just like other databases, the information is redundant if it is not utilised and it is this utilisation you are now considering.

The information you gather about movement/skills through observation allows you to analyse the movement/skills/performances of your pupils. When setting a task create a mental picture of the 'perfect' movement response. The clarity of the picture depends on your depth of knowledge and understanding of the task and the activity. Using your teaching points as a check-list, you need to bring about the meeting of what the pupils initially do and the 'perfect' response to the task set. The judgements are arrived at through a combination of:

- your understanding of the pre-requisites of the movement;
- your knowledge of the characteristics of the performance;
- what you know of any critical features of the activity and the movements involved;
- your personal skills of recognition of the movements by the pupils whilst participating in the activity;
- the expectations you have of the activity and of your pupils and their abilities.

When the pupils have been set a task you need to stand back and 'scan' the class to check the general level of success. It is particularly important that you can observe individuals and cope with the distractions taking place around you. You need to plan carefully how you are going to observe. Have a clear picture in your mind of what you are looking for and decide where it is best to stand to observe the pupils.

TASK 4.2 IMPROVING THE PERFORMANCE OF YOUR PUPILS

Observe and identify the teaching points for a skill within an activity you are teaching at the present time – for example, the front crawl in swimming, a handstand in gymnastics, a shot on goal in football. Create a movement 'picture' in your mind of a good performance of your selected movement/skill. Observe the performance of the pupils taking part in your lesson. How near are their performances to your 'good performance picture', based upon your knowledge and understanding? The nearer the two are, the more successful, efficient and effective the pupils should be.

Then ask yourself the following questions:

- which pupils need the most help in their movements?;
- why?;
- which teaching points are you going to select in order to improve the pupils' performance?

Complete the same task for three of the other activities you teach at present in your school experience school, including the ones in which you have less confidence.

Having gone through this process of acquiring sets of criteria and using them to determine the stage of learning and performance of your pupils, how do you make this information work for you and your teaching, to improve your effectiveness and efficiency and that of the pupils in your classes?

Progression and developments of movement

So far you have gained information about the activities you teach and the movement skills each requires. You are using your developing observation skills to collect knowledge about your pupils and their possible movement/performance needs. You should not only be comparing their performances with the 'good pictures' in your mind, but also prioritising the appropriate teaching points. Which aspect of their movement needs to be addressed first and would make their participation/performance more efficient and effective? Some of their movement needs could be addressed almost immediately – for example, stressing the need to focus on one point at eye line to create and maintain a balance; to keep the head over the ball to prevent the ball rising off the floor when kicked. Remember, though, care must be taken not to overload pupils with too much information at one time. It is important when giving feedback to pupils to focus on the teaching points that were introduced prior to the practice of the task, although you can give some additional information to pupils who are having difficulties or differentiate the task for one who is finding it too easy. You must be careful how you do this as to add extra teaching points to a task after it is started can lead to confusion. See also 'Feedback' in Chapter 9.

Skill improvement may need to be planned for over a longer period of time. Pupils may need time to practise the movements/skills, to develop an understanding of the concepts and principles involved in the movements/skills and to grow physically in order to co-ordinate the movement skills as young adults instead of children. Developments could take six to eight weeks, as in a unit of work, or even the three years for KS3 and the two years for KS4.

TASK 4.3 PLANNING A PROGRAMME OF SKILL/ PERFORMANCE IMPROVEMENT

Select a pupil in a class that you are teaching who requires help in an aspect of an activity that you know and understand well. Prioritise that pupil's movement needs in terms of:

- those which could be addressed immediately to give significant improvements in skill/performance;
- the more complex or co-ordinated movements/skills which will need a little more time to develop;
- those which will take considerably more time as the pupil's understanding, cognition and physique need to mature.

Decide which of these should be addressed:

- in the lesson;
- in the unit of work;
- over the year;
- over the key stage.

Plan how you can meet the immediate needs in your next lesson with the class. Discuss with your tutor how you can begin to address the longer-term needs. Record this in your professional portfolio for later reference.

SUMMARY

Good observation of movement in PE demands an awareness of how individuals move in different physical activities. Your acquisition and development of skills of observation of movement can be aided and extended through having/acquiring a substantial knowledge and understanding of the activities you teach. It is also essential for you to develop your knowledge of the supporting disciplines of biomechanics, kinesiology, physiology, psychology and sociology which you may have studied in your degree course. You need to use these disciplines to compare, interpret and analyse your observations so you can plan appropriate programmes of work for your pupils. Observation is a continuous process. What you observe increases the knowledge which you apply to your teaching, creating a more effective learning environment for your classes.

FURTHER READING

Schmidt, R.A. (1991) *Motor Control and Learning: A Behavioral Emphasis* (2nd edn), Champaign Ill.: Human Kinetics Books.
A theoretical book, but it contains information relevant to developing observation of movement and teaching skills. See specifically Chapters 9, 10, 13 and 14.

5 Communicating in PE

INTRODUCTION

This chapter is concerned with effective communication in PE. Clearly, communication is crucial in all teaching. Without communication teaching cannot take place and poor communication leads to garbled and incomplete messages which result in inadequate learning.

Each subject makes specific communication demands. The PE teacher has to contend with a variety of contexts (classroom, gymnasium, sports hall, playing field), and must also recognise the intrinsically practical nature of the subject. Non-verbal signals and demonstration are both important elements in the PE teacher's communication repertoire and although good use of spoken language is essential, over-talking is unforgivable because it can deny the pupil valuable activity time. Explanations and instructions should be succinct. You have almost certainly had the experience of listening to a teacher droning on when what you wanted to do was to get going on a physical exercise. Pupil talk can also be used effectively in PE lessons to deepen and extend learning but, again, talk must not dominate in practical sessions where your duty is to get the class moving. Pupils also use the non-verbal channel, and signals they send, either intentionally or unintentionally, are picked up by a perceptive teacher and the information gleaned is used to improve lessons.

PE like all subjects has its own technical vocabulary and part of the pleasure of being an expert in a subject is knowing subject-specific words and phrases and using them with other experts. Most pupils, however, are not experts and your teaching language must not confuse them. Of course, if you have GCSE or GCE A level classes they will expect to hear subject language, but with a year 7 group, for example, you must use a way of speaking appropriate to their level of understanding. If you are going to include a technical term, it must be carefully explained or have an obvious meaning in context.

OBJECTIVES

At the end of this chapter you should have:

- a good idea of the quality and flexibility of your voice;
- realised the importance of non-verbal communication in PE teaching;
- understood the role of teacher language in the teaching and learning of PE;
- understood the role of pupil language in PE lessons.

THE PE TEACHER'S VOICE

As a PE teacher you need a good voice which can be adapted to a variety of settings, some of which are difficult and demanding. It is sensible to get to know what your voice sounds like by recording yourself talking on a decent tape recorder.

TASK 5.1 YOUR VOICE

Record yourself reading a piece of text in a natural voice or having an ordinary conversation with a friend. If you have not heard yourself on tape before, prepare for a shock. You may sound quite different from what you expect. Remember though that you hear your voice coming 'back' from your mouth whereas most people hear it coming 'forward'.

Listen to your voice positively and discover your strengths. Is the tone pleasant? Do you vary the pitch to give interest? Do you sound like a friendly individual?

Vary the recording context to include different spaces where you teach. How do you sound in the gym?, the sports hall?, outside?

When you have become accustomed to the sound of you speaking and have grown to like what you hear, think about the ways you could vary your voice. You can experiment with:

- pitch;
- speed;
- pause;
- stress;
- volume.

All of these variations have an effect on the pupils you teach. A high voice generates more excitement; a deep voice is calming. Speed can give pace to a lesson, whereas a slow delivery has the opposite effect. If you are teaching gymnastics with a large class using apparatus in a small space, you may choose to speak slowly to create a safe, careful environment. A speedy delivery might be needed with a small group in a sports hall if you want to create enthusiasm and evoke an energetic response.

Your normal voice can vary considerably in pitch without discomfort. A lower voice is usually better indoors whereas a higher tone will carry better outside.

You can find more information about use of voice and language in Capel, Leask and Turner, (1995, unit 3.1).

Pause can be an effective strategy for teachers. Very often, instead of allowing a brief silence, a teacher uses a filler like 'er' or 'um'. One filler, much loved by PE teachers, is 'right', said with purpose and emphasis. There is nothing wrong with that but over-use of the same filler can be damaging. Pupils may concentrate on how many times you say 'right' and could ignore any important points you make.

Pause is also valuable as a gentle form of discipline. If you are talking to the class and a pupil is not listening, a pause in your delivery linked to a pointed look can bring the offender onside.

Stress is a useful tool as well because it is a way of highlighting important information. Stress must be used sparingly though. It is tiring to listen to somebody who is continually stressing words. Instructions about safety and key elements in a skill can be stressed so they stand out from the normal more relaxed delivery. This 'baseline' voice should be audible, pleasant to listen to and unforced.

Pupils often take more notice of how something is said rather than what is said. If you praise a pupil but deliver the praise in a flat unenthusiastic way, the pupil will not be convinced you mean it. Equally, if you discipline someone, your voice should indicate firmness or displeasure at some bad behaviour.

It is obviously vital that what a teacher says is audible and audibility is sometimes linked to volume. PE teachers have to cope with large spaces and classes outside where wind and traffic noise compete. A simplistic deduction suggests that you should shout or roar to be heard by your pupils. It is certainly helpful to have volume available if needed, but audibility is based on a number of factors. If you have a lot to say to your class, then they should be close to you not dispersed. You should always position yourself so all the pupils are in front of you. It is very hard to hear somebody whose back is to you. In general, if you are behind somebody, audibility is reduced by 75 per cent.

If you do have to talk to a scattered class, you must first ensure that they are quiet and attentive. You then use good projection to make yourself heard by the pupils furthest from you. Projection involves careful enunciation and a concentration on reaching the remotest pupils by pushing the voice out with conviction. This sounds somewhat painful, but good projection becomes a habit and then it is easy to make even a whisper carry a long way.

Sometimes, even when pupils are gathered round, you have to gain silence by a loud 'quiet, please'. Once, you have silence, the golden rule is not to shout into it. Moderate your voice and speak naturally to the class. You do not want to become the sort of PE teacher who **always** speaks loudly even in social settings.

TASK 5.2 VOICE VARIATION

It is worth while practising voice variation. Use a tape recorder to explore pitch and speed variation. Read a passage from a book and use pause for effect. Add stress to highlight certain words or phrases. You will probably feel silly doing this but the practice is invaluable. It has been said that somebody who can tell a story well will make a good teacher. This may be an exaggerated claim, but certainly an expressive and flexible voice is a tremendous asset in teaching.

You should also use real lessons for voice practice. A radio microphone would be ideal but you could ask your tutor to concentrate on your use of voice during some lessons and to provide you with feedback. You want positive comment as well as suggestions for improvement.

NON-VERBAL COMMUNICATION

Non-verbal cues are very important in communication. Just consider the power of a smile or a pat on the back. We are sending non-verbal cues the whole time, both intentionally and unintentionally. You are making decisions about what messages you want to send to others when you choose your clothes in the morning; when you decide to grow a beard; when you change the colour of your hair. As a PE teacher, you have a central role in health education so if you smoke or are noticeably overweight, you could be transmitting messages non-verbally which contradict your verbal promotion of a healthy lifestyle.

What you wear is noticed by the pupils. There is not one right way to dress as a PE teacher but it is sensible to wear a different colour from the pupils so that you can be quickly located if necessary. A smart turnout obviously creates a different image from that produced by a rather scruffy appearance. You might also like to consider whether you should wear PE kit in a classroom lesson, although changing can be difficult if you have a tight timetable schedule. How would you feel about a teacher covering a PE lesson wearing a suit? How would the pupils react?

TASK 5.3 THE CLOTHES YOU WEAR

Consider what you wear when you are teaching and what messages the various outfits might send to the pupils. You might like to compare what you wear with other PE staff and, more widely, with other teachers in the school. There is no suggestion here that there is a right or wrong way to dress in school, but dress is an area of choice and you have some control over the messages sent. You may also find that your headteacher or head of department has views about what you should wear in different school contexts, for example in PE lessons, in classroom lessons, at parents' evenings.

Gesture is another non-verbal tactic used by all teachers, but especially by PE staff. Gesture can emphasise points being made verbally and it is common for gesture to translate into partial demonstrations. Watch someone teaching swimming exemplify arm movements, often with exaggeration for greater effect. Hands are often employed to show how the feet should be moving in a particular stroke. The use of gesture also shows pupils how involved the teacher is in the lesson and how committed to their improvement.

Body hold and posture can also send strong signals. Pupils may receive these subconsciously, but the effects can be dramatic. If you look tense, you may communicate that tension to the class or indicate to potential troublemakers that you are nervous and expecting problems. The ideal body hold is relaxed but purposeful, confident but not cocky, approachable but not weak.

TASK 5.4 OBSERVATION OF PEOPLE

Observe people generally and teachers particularly. You might like to compare notes with somebody else. What can you learn from the way people hold themselves? Contrast confident and insecure individuals.

What are the clues to make such judgements? Can you get any tips from others which could help you improve? Obviously, you cannot change your personality by flicking the fingers but there are a host of adaptations possible which, while not making you a different person, enable you to improve your self-presentation.

Facial expression is also a strong indicator. Your normal expression should convey confidence, purpose and reliability. Smiling and laughing are not taboo, but too much obvious humour and affability early on with a class can make the pupils see you as 'soft'. It does no harm in the early encounters with a class to be firm and serious in demeanour and to relax gradually as you become secure in your basic authority. See Chapter 7 for further information about smiling and use of humour in your lessons.

Gaze is another element of non-verbal communication and eye contact can send a variety of messages. If a pupil is misbehaving mildly, then eye contact allied to a slightly disapproving expression can sometimes be enough to stop the misbehaviour.

When you are talking to a group in a classroom or gathered round you in a large space, you need to spread eye contact widely. You should not dwell for long in one contact unless you have a specific message to send. Equally, you should not avoid eye contact with any pupil. Avoidance sends out a message of rejection or apprehension, either of which can cause subsequent problems.

TASK 5.5 YOUR NON-VERBAL BEHAVIOUR

Ask your tutor to observe your non-verbal behaviour in a particular lesson. How do you hold yourself? How do you use gesture?, facial expression?, gaze?, eye contact? Are you transmitting appropriate non-verbal messages?

Use the feedback to improve your non-verbal behaviour and monitor the improvement by asking your tutor to observe you again.

Again, there is more information on non-verbal communication in Capel, Leask and Turner (1995, unit 3.1).

As a PE teacher you often patrol a large area where pupils are working in groups. As you move, the proximity pattern with the pupils changes. The influence of the teacher increases with proximity and it is noticeable that teachers sometimes spend more time closer to some pupils than others. The reasons may vary. One teacher may avoid the badly behaved pupils; another may be nervous of the able group; a third may prefer to be nearer to pupils of the same or the opposite gender. A confident teacher, however, moves freely around the class sharing proximity democratically without fear or favour. See also 'Positioning yourself in a PE lesson' in Chapter 6.

If you get too close to somebody, you invade personal space. This may well be interpreted as a statement of intimidation or affection so you need to be very careful not to make such an invasion unless you have a clear idea of why you are doing it.

Touching is the ultimate proximity. Touch is a potent non-verbal tool and if used with sensitivity can be highly effective. A hand on the shoulder can transmit strong approval, and teacher support in gymnastic exercises or scrummaging practice is reassuring. Research shows that even casual and almost imperceptible touch is a powerful tool in achieving a positive response from individuals. You must remember though that touch is subject to strong taboos. You must be very careful when touching pupils that you are aware of the restrictions implied by their gender or culture. This particular sensitivity is important in the PE teacher who goes into changing rooms; who meets mixed groups in brief clothing; and whose role can present valid opportunities for physical contact with pupils.

One particular non-verbal instrument used regularly by PE teachers is the whistle. The pupils should be taught that a blast on the whistle demands an immediate response of still and silent attention. It is effectively a discipline signal but it does not appear to be a statement of the teacher's will and is therefore less likely to produce rebellion. The pupils are already conditioned to the whistle's authority when used by a referee or police constable. In dance lessons, a drum can be used to similar effect. You can indicate that silent stillness is a dance skill and use a drumbeat as a non-verbal command to freeze. Again the class will not see this as an order from the teacher.

TASK 5.6 YOUR MOVEMENT IN A LESSON

Ask your tutor or another student teacher to observe a sequence of lessons and plot your movement around the space where you are teaching. What do the results tell you? Do you have a favourite spot where you stand most of the time? Do you avoid certain pupils? Do you prefer to be close to particular pupils?

Once you have considered the results, think what effects your movement patterns might have on the class. How might you change your habits to improve?

The whole topic of non-verbal communication is fascinating and many would claim that using the non-verbal channels with competence and sensitivity almost guarantees successful teaching. The Argyle book included in the Further Reading section of this chapter gives more information.

THE TECHNICAL LANGUAGE OF PE

Like all disciplines, PE has its own specialist language. This language is invaluable because it helps experts in PE to communicate succinctly with each other. Part of the development of any discipline is this accumulation of specific terminology.

PE teachers are familiar with the words and phrases of their subject, but their pupils may not have met the vocabulary before or may have only a hazy idea of what the various terms mean. These should be introduced gradually and explained or, better, exemplified in practical situations. If the class see a lay-up shot performed and labelled, they will have learnt the phrase and the meaning in the most effective way. Of course, many will need to have the learning reinforced by questions or repetitions.

TASK 5.7 TECHNICAL LANGUAGE

Select one activity which you are teaching (for example, cricket or gymnastics) and make a list of technical terms associated with that activity. Do not forget that you are an 'expert'. What seems to have an obvious meaning to you, may well be much less obvious to a pupil in year 7 (for example, a straight drive or a head stand). When you have completed your list, which in both the activities cited would be very long, consider how you might explain the terms to pupils. With a verbal description? By a demonstration? By use of a diagram?, a video? Try this out in one of your lessons teaching this activity.

TEACHING THE LANGUAGE OF PE

PE covers a range of activities taught in a variety of contexts and each particular blend of activity and context should have an effect on your use of language. One of the simplest polarities is indoors/outdoors. If you are teaching a games lesson outside on a cold winter's morning, your instructions and explanations must be concise. It might even be advantageous to consider how much of your verbal input could be given in the changing rooms beforehand.

Some activities taught in PE (for example, swimming) are very skills-based and also potentially dangerous. The swimming pool is also a difficult setting acoustically. Language is likely to be command-style in tone and wording, associated with a strong motivational element – praise linked to skill acquisition.

Dance, on the other hand, is about creative movement, and the risk factor in a well-ordered class is small. This does not mean that as a teacher you have a licence for verbosity, but your language is likely to be more expressive, based on stimulating description and open questions aimed at encouraging diverse responses.

Chapter 17 gives examples of language appropriate to the process of learning in PE, specifically developing pupils, ability to plan, perform and evaluate.

Questioning is a universal feature of teacher language in all subjects. Research studies (for example, Wragg, 1984) have shown that the average teacher can ask up to 400 questions a day. The majority of these will be checks on knowledge recall. For example:

- How many players are there in a volleyball team?
- What do we call a tennis shot made before the ball bounces?

In a PE lesson, the response to such questions could be linked to a pupil movement or demonstration. For example:

- Which part of the foot do you use to pass the ball?
- At what point do you release the discus?

All the questions quoted above are closed; there is only one correct answer, which the pupils should already have been taught. It is unfair to regularly ask pupils closed questions on topics they have not covered.

There are other questions you can ask which demand more thought of the pupils. It is not sensible to make all the questions you ask searching because if you do lessons move slowly. However, in one-to-one contexts and as pupils progress in PE, you will want to make them think and you might use evaluative questions like:

- What do you think is more effective – the cross cut back to the forwards or the pass lofted forward to them?

or questions which call for understanding like:

- Why do you pass with the side of the foot not the toe?
- What is the point of the follow through?

TASK 5.8 POSING QUESTIONS

You will need help on this task. Ask your tutor or another student teacher to observe one of your lessons and to write down all the questions you ask. This is not easy and some are likely to be missed. That does not much matter because the record obtained should still give you a flavour of your questioning approach.

Check how many questions you ask and what type of questions they are. Who answers them? You? Nobody? A range of pupils? Just one or two pupils?

You might also like to carry out a check on the amount of time you talk in lessons by getting your observer to use a stop watch. This might seem a fairly crude measure, but it gives you an idea of how much you talk and whether you may want to try and reduce the input. Of course, some talk is to static pupils (for example, giving instructions) while some is to active ones (for example, giving feedback to pupils while working on a task). You might like to differentiate these.

The protocol of answering questions needs to be defined and enforced. Some teachers ask named pupils and redirect unanswered questions to other named pupils. Another technique is to ask a pupil who puts a hand up. The problem with using this strategy is that some pupils never put their hand up and others do so without knowing the answer because they wish to be seen as keen or knowledgeable.

Pupils also ask you questions. Sometimes a brief response suffices. In some instances, you can relay the question to the class and get them to think about possible answers. On occasion, the question will be a challenge to your authority and you will have to use techniques like humour or deflection.

WRITTEN LANGUAGE IN PE TEACHING

Because PE is seen as a practical subject involving a great deal of movement from teachers and pupils, talk can be seen as the exclusive medium of teaching. This would be a pity because there are many instances where the written word is useful. If there is a whiteboard or an overhead projector (OHP) in the gymnasium or sports hall, you can write up the key teaching points or the elements of a practice for pupils. Transparencies can be prepared beforehand and filed for individual or department reference. If you are writing in the lesson, you need to develop a clear boardwriting style. Diagrams can also be drawn or displayed. A flexible jointed figure can be used on an OHP to illustrate body positions.

Of course, with examination classes there is more emphasis on writing. You have to develop an acceptable boardwriting style – clear, neat, even and of a size which can be read by a pupil at the back or one with poor sight. Avoid misspellings. If you are not sure of a word, check it before the lesson. Your pupils should also be encouraged to write accurately and accessibly.

Many PE teachers use work cards and these can be valuable resources. It is important that they are well-presented and preferably laminated to last. You should check your spellings and grammar. Written materials can also be valuable in wet weather lessons, or with pupils who are not participating in lessons or who are off school for an extended period. Again, get into the habit of filing all your materials for easy access.

Another writing task for you as a PE teacher is the production of notices. Again, the clarity, correctness and presentation quality are all important and the notice board in a PE department sends out non-verbal messages to pupils and visitors to the school (like OFSTED inspectors). Are they the messages you want?

TASK 5.9 USING WRITTEN LANGUAGE

In one of your next indoor lessons, see if you can use a whiteboard or OHP to illustrate and extend your teaching. You might want to list the sections of the lesson, stress the teaching points or put up some pupil ideas.

Ask your tutor or another student teacher to watch and comment on how the tactic worked. Did you seem easy with the writing role? Was your writing clear? Did the pupils react well? Did any look at what was written later to check? How could you improve your use of the board or OHP in future? Practise these and try to incorporate them into the next lesson in which you use a board or OHP.

PUPIL TALK IN PE LESSONS

Pupils inevitably talk in all lessons. It is part of the socialising process. They talk subversively when the teacher is not watching, but it is clearly better to channel the need to talk into a constructive channel. Silence, of course, is important too. Pupils should watch a demonstration in silence and they should not talk when the teacher is giving instructions or explanations. You should not start talking until all pupils are silent and attentive.

Some activities taught in PE make pupil-to-pupil talk very difficult. Pupils in the swimming pool tend not to talk to each other because the setting makes that difficult. They might squeal when they enter the cold water or shout with the pleasure of the experience. A strenuous game of football or hockey can also make pupil conversation difficult. Language tends to be used to call for the ball or to indicate the proximity of an unseen opponent. Indeed, if you find that there is a lot of pupil chat going on not related to the activity, you might need to condition the game in some way to increase the participation level.

Pupil talk, however, is a valuable part of PE. Talk can be used in a variety of ways to assist learning and deepen understanding.

One obvious way for pupils to learn is by asking the teacher questions; but they are generally reluctant to do that. Asking questions can make a pupil seem 'stupid' and could be interpreted as 'creepy' behaviour by the pupil's peer group.

Answering questions can help learning, especially if the pupil is encouraged by being given time to think and if initial answers are followed by further probing. Such a process is best done at an individual or small group level and can be time-consuming. It is to be encouraged and all pupils should benefit from such focused attention from time to time, but the reality of PE of teaching in large spaces where vigilance is essential means that it cannot happen more than once or twice a lesson.

Discussion is the most available form of pupil talk to encourage learning. A number of activities can benefit from pupil discussion – the construction of a group sequence in gymnastics; a problem-solving exercise in outdoor education; the planning of a dance to given music. All of these inevitably demand pupil interaction with ideas being voiced; perhaps tried practically; then adapted and developed with the help of further discussion.

The problem for you as a PE teacher in such situations is to control the balance between talk and physical activity and to ensure that the talk is task-directed and not merely social.

The make-up of a group is important. Friends may work well together and discuss productively; they may, however, be tempted to chat as friends do. A mixed ability group may operate effectively, but there is the danger of the able being held back and the less able being ignored. There is no formula guaranteed to achieve results. You must monitor the progress of groups and mix and match accordingly. Remember though that if you define a number of groups over a period of time there will probably be a marked reluctance to change that system. If you want flexibility tell the pupils that you intend to vary groupings, and establish the principle by making regular changes.

Another important factor in achieving a good discussion environment is the clarity and nature of the tasks set. Imprecisely defined tasks lead to woolly and unfocused discussion. That does not mean that all tasks need to be closed. PE has a number of areas which demand open-ended tasks, especially with older and more experienced pupils. But open-ended tasks can still be couched in precise accessible language thus: 'This music is called "The Market Place". Listen to it carefully and then work out in your group what is going on in this market. Use your ideas to make up a dance to fit the mood and rhythm of the music.'

TASK 5.10 GROUP TALK

Plan to have a group task in one of your next lessons. Your specific observation task is to check on the discussion pattern of individual groups. Is there a dominant pupil? Is there a non-contributor? Is talk task-focused? Is there enough physical activity? Should you think of re-jigging the groups next time to improve the quality of discussion? How can you improve the quality of the discussion in the groups in future? Discuss this with your tutor and try to put any changes identified into practice.

In PE, talk has a valuable role in testing hypotheses, suggesting tactics, exploring the consequences of physical initiatives. The imagination is an important element in successful physical activity and, although skills learning is fundamental, pupils should be encouraged to use their imaginations, to make suggestions, and, where possible, to test ideas in practice.

Reciprocal learning can be used to good effect in PE lessons. The pupils work in pairs with one acting as the teacher and the other as the learner. The 'teacher' needs to be clearly briefed about the nature of what is to be learnt. The skill may need to be broken down and teaching points given. The best way to do this may be a work card. Inevitably, this process involves pupil talk, with the 'teacher' giving instructions, providing feedback, and praising effort and competent performance. See Chapter 9 for more information about teaching strategies.

When pupils are engaged in group tasks and are talking constructively about what they will do, the teacher has a monitoring role. It is important to give the groups some initial time to get their ideas going. If you intervene too quickly into a group, you may hinder rather than help. Your job is to assess when a group has stalled or broken down and to help by question or advice.

AN EXAMPLE OF COMMUNICATION AND ITS LINKS TO OBSERVATION: DEMONSTRATION

It is said that 'a picture is worth a thousand words', which suggests that we, as sighted people, gain much information through our eyes. In practical subjects such as PE good demonstration is an invaluable teaching aid. There are many reasons why demonstrations are used – for example, to explain, to encourage, to enforce and to evaluate. The following examples show some of the reasons for which you could use demonstration in your teaching:

- to **swet a task**. This is usually better than just a lengthy verbal explanation and is very economic on the teacher's time. A good strategy is to set up the activity with one group while the rest of the class is working and then stop the class and show the demonstration;
- to **teach a new skill/activity**. For example, a push pass in hockey, dance step or a headstand, where you pick out specific features, teaching/movement observation points, such as where to place hands in relation to the head in a headstand;
- to **emphasise a particular aspect/help pupils' understanding**. For example, to show a change of speed, direction, flexibility, strength;
- to **improve quality/set standards**. The teacher pinpoints observations 'look at stretched feet . . .', starting, finishing positions, variety in movement, such as use of fingers in basketball dribble, to show what is expected;
- to **show variety**, especially to show **creativity** in gymnastics, dance, and different manoeuvres in games;
- to **reward improved/well done work**, especially by pupils or groups who are not outstanding but always work to the best of their ability and deserve recognition;
- to **stimulate/motivate**. To show pupils' flair, individuality, to motivate all pupils, to challenge more able pupils to be ambitious – for example to do a slice serve in tennis or a headspring in gymnastics;
- to **show completed work**. At the end of a unit of work you can show and reward individual pupil, pair, groups, half-class. Knowing they may be asked to demonstrate may stimulate pupils to work on quality.

There are many aspects you need to consider when setting up a demonstration, as Figure 5.1 illustrates.

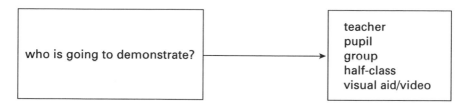

Figure 5.1 Who is going to demonstrate?

You have to decide **who** is going to demonstrate and **why**. Generally it is more motivating for the class if a pupil demonstrates, but it may be more appropriate for the teacher to demonstrate if a pupil is not capable, or if a new or difficult skill is being demonstrated. Consider which pupil(s) to ask to demonstrate. Remember not to use the same pupil(s) to demonstrate all the time. Do not always ask the most able pupil as this may demoralise the others. It is important sometimes to use an 'average' pupil to demonstrate. A group can show their expertise, or to save time half the class may demonstrate. Visual aids such as posters of good gymnastic movement, work cards for games tactics and video can also be effective tools to show good form and movement to a class.

Before you use demonstration consider some of the following:

- Have you asked the pupils if they mind demonstrating in front of a class?
- Do the pupils know what is expected of them? Have you briefed them, have they practised the demonstration, do they feel confident in demonstrating?
- What role is the pupil to take in the demonstration? You need to know your pupils, their strengths, for example, if they are taking on the role of the feeder in a practice.
- Is the situation safe?
- If they make an error let them try again, do not allow other pupils/yourself to laugh at the error.
- Always remember to praise; thank the demonstrators afterwards.

Should you demonstrate?

There are times when it is not wise to use demonstration, such as at the beginning of a lesson when the class needs to get tuned in and active quickly, or on a very cold day, or when the quality of the work is not good enough.

How can pupils get the most out of a demonstration?

In the examples of reasons for using demonstration above, the word 'show' is repeated and this indicates that a most important part of demonstration is **observation**, especially for the viewer (see also Chapter 4 on observing pupils in PE). In the case of the pupils who are 'looking at' the demonstration, they must **see** and **understand**. It is important to train pupils to **observe** intelligently by:

- directing the attention of pupil/class to particular aspects of the demonstration;
- asking questions about the demonstration;
- focusing pupils' attention on the quality of the work observed;
- helping pupils develop the ability to assess similarities, differences in the work demonstrated.

Figure 5.2 shows some of the things you need to be aware of for pupils **observing a demonstration**. The first priority is safety (Chapter 8 addresses safety). You must also consider the best position for the pupils to view the demonstration. A number of factors should be taken into account – for example, whether the demonstrator is right or left handed, the position of the sun if outdoors (you should be facing/looking into the sun, with the sun behind the pupils so that they can see the demonstration), or whether there are any distractions (pupils should not be facing any distractions, therefore should have their backs to another group or to a classroom). You also need to consider the speed of the demonstration (beginning slowly) and that some pupils may need to see the demonstration more than once.

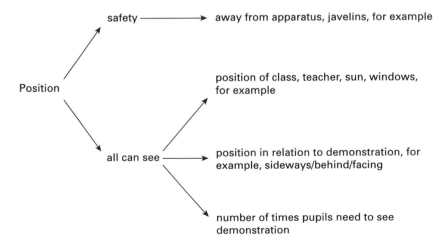

safety ───────► away from apparatus, javelins, for example

Position

position of class, teacher, sun, windows, for example

all can see ───────► position in relation to demonstration, for example, sideways/behind/facing

number of times pupils need to see demonstration

Figure 5.2 Observing a demonstration

Before you set up the demonstration consider the environmental conditions, especially whether they affect pupils' ability to **hear the demonstration** (see Figure 5.3). Is it very windy? if so bring the group up to you. As you give the demonstration also state the most important teaching points in clear, concise language. Always remember to follow up the demonstration with question and answers and positive feedback on the pupils' performance.

You also need to **focus the pupils' attention** on a specific aspect of the demonstration (see Figure 5.4) so they are sure about what they are looking for. This is important in improving pupils' evaluation skills.

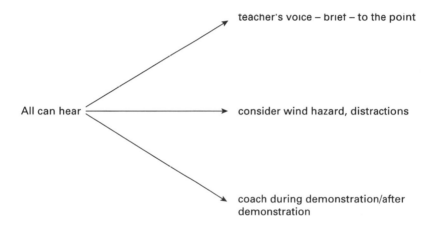

Figure 5.3 Hearing a demonstration

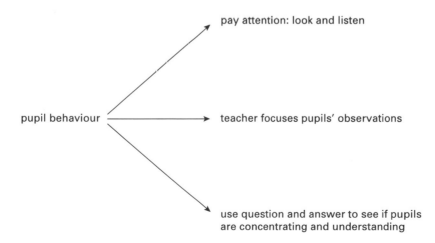

Figure 5.4 Focusing pupils' attention in a demonstration

TASK 5.11 OBSERVATION OF A DEMONSTRATION

Devise an observation sheet that focuses on the use of demonstration. Use the information above to identify the important aspects of demonstration that you want to be included on the observation sheet. You may want also to look at some of the observation sheets in Appendix 1 to help you develop this observation sheet. Ask your tutor to use this observation sheet to observe your use of demonstration in a lesson. Discuss the outcome of the observation with your tutor after the lesson and try to put into practice in future lessons what you learn from this experience. Also try to incorporate any feedback on the observation sheet into future observation sheets to aid your observation of teaching and learning.

It is important for you as the teacher to be knowledgeable and to be able to demonstrate well, because pupils imitate good practice in order to become more proficient; sometimes this process is called 'modelling' (see your sport psychology notes from your first degree for more information about this). Also remember that 'practice' makes 'permanent', so demonstrations do need to be 'perfect'!

SUMMARY

This chapter has explored language and how language is used in PE lessons. It has stressed the importance of:
an audible voice;

- a varied and flexible delivery which can adapt to different contexts;
- an understanding of your non-verbal communication;
- a sensitivity to pupil non-verbal cues;
- a careful use of the technical language of PE;
- the intelligent use of questions;
- care in responding to pupils' questions;
- the neat and accurate use of written language;
- pupil talk as a part of the learning process.

If you can develop these aspects of your communication you are well on the way to being a good communicator.

The chapter has also given one example of communication in practice: demonstration. We hope that you now appreciate how useful good demonstration can be to set up tasks quickly, to help pupils to understand the task and its value in the learning process. We hope also that you can see the importance of communcation and observation in demonstration, both individually and in relationship to each other. Communication and observation are important in other aspects of your teaching. You may want to consider these in relation to other teaching skills you use as you work through the next chapters of this book.

FURTHER READING

Argyle, M. (1988) *Bodily Communication* (2nd edn), London: Methuen.
This is a fascinating book which covers all aspects of non-verbal communication in a lively accessible way. It is not specifically aimed at teaching but it is full of valuable information. It also provides a useful bibliography.

Godefroy, H. and Barrat, S. (1993) *Confident Speaking*, London: Judy Piatkus.
This book gives some helpful practical tips about how to use your voice and language effectively.

Young, R. (1992) *Critical Theory and Classroom Talk*, Clevedon: Multilingual Matters Ltd.
This book provides some insights into how teaching language and teaching voice can affect pupil response to subject and teacher.

6 Lesson organisation and management

INTRODUCTION

The more time pupils spend 'on-task' (i.e. time in which pupils are engaged in motor and other activities related to the subject matter in such a way as to produce a high degree of success, and hence for lesson objectives to be met) the more opportunity there is for increasing physical development and physical competence. However, pupils also spend time in lessons on a number of other activities (for example, moving from one task to another, waiting and receiving information). In some lessons pupils spend little time actually on-task. This may be for a variety of reasons – for example, conjestion caused when pupils are asked to collect and put away hockey sticks in a cupboard with one small door or to listen to a long explanation from a teacher about a practice or instructions that are confused on a cold day, or because their behaviour is not managed effectively. Pupils are often more disruptive when they are not on-task. In order to maximise the time pupils spend on-task and to reduce the possibility of disruption, you need to consider how to minimise the time spent on these other activities. You can, for example, cut the amount of time pupils spend moving from one task to another by reducing the number of different tasks in the lesson or by having effective routines for the transition from one task to another. This requires you to be able effectively to:

- organise (people, the space, the equipment and time);
- establish rules and routines;
- manage the class; and
- maintain discipline.

Organisation and management should be integral parts of your lesson planning. In this chapter we look at some organisation and management skills.

OBJECTIVES

By the end of this chapter you should be able to:

- understand how to increase time on-task in lessons;
- organise people, the space, the equipment and time in lessons;
- establish effective rules and routines;
- manage pupils' behaviour and maintain discipline and control.

ACADEMIC LEARNING TIME IN PE

TASK 6.1 TIME SPENT ON DIFFERENT TASKS

Ask your tutor or another student teacher to observe one of your lessons and record the amount of time in which pupils are:

1 actively engaged in motor tasks (for example, practising a skill, playing a game);
2 actively engaged in non-motor learning tasks (for example, choreographing a dance with a partner or watching a video of particular skills being learned);
3 supporting others in learning motor activities (for example, holding equipment, supporting a partner);
4 moving from one task to another;
5 waiting;
6 receiving information;
7 engaged in other organisational tasks;
8 engaged in other tasks not contributing to the achievement of lesson objectives.

How much time is spent on each of these eight types of task (a) individually and (b) on 1 to 3, and on 4 to 8, respectively?

What is the relative percentage of time pupils spend working directly to achieve lesson objectives (1–3) and on other tasks (4–8) in the lesson? Do you think this is acceptable? Discuss these with the observer. Work to change the time allocation in your lessons if appropriate. Repeat this task later in your initial teacher education (ITE) course to check if the time spent on different tasks has changed.

Research on academic learning time-physical education (ALT–PE) has divided activity time in lessons into:

- that time in which pupils are engaged in motor and other activities related to the subject matter in such a way as to produce a high degree of success, and hence for lesson objectives to be met. This has been called time 'on-task', or 'functional' time (Metzler, 1989). It is often seen as a determinant of effective teaching in PE; and
- other time in which pupils are engaged in motor tasks but which is not time on-task – for example, the task is too hard or too easy or pupils do not apply themselves to learning (they may, for example, hit a shuttle over the net in a badminton lesson but not work to achieve the objective set, such as use a particular stroke or practice a specific tactic).

Siedentop (1991) reported results of research which show that these two account for, on average, 25–30 per cent of total lesson time. However, time on-task may account for only 10–20 per cent of total lesson time (Metzler, 1989). Siedentop also identified differences in the amount of time on-task in lessons in which different activities are being taught. Least time on-task was found in lessons in gymnastics and team games, with time on-task rising in lessons in individual activities and highest time on-task in lessons in dance and fitness activities.

TASK 6.2 REASONS FOR DIFFERENCES IN TIME ON-TASK IN LESSONS IN DIFFERENT ACTIVITIES

What reasons can you identify for differences in the amount of time on-task in lessons in different activities identifed above? Consider ways pupils spend their time in lessons – for example, organisational time, time waiting and receiving information.

   Discuss your reasons with another student teacher, along with the implications for you as a student teacher. Refer to these issues when your are preparing lessons in each of these activities.

Task 6.2 should have highlighted the interactions between different aspects of a lesson; for example, if you spend a great deal of time organising, the less time pupils can spend on-task. Hence, increases in time on-task in your lessons cannot be achieved without effective organisation.

At this point it should be emphasised that effective organisation and management enable your lessons to run smoothly, help to provide an effective learning environment and maximise the time available for learning, but themselves do not lead to an increase in learning by pupils. They must be accompanied by good teaching if learning is to be achieved. Below we consider organisation of the learning environment, management of pupils' behaviour and maintaining discipline and control.

TASK 6.3 ACADEMIC LEARNING TIME

Ask your tutor to complete the ALT–PE observation schedule (Siedentop, Tousignant and Parker, 1982) whilst observing a couple of lessons in which different activities are being taught to see if there are any differences in time on-task between lessons in different activities. This schedule can be found in Appendix 1 on page 300.

After each lesson reflect on the results and discuss them with your tutor, to inform your evaluation of the lesson(s) and to identify what you can do to increase time on-task in the lessons. You may be better able to undertake this part of the task after you have read the next sections of this chapter. Ask your tutor to undertake the same observations after you have had time to try to increase pupils' time on-task in the lesson. After all the observations compare the time on-task in lessons in different activities.

ORGANISING PEOPLE, THE SPACE, THE EQUIPMENT AND TIME

Before, during and after a lesson you need to consider organisation of:

- yourself;
- the environment/working space;
- the pupils/equipment; and
- the timing of the lesson.

Organising yourself

As the teacher you are expected to be a positive role model, therefore you need to organise yourself before the lesson begins. Your behaviour influences the pupils' behaviour, and aspects of self-presentation (addressed further in Chapter 7) are very important – for example, your time-keeping/punctuality affects the pupils' time-keeping and expectations.

An important aspect of organising yourself is obviously your planning and preparation of the lesson (see also Chapter 3):

> Evidence that you have thought carefully about your preparation
> and planning shows the care and effort you have taken over prepa-
> ration and this can have a major positive impact on pupils' sense that
> the teacher cares about their learning and the activities to be taken
> are worthwhile and important.
>
> (Kyriacou, 1991, p. 27)

Organising the lesson

The following is a check list for you, the PE teacher, for organising the
lesson *before* it starts. You should have:

- prepared the lesson. It is essential to plan each lesson well before it is
  taught as it is very important to have a clear understanding of what
  you want to achieve in every lesson you teach (see Chapter 3);
- marked homework. It is important that you meet deadlines and return
  homework with appropriate feedback for the pupils. This is also very
  important for pupil motivation (see Chapter 7);
- checked the working space. Is it available and safe for use? At the
  beginning of the day it is important to check your working space so
  that you have a smooth start to your lesson. It may, for example, have
  been used for evening classes and equipment (for example, badminton
  posts/nets) may not have been put away;
- checked and counted all equipment. Is it readily available and in good
  order? You may delegate this task to pupils in your lesson, but it is
  important to ensure the equipment is ready (for example, that basket-
  balls are inflated) for your lesson. Perhaps set aside a time in which
  this is done every week;
- established pupils' entry into the changing room. This should be
  orderly and quiet. Teachers establish their own routines; for example,
  pupils line up quietly outside the changing room (see Chapter 3). It is
  essential that you arrive on time to let pupils into the changing room;
- established routines for attending to such tasks as collecting pupils'
  valuables, excuse notes and giving out kit to pupils who have forgotten
  theirs. Routines prevent time being wasted at the beginning of a lesson;
- set work for pupils missing the lesson through injury, illness or other
  reasons. This may depend on the weather. If it is very cold it may be
  more appropriate for pupils to do some theory work indoors on the
  specific activity being taught. Each school/department has its own
  policies on such procedures;

- taken the register. This needs to be done without wasting too much time (for example, while pupils change or in the working space before the lesson starts);
- established routines for organising the taking out of equipment. There are many different methods for doing this (see later in this chapter);
- set a task from the work in the previous lesson so that pupils start working quickly. For example, in hockey, you can ask pupils to 'remember the practice of beating your opponent that we covered in last week's lesson; practice this when you get to the pitch'. Pupils can therefore start as soon as they are ready;
- have team lists, visual aids, work cards, spare whistles. As part of your preparation it may be advantageous to prepare team lists for when you move to the game section of your lesson, visual aids to give pupils more ideas, work cards to help pupils complete a task and spare whistles so that pupils can take on the role and responsibility of umpiring/refereeing in your lessons. This makes for smooth transitions and little wasted time;
- checked that all the pupils are out of the changing room and lock the door. Most changing rooms are locked for security. It is your responsibility to check that all pupils are changed and have left the changing room.

Can you add to the above list?

The rules and routines listed in Task 6.4 lead to more efficient use of your lesson time.

Organising the working space

From your first meetings with classes you need to establish your authority and your expectations and encourage pupils to use safe organisational routines within your lessons. You, as a PE teacher, work in many differing spaces – for example, gymnasium (confined), games field (large/muddy/cold/windy), swimming pool (confined, acoustics poor?, potential danger), classroom (confined, seating). Therefore you need to be aware of how best to use the specific working space to maximise safety (see Chapter 8), pupil involvement and efficiency.

Each space you are using has a working potential with specific space, walls, lines, markings, grids, apparatus, which you need to consider in planning and organisation (you should have collected such information on your preliminary visits to the school, see Chapter 1). The working

---

TASK 6.4 RULES AND ROUTINES IN PE LESSONS

Read the school and PE department rules for your school experience school, then discuss them with your tutor. Ask if there are any additional rules for specific activities you are teaching.

Examples of aspects of PE lessons for which routines are advantageous are:

- entering the changing rooms;
- taking the register;
- entering the working space;
- giving instructions;
- collecting equipment;
- moving into groups;
- starting work;

- gaining attention;
- changing;
- finishing a task;
- putting away equipment;
- leaving the space;
- leaving the changing rooms.

Can you think of any more? If so, add them to the list.

Observe different members of the PE department in your school experience school teaching lessons, specifically looking at the way they enforce the rules and what routines they have for those tasks and behaviours which occur frequently. How are the routines different? How are they the same? Why? How can you apply these in your lessons? You may want to use the observation sheets in Appendix 1 to help you with this task.

---

space should be utilised as appropriate for a specific lesson (for example, using grids for practices, setting up equipment for a circuit). If you are in a confined space using apparatus/equipment your organisation has to be planned carefully to ensure that:

- the environment is safe at all times;
- the apparatus is not too close to walls;
- you are aware where misplaced balls/shuttles may go;
- it accommodates large groups for activity (for example, badminton);
- equipment/apparatus is stored and accessible;
- you are using the space most effectively for the activity and the performers.

You also need to think very carefully about contingency plans, and adaptations to your lesson to suit any changed conditions you may find yourself in (for example, an outdoor lesson moved indoors due to weather).

These are general principles which apply and can be used in organising most tasks.

Some examples of how to use the available space are given in Figure 6.1 (progressions in groupings and use of working space in volleyball) and Figure 6.2 (organisation of your working space in netball). Examples of how to organise gymnastic apparatus for different themes are given in Appendix 2.

TASK 6.5 ORGANISATION OF YOUR WORKING SPACE

Design an indoor circuit for a class of 30 pupils for an activity and year group of your choosing. In your planning consider safety, activity levels for the pupils and methods of scoring pupils' results. After completing this task teach the lesson and use this experience to design further circuits.

Organising the pupils and the equipment

Before planning any lesson you need to know how many pupils are in the class and how much equipment/apparatus is available for a particular activity (for example, rugby, athletics or hockey), as this determines how you organise tasks/practices/games. It is important in your planning to develop strategies for grouping pupils and for organising the getting out of equipment in your lessons.

There are many reasons for specific groupings of pupils – for example, mixed ability groups where there are a wide range of abilities working together, or to promote leadership, co-operative skills, sharing and developing pupils' self-esteem, or same ability groups for specific activities such as swimming or having similar somatotypes for rugby. You may consider utilising the strengths of more able pupils to influence other pupils' performance, effort or behaviour in positive ways. It is important sometimes to use social friendship groups with older pupils to encourage motivation. It is your responsibility to devise methods of putting pupils into groups and to check that all pupils have a group, as the quiet, shy pupil may not tell you.

You need to plan how you develop the use of equipment and of pupils' groupings throughout the lesson (for example, developing from 1's to 2's or 3's; 2's to 4's or 6's; or 3's to 6's) so that there are smooth transitions and continuity to the lesson's structure. This is particularly important outside on cold days. In addition you must be prepared to adapt tasks and practices to accommodate one less or one more pupil. Alternatively you could set the pupils the task of doing this. Generally try and avoid the

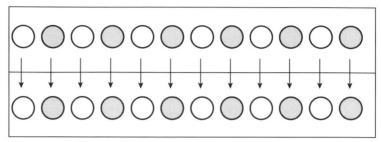

1 v. 1 warm up activity – volleying to partner over net down centre of space

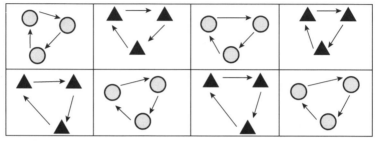

Into 3's – divide space equally. Set a practice for continuous volley, dig, etc.

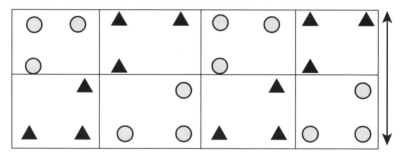

3 v. 3 – set up a conditioned game – serve, receive, set, spike, etc.

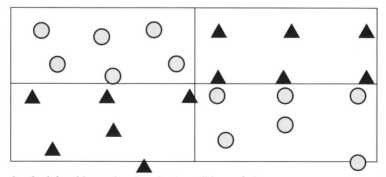

6 v. 6 – join with another 3 and set conditions of play

Figure 6.1 Progressions in groupings and use of working space in volleyball

Source: Adapted from National Coaching Foundation (1994)

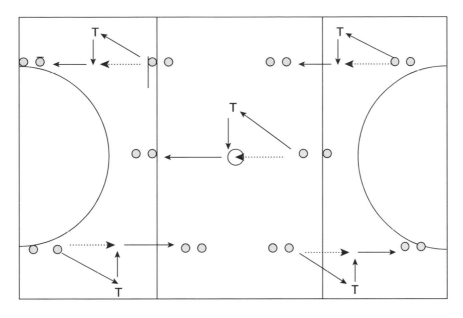

Organisation on netball court: 5 groups of 5 players

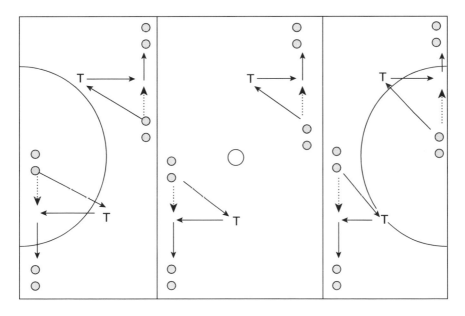

Organisation on netball court: 6 groups of 5 players

Figure 6.2 Organisation of your working space in netball
Source: Adapted from Crouch (1984, p. 123)

pupils picking groups, which can result in a lot of wasted time and poor self-esteem for some pupils as the following poem illustrates.

PICKING TEAMS
When we pick teams in the playground,
Whatever the game may be,
There's always somebody left till last
And usually it's me.

I stand there looking hopeful
And tapping myself on the chest,
But the captains pick the others first,
Starting, of course, with the best.

Maybe if teams were sometimes picked
Starting with the worst,
Once in his life a boy like me
Could end up being first!
(Ahlberg 1983, p. 35)

Some methods you may use for grouping pupils are:

- count heads as the pupils are warming up so you know the number in the class and can think of any adaptations you may need to make during the lesson;
- in 2's of similar height and build for a warm-up task;
- pupils jogging, teacher calls a number, for example, 2, 3, 5 or 7. Pupils quickly get into groups. Eventually the stated number go into first practice/apparatus/team group;
- if you know the class you may devise appropriate team lists/groupings/leaders before the lesson;
- into 2's, number yourselves 1 and 2, number 2 get a ball. Have balls in a designated area central to the working area;
- develop above practice to 4's with 1 ball. Join with another 2 and put one ball away as quickly as possible (the teacher may number pupils 1 to 4 and state a number, for example, 3, who puts the spare ball away);
- mixed ability – 28 pupils into teams of 7 – find a partner (into 2's), join with another 2 to make a 4 – in your 4's number off 1 to 4, all 1's together, all 2's together, all 3's together, etc., to form teams of 7.

Linked very closely to your groupings is the storage/use of equipment/apparatus in your lessons. If pupils learn when they are on-task, they should be given maximum opportunity to participate. This requires time spent (for example, on moving from one task to another, receiving information or waiting) to be kept to a minimum. Pupils learn little by practising a skill with one ball between a group of, say, ten pupils, as each pupil touches the ball very little during the practice. Count the number of balls (or other equipment) available and plan your tasks so that you use as much of the available equipment as you can, grouping pupils into as small groups as possible and cutting down on pupils queuing for their turn so that pupils have as many turns as possible, therefore giving them greater opportunity to learn.

TASK 6.6 ORGANISATION OF PUPILS AND EQUIPMENT I

Plan a games lesson for 30 pupils where each pupil can have a ball, implement or other equipment. Specifically highlight the development of your groupings, equipment, organisation throughout. Teach this lesson and record the outcomes of your thorough planning in your lesson evaluation. Try to correct any problems in the next lesson you teach with the class.

Your lesson should develop logically so that you are not putting away equipment and then getting it out again. Some general aspects to consider are where is the equipment stored and what are the best or most appropriate methods for getting it out and putting it away?
Some methods you may use are:

- first pupils ready take equipment out. Equipment is always counted;
- pupils line up outside store room individually, in 2's or other numbers and collect when told;
- certain groups always take equipment out, others always bring in;
- as numbers develop, any spare equipment (for example, spare hockey balls) must be put away for safety reasons. Have containers near to the working area to put these in. Decide how/who is to put these in;
- at the end of a games lesson make sure you organise, and make pupils responsible for, bringing in all equipment (for example, bins, cones, balls, posts and any other equipment).

There are general principles for organising equipment, but you should appreciate that you need specific rules and routines for organising equipment for each activity. In gymnastics, for example, pupils line up in 2's by the mat trolley, the first mat to go to the furthest part of the gym. Pupils should be made responsible for caring for the equipment and at all times safety procedures must be adhered to.

TASK 6.7 ORGANISATION OF PUPILS AND EQUIPMENT II

Observe several different teachers' lessons in different activities and record the processes they use to organise the pupils and the equipment. At the end of this task you should appreciate how important organisation is to smooth transitions in PE lessons.

Managing time

An essential item for all PE teachers to wear is a watch! Lessons can vary from 35 minutes to 70 minutes or longer. Planning how you use the time allocated to your lesson is vital in maximising learning. The tempo of the lesson should ensure logical, smooth transitions, avoiding over-dwelling on a particular task. When you are inexperienced it is sometimes difficult to judge how much time to spend on a task. This ultimately depends on the pupils' responses to your material, and you, as the teacher, must be aware of pupils who work at different rates. You observe pupils' responses and note whether they are on- or off-task (for example, because it is too difficult or too easy or because they have finished the task) and respond appropriately to this. Your response may not always be to change the task, but may be to give supportive feedback to help a pupil off-task to get back on-task. On the other hand, you may adjust your lesson plan after monitoring the class. During the lesson you also manage, for example, pupils' movement, noise levels and behaviour. The allocation of time in your lesson should allow time for:

- pupils to complete tasks and receive feedback from the teacher;
- pupils to use the apparatus and have time to put it away. It is pointless to get apparatus out in a gymnastics lesson if pupils do not then have enough time to use it effectively. At the end of your lesson you need to allow sufficient time to put the apparatus away safely, without hurrying;
- pupils to have a game if they have practised skills/small-sided games. Pupils need time to experience how well they can apply their earlier learning to a game situation. This may also inform you of the pupils' understanding of tasks set;
- pupils to complete a circuit and to collect scores. This again is important in giving feedback to pupils (see Chapter 9) and increasing their self-esteem (see Chapter 7) through completion and achievement of tasks set;
- you to give feedback about the lesson. It is important to highlight the

learning you hoped to achieve (for example, with a question and answer session) to conclude your lesson;
- you and the pupils to finish the lesson smoothly;
- the pupils to shower and dress after the lesson;
- you to ensure pupils are not late for their next lesson!

Positioning yourself in a PE lesson

Most teachers work in a classroom with seating and the teacher needs to plan the most effective seating for the task in hand. As a PE teacher, however, you work in many spaces without pupils in set places/seats. Good teacher positioning and movement is vital in establishing and maintaining learning, discipline, safety in your lessons (see also Chapter 5, p. 62). You need to position yourself so that your voice is audible, with the appropriate volume for the specific environment – for example, a swimming pool, a hockey pitch on a windy day or a sports hall with poor acoustics. You must always be aware of the whole class and avoid having your back to the group, standing in the middle of a group of pupils or having pupils behind you. Positioning is also important in monitoring. Good positioning enables you to observe effectively so that you can monitor, for example, pupils' progress or behaviour and give them feedback either as individuals, groups within the class or as a whole class (see Chapter 4 for observation of pupils in PE).

TASK 6.8 TEACHER POSITIONING

Ask your tutor or another student teacher to observe how effectively you position yourself when teaching three different activities (for example, gymnastics, swimming and outdoor games). At the end of this task you should be able to draw up a list of ways in which teaching position influences outcomes and appreciate how different activities in PE require different teaching positions. Try to use this knowledge to improve your positioning in your next lessons.

With experience you learn to vary your positioning by changing the class's focus and addressing the whole group from different positions so that **everyone** is always aware that you are nearby and can see them! Linked closely to this, it is important for you to devise ways of learning pupils' names so that you establish contact from wherever you may be in the working space. Refer to Chapter 7 and unit 2.3 in Capel,

Leask and Turner (1995) for further information about learning pupils' names.

Your positioning constantly changes depending on your working space and the purpose of a task (for example, setting up a practice or demonstrating). You need to be aware of your positioning in relation to the class and also of the class in relation to you, other groups, the sun and any other important factors. The following are some examples of the many different situations you experience when teaching PE and where effective positioning is important in your lesson organisation and management:

- when setting a class task you need to be able to see everyone and to ensure that all the class can see and hear you. This is much easier to do in a smaller indoor space than in an outdoor space. In your outdoor lessons define the working area for pupils (for example, refer to the use of lines on the court or pitch) so that you do not lose contact with your class;
- monitoring your class. This is best done from the perimeters (for example, from the corners of an indoor space, from the back of a tennis or badminton court). From your observations you are able to assess whether the whole class understands the task. If most of the pupils are doing one thing incorrectly or the task is too easy, you need to stop the whole class and give them some form of feedback (see also Chapter 9);
- when getting the equipment/apparatus out you need to establish set routines and give the class clear instructions. Then make the pupils responsible, standing back where you can see everyone and watching, only helping when and where necessary;
- helping individuals/small groups. Here you may be supporting a pupil in gymnastics or dividing your attention between several small 4 v. 4 football games. At all times you must be able to see the rest of your class. This is best achieved by monitoring from the perimeter and looking in towards the class;
- setting up a demonstration (see Chapter 5);
- when setting a class competition ensure that you are in a position, before you begin the competition, where your peripheral vision enables you to see all the pupils and to see who wins the competition;
- being near to a misbehaving pupil. It is important to circulate and be near to the trouble zone. Knowing your pupils and their names helps you control potential disruption (see Chapter 7);
- it is important to be aware of any pupils with special educational needs and the nature of their specific needs (for example, poor hearing or eye-

sight) so you can position them advantageously in your lessons (see Chapter 10).

MANAGING PUPILS' BEHAVIOUR AND USING DISCIPLINE AND CONTROL EFFECTIVELY

> Teachers are expected to be good classroom managers. Administrators often consider teachers who exert strong control to be their best teachers, while parents and the community expect students to be taught self-control. Likewise students expect teachers to exert control and establish a positive learning environment.
>
> (Cruickshank, Bainer and Metcalf, 1995, p. 393)

You may want to refer to unit 3.3 in Capel, Leask and Turner (1995) for an overview of managing classroom behaviour. Your colleagues, school management, parents and society expect you to manage pupils effectively. From experience of other student teachers, management skills are ones with which you are likely to be most concerned in your early school experiences. Without good management, pupil time on-task is reduced and you cannot concentrate on those aspects of teaching which promote learning.

The task of establishing discipline and control is particularly challenging in PE, both because safety is a key issue and because in relatively unrestricted spaces (such as a games field or sports hall) there is considerable opportunity for misbehaviour.

One way to approach discipline and control is to start from a positive standpoint. Rather than looking to avoid problems a useful goal is to set yourself the objective of keeping pupils on-task. Pupils who are on-task are both less likely to misbehave and more likely to master the intended learning obectives.

Keeping pupils on-task demands a range of teaching skills, many of which have been referred to in other chapters. For the purpose of this section we focus on three main areas:

- appropriate planning;
- effective management; and
- building positive relationships with your classes.

Appropriate planning

It is often the case that pupils look forward to PE as a lesson they enjoy and it might follow that we should have few problems with disinterested pupils. However, pupils' interest in a lesson depends, in part, on the tasks you have planned for them. If the work set is too simple or too demanding pupils' effort is likely to wane (see also Chapter 1). Alternatively, if your organisational planning has not been carefully thought through, and there are prolonged awkward episodes during which no productive work is going on, pupils' attention wanders. This could happen if too long is spent on organising pupils into groups/teams or if the setting up of apparatus is lengthy. Careful planning of the structure of the lesson, of material and of organisation, goes a long way to ensure that pupils are actively engaged in learning and not causing problems.

TASK 6.9 PUPILS' TIME ON-TASK

Ask your tutor or another student teacher to observe one of your lessons and identify six instances of pupils not being on-task. After the lesson:

1 discuss with the observer how the lesson plan could have been devised to avoid the problems; and
2 together, plan the next lesson using the ideas proposed in 1 above.

Effective managment

While planning is carried out prior to a lesson, management is what occurs during a lesson. In well planned lessons you spend less of your time managing and more time promoting learning. The first requirement for effective management is a clear and purposeful implementation of the lesson plan. Following this, the two key skills you need to manage a lesson effectively are vigilance and rapid response. With the goal of keeping pupils on-task it is essential that you know what is going on in all corners of a gymnasium, swimming pool or rugby pitch. Taking time to see clearly what is happening in the class as a whole is critically important.

When a task is first set it is essential that you stand back and check that your instructions have been understood and are being followed. While pupils are working on a task it is again essential that you survey the whole class regularly to see if they are all on-task. You must be in constant touch with what is happening in the lesson as a whole and avoid spending too long working with individuals and groups. Having added vigilance to your skills, what are you looking for and how might you respond?

Figure 6.3 usefully maps out the pattern of observation and response (the numbers which follow refer to numbers on the figure). In (1) all pupils appear to be on-task. You are moving round the working space monitoring what is going on (2). While all pupils are on-task (3) you proceed to provide teaching points and encouragement. However, should you see some pupils moving off-task (4) you need to respond rapidly with preventive teacher action (5). This response could simply involve your moving close to the off-task pupils or it could be a private or public reminder to the pupils of the task they should be engaged in. Alternatively, you could ask the off-task pupils a question or take time to help them with their movement. However, if monitoring (2) reveals that a good many of the pupils are straying off-task, a different response may be needed. Perhaps the task is proving too easy or too hard, maybe the class are ready for a change or are needing feedback from you as to how well they are progressing. Here the preventive action (5) is to stop the

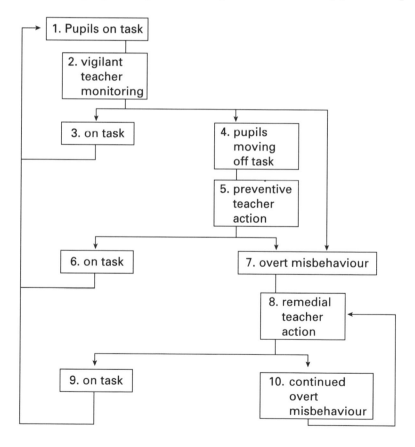

Figure 6.3 Pattern of observation and response in managerial behaviour
Source: Adapted from Morrison and McIntyre (1973)

whole class and redirect the work. Hopefully on-task behaviour (6) follows. If you do not pick up whole class problems it is very likely that passive off-task behaviour may turn into overt misbehaviour (7) by some pupils. Again rapid response is essential to avoid problems spreading to the whole class. It is useful to remember that there is some truth in the saying that misbehaving pupils are often telling you what others are too polite to say. So there are possibly, but not necessarily, two problems here: one the individual pupil and the other the nature of the whole class task. It is probable that you will have to repeat preventive action (5) with the whole class as above, but you must also enact a specific remedial action with specific individuals (8). This could be similar to that you effected when noticing earlier off-task behaviour of an individual, but it is likely to require firmer action. As far as possible avoid public confrontations and always identify the behaviour, not the pupil, as seriously out of order. Never resort to physical intervention. You may need to remove the pupil at once or require a private word with the transgressor after the lesson. An alternative is to issue a threat that a particular course of action will be taken if on-task behaviour is not resumed (9). This threat should be in line with school policy on punishment, but whatever the threat it must be carried out if overt misbehaviour persists (10). Whenever and whatever your response is throughout this whole cycle it is important that you stay calm. Adopt a stable symmetrical stance, an authoritative posture and a measured tone of voice. Give every impression that you expect to be obeyed.

TASK 6.10 MANAGING BEHAVIOUR

Ask your tutor or another student teacher to observe one of your lessons and tally the number of times you responded to observed problems in the categories 5, 8 and 10 in Figure 6.3. Discuss with the observer how effective your response was and what you can do in your next lesson(s) to increase your effectiveness.

Building positive relationships with your classes

While planning and management may be focused on an individual lesson, the relationship you have with a class develops over a number of weeks/terms. Building positive relationship with your classes is also addressed in Chapter 7.

When there is a positive relationship pupils feel secure and arrive at a lesson expecting to work, learn and be successful (see Chapter 7). Security results from the formulation and enactment of clear rules, routines and procedures. These are concerned with such issues as conduct on entering the working space, safety rules to be observed and clothing to be worn. Some examples are given in Figure 6.4.

Activity	Rule/routine/procedure
Gymnastics	No large apparatus to be used until it has been checked for safety by the teacher. No running at times when apparatus is being put out or dismantled.
Swimming	No one should enter the pool without permission. No running on pool-side. No screaming in pool.
Hockey	One short sharp whistle, stand still, face the teacher and listen.
Javelin	Always walk when carrying a javelin. Have the sharp end pointing down. Never throw unless given permission by the teacher.
Add your own for other activities	

Figure 6.4 Some examples of rules, routines and procedures

Security also results from the experience of fair, consistent and firm teaching, and from teaching which accommodates, as appropriate, the needs of individuals and of the whole class in particular situations (see Chapter 10). Pupils should not be afraid to come to you with problems before or during the lesson and, where appropriate, you should modify your demands on a particular pupil. A pupil may, for example, report it is her first day back after illness. She wants to take part but is worried she may tire. Another pupil has had her kit stolen for the third time and asks not to be punished for not having the necessary clothing.

SUMMARY

Although teachers of all subjects have to organise and manage their lessons, organisation and management in PE lessons need specific consideration as pupils are working in large spaces, using a variety of equipment, with limited time. All teachers need to be able to give clear, precise instructions and explanations, and PE teachers need to consider how they can give these to pupils who are not sitting in neat rows behind desks, but moving around in a large space, often at considerable distances from the teacher. As a PE teacher both organising and managing lessons effectively is especially important because of the safety implications of activities and the large space in which you work.

In an effective lesson as little time as possible should be spent on organisation and management. Although effective lesson organisation and management are clearly important, they are not everything and alone they are not enough. They can create the time when learning can take place and an environment suitable for productive activity, but you need to use that time effectively for learning to occur. Effective lessons are those in which the time pupils are on-task is maximised. The teacher has planned thoroughly what and how she is going to teach and how she is going to organise and manage the lesson (anticipating where problems are likely to occur in the lesson, having planned especially carefully for these but having contingencies for overcoming these should they occur). You must be careful not to focus too much on effective organisation and management (especially in the early stages of your school experiences), but see these as providing time and opportunity for effective teaching to occur.

FURTHER READING

Department of Education and Science and the Welsh Office (1989) *Discipline in Schools. Report of the Committee of Inquiry Chaired by Lord Elton (The Elton Report)*, London: HMSO.
This report is the outcome of an inquiry into discipline in schools in response to concern about the problems facing the teaching profession. It covers a wide range of aspects of the problem and contains examples of behaviour policies from schools.

Mawer, M. (1995) *The Effective Teaching of Physical Education*, London: Longman.
Chapters 6 and 7 in this book focus on aspects of organisation and management in PE lessons.

Siedentop, D. (1991) *Developing Teaching Skills in Physical Education* (3rd edn), Mountain View, Calif: Mayfield Publishing Co.
Chapters 6 and 7 focus on preventive class management and discipline in PE lessons.

Smith, C. J. and Laslett, R. (1993) *Effective Classroom Management: A Teacher's Guide*, London: Routledge.
This book considers many aspects of discipline in the classroom, from minor disruption to confrontation. It includes some very good case studies of how confrontations can occur and how they can be managed well, or, alternatively, how they can get out of hand. It includes a section on working with pupils with emotional and behavioural difficulties in mainstream classrooms.

7 Developing and maintaining an effective learning environment

INTRODUCTION

In this chapter we introduce you to aspects of your work as a teacher designed to create and maintain an effective learning environment to support other aspects of your teaching. We try to address questions such as: What messages are you sending to pupils? Do you convey messages that PE and learning are fun, that pupils can achieve the objectives of the lesson, that you care about pupils and their learning, and that you value your pupils as people? Do you send any hidden messages to pupils? Do your verbal and non-verbal communications send the same message? Are you enthusiastic? Do you convey this to pupils? Are your interactions mostly positive or negative? Are they consistent? Do you motivate pupils? Developing and maintaining a positive, supportive learning environment does not happen by chance, you need to plan for it.

TASK 7.1 WHAT MESSAGES ARE PE TEACHERS SENDING?

Read the situations below and identify what messages you think the teacher is sending. Discuss your perceptions with another student teacher. Record your findings in your professional portfolio to return to at the end of the chapter.

- a teacher arrives at the lesson dressed in a tracksuit that he wore to train for rugby the night before;
- it is a cold, wet day in the middle of January, the playing fields are waterlogged and cannot be used. The teacher sends the pupils on a cross-country run and returns to the changing room for a cup of coffee;
- it is a cold, but dry day, the teacher decides to take the class outside for a netball lesson. She does not allow the pupils to wear tracksuit trousers or gloves, but she wears a tracksuit and a thick ski-jacket;

- at the same time, another teacher is taking the pupils outside and although she does not allow them to wear tracksuit trousers or gloves she goes outside dressed in the same way as the pupils;
- in a high jump lesson the pupils are taking turns to jump over the bar. The height of the bar is increased at the end of every round. Pupils who did not jump the previous height are not allowed to have another turn at the new height, therefore sit at the side of the pit and watch as the lesson continues;
- the bell goes for the start of lessons after the lunch break. The teacher has been coaching the rugby team at lunch-time in preparation for an important cup game. He has not had any lunch, therefore goes to the staff room for some lunch whilst the pupils get changed and wait for him to start the lesson.

We have seen such scenarios in PE lessons. Most of these situations do not help to create a learning environment which encourages pupils' learning, but lead to the creation of a negative climate in the lesson. They also have implications for safety (see Chapter 8).

A positive lesson climate provides the most effective learning environment. There are many factors which contribute to establishing a positive lesson climate, including the self-presentation of the teacher and the presentation of the working space, the purposefulness of the lesson, the inter-personal relationships between teacher and pupils and between pupils, the motivation of pupils and the self-esteem of pupils. In this chapter we consider these aspects of your teaching. In developing these aspects of your teaching you use some of the skills identified in earlier chapters. You should therefore refer back to earlier chapters, where appropriate.

OBJECTIVES

By the end of this chapter you should:

- understand the importance of creating a positive lesson climate and an effective learning environment;
- appreciate some aspects of self-presentation that are important to PE teachers;
- appreciate how the appearance of the working space contributes to the lesson climate;

● understand some of the personal and inter-personal factors that influence this climate, including inter-personal relationships, motivation
and self-esteem.

DEVELOPING A POSITIVE CLIMATE IN YOUR LESSONS

A lesson with an effective learning environment has a positive climate.
What is the climate of a lesson? What do we mean by a positive climate? Why is this important? When we talk about the lesson climate
we are referring to the prevailing mood of the lesson. Pupils and their
learning are put at the centre of your lesson planning and delivery.
The lesson has a relaxed but purposeful atmosphere. Pupils are
expected to learn and to be on-task (see Chapter 6), supported by a
caring, enthusiastic teacher. The teacher uses a positive teaching style,
identifying and providing feedback on appropriate work, the positive
reinforcement motivating pupils to learn and enhancing their self-
esteem. Thus, much of the interaction in the class is positive, creating
effective inter-personal relationships. A climate is not positive if it has
all of the above, but no learning is taking place. You have, no doubt,
seen lessons in which there was a good atmosphere, but no learning
was taking place.

TASK 7.2 POSITIVE AND NEGATIVE COMMUNICATION

Audiotape one of your lessons. You may want to attach a
microphone to yourself to ensure you record all your
communications. As you listen to the tape answer the following
questions. Was your communication mostly positive or mostly
negative? Was there any pattern to positive and negative
communication, for example, positive when providing feedback:
about work but not about behaviour; to able pupils but not to less
able pupils; to boys but not girls? How did your pupils respond to
the communication? Discuss with your tutor the pattern of your
communication, your pupils' response and the implications of this.
Identify how you can increase the amount of positive
communication, if appropriate. Try to put this into practice in your
next lessons.

Your self-presentation: what impression do you create on your pupils?

TASK 7.3 AN EFFECTIVE PE TEACHER

Write down 12–15 adjectives or phrases that you might use to describe an effective PE teacher (for example, 'patient', 'well organised'). Underline all those that refer to how you might **present yourself** as a PE teacher. Compare your list with that of another student teacher doing the same task.

  Keep this information in your professional portfolio to refer back to in Task 7.5.

Teacher self-presentation always depends on the personality of each individual. However, it would be surprising if your list of adjectives or phrases to describe an effective PE teacher differed radically from that of another student teacher doing the same task. Such is the particular nature of the subject of PE that to be a successful teacher you need to exhibit key characteristics. These help you to gain the respect of pupils, motivate them to work and promote learning on the part of each individual.

First, a PE teacher needs to be **confident, authoritative** and clearly **in control of the situation**. These self-presentational attributes are necessary because you are working in a large space, at some distance from many of the pupils and in an environment that may contain safety hazards (see also Chapter 8). To retain your authority you must clearly convey an assured and business-like self-presentation. Appropriate and smart clothing are also essential (see also Chapter 5). You are in part an organiser and safety manager and your presentation must reinforce these roles.

Second, a PE teacher needs to be **energetic** and **enthusiastic**. While all teachers have to engage and interest pupils, you have to motivate pupils to expend considerable effort to gain most from the lesson. A lethargic teacher is hardly likely to have a dynamic and determined class. In everything you do, you need to be alert, lively and encouraging. Do you convey to your pupils your enthusiasm for your subject content, for them and their learning or improvement in performance to your pupils? How do you do this?

As an enthusiastic teacher you prepare each lesson thoroughly, plan learning tasks appropriate to the needs of individual pupils, arrive early for the lesson, provide a quick pace to the lesson, do not let minor interruptions interfere with the lesson. You have a positive approach and teaching style, smile a lot, praise pupils for effort or performance, give specific, positive feedback whenever possible and encourage pupils to achieve obtainable, appropriate and challenging objectives, and therefore develop a positive lesson climate. Further, you dress and act as though you are enthusiastic about, and participate in, physical activity yourself. It is also an advantage to be a positive role model in your skilful execution of movement skills, and it is certainly the case that teacher demonstrations can help to inspire and enthuse pupils. Although it is difficult to define precisely how enthusiasm is shown, as this is unique to each of you, it is important that as an enthusiastic PE teacher you convey your enthusiasm to the pupils; therefore enthuse and motivate pupils to participate.

Third, a PE teacher needs to convey in his self-presentation that he is more than an authoritarian, able sports person. The movement skills that are often the focus of the lesson are performed by the pupils for all to see, and so there is a danger of self-consciousness, as the pupils' very selves, their bodies, are the subjects of observation and comment. The work in PE is therefore of a very personal nature and you need self-presentational skills that demonstrate a dimension of **understanding** and **sensitivity**. Furthermore, you need to convey to the pupils that you are approachable, sympathetic and caring. The teacher should show both verbally and non-verbally, that concern for the pupils and their efforts are at the heart of the lesson. If, for example, you learn pupils' names quickly, you send a message to pupils that you care about them and their learning. However, it is not easy to learn pupils' names in PE lessons as they are not sitting at desks. We have experienced the difficulties ourselves. For example, in one school in which one of us taught, the pupils were taught swimming for the first half of the first term. All girls were required to wear navy blue costumes and swimming caps. Therefore, as a new teacher in the school a special effort had to be made to learn pupils' names. This was done mostly by talking to pupils at the beginning and end of lessons. Some of the techniques often used by teachers to learn names are difficult to apply in PE lessons, or in some activities in PE. It is suggested, for example, that pupils say their name when you talk to them or you set a goal of using pupils' names in, say, 50 per cent of interactions with them. It is difficult to hear what is being said in, say, a swimming pool or when pupils are scattered in a large area, therefore you need to find techniques appropriate for the situation. However, what is important is that as a student teacher you learn pupils' names.

TASK 7.4 LEARNING PUPILS' NAMES

As soon as you can, get a register of all pupils in your classes. Ask experienced PE teachers what techniques they use to learn names (see also unit 2.3 in Capel, Leask and Turner, 1995). Make a particular effort to learn the names of pupils in your classes as soon as you can. If one technique is not working, try another one until you have found a technique which works for you.

In Capel, Leask and Turner (1995), unit 3.1 addresses how to convey attributes of confidence, enthusiasm and involved sensitivity and unit 1.2 addresses the school's expectations of the student teacher, which relates closely to self-presentation. This unit also includes consideration of professionalism. It is certainly the case that your self-presentation should at all times demonstrate your professionalism.

TASK 7.5 EFFECTIVE SELF-PRESENTATION

Return to Task 7.3 and compare the three key features identified above (confident, authoritative and clearly in control of the situation; energetic and enthusiastic; understanding and sensitive) with your list and those aspects you underlined. Discuss with another student teacher how far you agree with the priority given to these three. Set yourself the challenge to convey these three attributes during your next week of teaching. Ask your tutor to give you feedback on your mastery of each.

It is worth taking time to check aspects of your self-presentation; for example, use of your voice, the clothes you wear, confidence, your non-verbal communication and your movement in a lesson (see particularly Tasks 5.1 to 5.6). You might also want to check other aspects of how you present yourself – for example, whether you have any habits or mannerisms such as brushing your hair back from your face whilst teaching, which may detract from your ability to communicate with pupils effectively. You might find pupils spending more time counting how many times you brush your hair back than they spend listening to you.

TASK 7.6 YOUR HABITS AND MANNERISMS

Early on in your teaching ask another student teacher or your tutor to videotape one of your lessons. After the lesson watch the videotape and try to detect any habits or mannerisms which could be distracting in lessons and prevent effective communication. Work hard to eliminate or at least reduce any such habits or mannerisms. Ask the same person to videotape another lesson after you have worked to eliminate any habits and mannerisms and see if there is any difference.

What impression do the PE facilities create?

The general appearance of the working space is also an important factor in creating an effective learning environment. You need to ensure that the space is clean and tidy and conveys care and attention to pupils and their learning.

It is obviously hard to keep working spaces clean and tidy if a large number of groups and teachers are using the space. This is made harder if the space is let to outside users. If you arrive for a lesson in a space which is untidy, it is worth tidying it up before the lesson starts. You should also mention this to your tutor so that she can talk to the person who used the space previously to prevent the same from happening again.

Each time you use the space you must check that it is safe (see also Chapter 8). This requires equipment to be well maintained and in good order. There should not be any equipment left in the working space. Likewise, as your lesson progresses, you should make sure that spare equipment is put away safely and not left lying around. Also ensure that equipment is put away properly after the lesson so that it is tidy and easily accessible and that the space and the changing rooms are left in a suitable state for the next group.

TASK 7.7 THE PE SPACES

Are the PE facilities in your school experience school attractive? Clean? Tidy? Well looked after? Do they invite participation? What can you learn that you can apply when you are in your own school? How can you create an attractive, motivating PE environment in your school? Record this information in your professional portfolio for reference when you are in your first post.

You can enhance the space by using neat, tidy and well presented visual displays such as posters, notices and results sheets. There are several books that you can refer to for advice on how to create good visual displays (the technical or library staff in your higher education institution (HEI) should be able to point you towards some). All of these help to create a positive feeling among pupils about the lesson.

Purposefulness of your lesson

In a purposeful lesson pupils expect to work, learn and be successful. In order to create a sense of purposefulness you, as the teacher, must create as much time as possible for learning (time on-task, see Chapter 6) and not allow time to be wasted. You can achieve this by good organisation and management skills (see Chapter 6) and establishing a good pace to the lesson. For example, make sure that pupils do not spend too long in the changing rooms before the lesson, that the lesson starts as promptly as possible and that your organisation enables each task or change of task to proceed smoothly and efficiently. You also create a sense of urgency in the lesson, encouraging pupils to do things quickly rather than dawdling; for example, pupils should run to the outside space in which they are working rather than walk along chatting to a friend. They should also have been set a task to start when they get there. Further, you should not allow the pace of the lesson to slow by, for example, taking too long to explain what pupils are to do next or to deal with a minor problem or unnecessary interruption such as a telephone call in the office (you must not leave a class alone to take a call).

TASK 7.8 PURPOSEFULNESS OF A LESSON

Observe two or three lessons taught by experienced teachers, focusing on the purposefulness of the lesson. For example, how long it takes for pupils to change for the lesson; what techniques the teacher uses and what she says to maintain a good pace to the lesson; how the teacher deals with unnecessary interruptions; how long it takes to move from one task to another and how the teacher keeps this time to a minimum.

How do these compare with your own lessons? Ask another student teacher or your tutor to observe one or some of your lessons in relation to the same points. Do you need to change your practice to create a more purposeful lesson? If so, how can you do this? Are there aspects of good practice you can adopt in your lessons? Try these out in your lessons.

Inter-personal relationships

In a lesson with a positive climate pupils are supported in their learning by a teacher who cares about them and their learning (see page 99). You need to know pupils personally in order to build up a relationship with them. You and your pupils must develop mutual respect for each other, accepting each other and valuing each other's viewpoints. All aspects of your teaching are important in showing you value pupils, including such aspects as questioning techniques. A teacher may, for example, ask a question such as 'how can you get over a box without putting your feet on it?' If you only want and accept one possible answer 'a vault', you may discount an answer from a pupil which answers the question but is not the answer you wanted. Hence, the pupil's answer is not valued and the pupil is not given the opportunity to make an effective contribution to the lesson.

You must not become too friendly with your pupils. We have seen some student teachers on their initial school experience adopting a friendly approach to their pupils and then they have not been able to establish their authority. You must maintain your status as a teacher so that your authority is not undermined and so that pupils do not lose respect for you. If you establish a good relationship with your pupils you can exert your authority when you need to.

Siedentop (1991, p. 132) identified the following components of good relationships:

- know your pupils;
- appreciate your pupils;
- acknowledge their efforts;
- be a careful listener;
- include pupils in decisions;
- make some concessions when appropriate;
- always show respect for pupils;
- show honesty and integrity;
- develop a sense of community, of belonging to the class.

As with all other aspects of your teaching you need to monitor your relationship with your pupils. You can do this by observing pupils' reactions to you and your lessons. If pupils get to class early, are enthusiastic, do things quickly and willingly, ask you questions to enhance their learning, follow established rules and routines, treat you and other pupils with respect, and help one another without being prompted, this suggests that you have or are establishing a good relationship with your pupils.

Being relaxed

In a lesson with a positive climate you are likely to be relaxed. If you are relaxed, your pupils are likely to be relaxed. When pupils are relaxed, they can concentrate on the learning tasks and are more likely to behave appropriately. When you are relaxed, you are more likely to smile, conveying that you are relaxed and sustaining the relaxed atmosphere already created. This can be aided by using humour effectively.

Using humour

As with other teaching skills, humour must be used appropriately. In the early stages of learning to teach you may wonder whether, when and how you should use humour. However, as you develop as a teacher, you should become more confident. Humour can be used to laugh at yourself when you have said or done something silly, to reassure a pupil who is anxious, to defuse a situation in which there is potential conflict, to laugh with pupils at something they find amusing (as long as that is appropriate for you as a teacher) – for example, a hockey ball breaks in two and the pupils laugh about which part to use.

Although using humour well can be effective, using humour badly can make lessons go badly wrong. You must not use humour at a pupil's, expense, for example. If you use humour too much pupils may see you as trying to be their friend, therefore you may become too familiar with pupils (see above). Thus, effective use of humour can help you to establish a positive climate in your lessons, but if you do not use it effectively it can destroy your working relationship with your pupils and undermine your authority. It should therefore be used with care and treated as a teaching skill to be developed as you do with any other skill.

TASK 7.9 LESSON CLIMATE

Observe two or three lessons, each taught by a different teacher. Focus on how the teacher establishes and maintains a positive lesson climate. Record aspects of both verbal and non–verbal behaviour and the responses of the pupils to this behaviour. Record examples of good practice in your professional portfolio so that you can incorporate some of them into your own teaching, where appropriate.

The Flanders Interaction Analysis System (FIAS)(Flanders, 1960) is an observation schedule which focuses on interactions between teachers and pupils and therefore measures classroom climate. The Cheffers Adaptation of the Flanders Interaction Analysis System (CAFIAS)(Cheffers, Amidon and Rogers, 1974) is an adaptation of this for use in PE lessons. This has been widely used in studies designed to describe the climate of the gymnasium. If you are interested in this aspect of teaching you may want to obtain a copy of the CAFIAS to gather information as the basis for an assignment on your course.

MOTIVATION

As a teacher you must try to motivate pupils towards learning. Unit 3.2 in Capel, Leask and Turner (1995) covers motivation in detail and you should refer to that chapter for further information.

Motivating pupils is not always an easy task. An understanding of what motivates pupils helps you. Pupils are motivated by activities and tasks which are meaningful, interesting and enjoyable to them. Pupils may be intrinsically motivated in PE to learn or develop a skill, to achieve something difficult, to develop their self-esteem or to have fun. They may be extrinsically motivated by some reward or recognition, such as status, approval, acceptance by peers or teachers. It may be that a few of your pupils are motivated to increase their skill to become professional footballers with the large rewards that can bring. The obtainable, appropriate and challenging objectives you set for pupils should therefore be differentiated to meet the needs of different pupils and to be meaningful to individuals.

An understanding of how pupils learn is also important in helping you to motivate them. Pupils' learning is affected by a number of factors, including their previous knowledge and experience of an activity, the relationship with the teacher, the learning situations which the teacher organises, the social context and their motivation to learn. An understanding of theories of learning – for example, Piaget (1962), Vygotsky (1962) and Bruner (1960) – helps you to develop teaching tasks which are appropriate to pupils' learning needs, which actively engage them in their own learning and which are motivating for pupils. Piaget's theory (Piaget, 1962), for example, particularly the notion of readiness (i.e. that children only learn effectively if their educational experiences are suitably matched to their current level of understanding), can help you to see the need to identify the intellectual demands a task makes on pupils so that it can be matched to pupils' performance. Refer to unit 5.1 'Ways pupils learn' and unit 5.2 'Active learning' in Capel, Leask and Turner (1995) and try to apply the information to PE.

Perhaps most important to remember is that the best motivator is success. If you know your pupils you can establish objectives which allow them to achieve success (Chapter 10 looks at differentiation). You should adopt teaching strategies that actively involve pupils in their own learning and which help them achieve a specific objective (see also Chapter 9). If learning objectives and tasks are too easy or too difficult pupils' motivation to achieve them is reduced. It is especially important to set obtainable, appropriate and challenging objectives in PE because pupils' performance is on show, therefore failure in PE is particularly obvious. Physical actions and the success or otherwise of a pupil in accomplishing a task can be seen immediately by the rest of the class, the teacher and anyone else who is able to observe the class. To team-mates a mistake is obvious; for example, if a pupil drops a catch and the opposition gains possession or a pupil cannot get into a handstand. Failure in front of a class of peers can be particularly demotivating, especially as it is likely to decrease self-esteem (see below).

This can be made worse by the situation – for example, a hockey lesson on a pitch being overlooked by pupils in a classroom or another 'public' place. Pupils may lose interest in the lesson if they feel conspicuous; for example, if girls wear kit for PE in which they feel embarrassed, they are likely to spend more time worrying about their kit than about achieving the task.

The focus of lessons may also make pupils feel failures. In tennis, for example, teachers have tended to focus on skills and technique (i.e. how to execute a stroke technically correctly), rather than on pupils achieving success by being able to hit the ball over the net. Although technique is important, should it be more important than being able to keep a rally going? How much emphasis should be put on good technique and how much on keeping a rally going? Can pupils enjoy a game of tennis in leisure time without being able to hit the ball correctly each time? PE teachers have different viewpoints on this. You might like to discuss this with your tutor. There is plenty of literature on teaching points for particular skills you might teach and, indeed, you include these in your lesson plans. However, there is also literature which encourages you to see that success can be achieved by adopting different approaches to teaching activities – not instead of traditional approaches but as additional approaches to teaching an activity. You might like to look at literature on 'games for understanding' (Thorpe, Bunker and Almond, 1986), for example. The literature on a health focus in PE also provides an alternative approach for teaching PE (see, for example, Almond, 1991). The model he proposes places health related exercise at the core of all physical activity during PE, for life and as a foundation for performance and excellence (see Chapter 16). You might like to read further about such issues and discuss them with your tutor.

You therefore need to understand what motivates your pupils and arrange the learning environment so that they are motivated to learn and are successful.

TASK 7.10 MOTIVATING PUPILS

Reflect on the section above and consider for one class you teach which is not highly motivated (if there is one), how you can increase pupil motivation in one lesson with the class. Discuss this with your tutor, then thoroughly plan and prepare how to motivate the pupils in the next lesson with this class. Implement this when you teach the lesson, then evaluate how successful your approach was.

Praise

White (1992, p. 5) states 'that the majority of teachers believe that being positive, honest and fair with pupils is fundamental to good classroom practice'. If you consider carefully how to use praise to motivate pupils you should receive positive responses from pupils. As a teacher you are a stimulus and praise is used to encourage, to reward, to give a sense of achievement, satisfaction, pleasure, and to establish positive behaviour in your lessons.

> It is easy to overlook the occasions for praise, and to react more rapidly to the need to censure. Each lesson, you should try to find some word of praise for a handful of fairly ordinary but commendable things: a well answered question, the good use of a word, a helpful act.
>
> (Marland, 1993, p. 23)

Most pupils prefer to be praised than criticised (see some exceptions in unit 3.2 in Capel, Leask and Turner, 1995). Praise can provide positive reinforcement, make pupils feel better, worth while and probably work to achieve more in the lesson. You should use praise when pupils do something well, put effort into their work, show persistence, exhibit appropriate behaviours. Remember that it is important to praise **effort** as well as **achievement**. To be effective praise needs to:

- sound convincing, with well chosen words accompanied by appropriate facial expressions;
- be clearly linked to what is being praised;
- be given only if deserved;
- come from someone with prestige.

There are some problems associated with the use of praise; for example, some pupils get all the praise. Do some pupils never deserve praise, and is one pupil's praise another pupil's absence of praise?

The general points to remember when using praise are:

- do not over-praise, as praise then becomes meaningless;
- make sure it is earned;
- don't say it if you don't mean it;
- if you mean it, **sound** and **look** as though you do: '**SAY** what you mean and **MEAN** what you say'.

TASK 7.11 USE OF PRAISE

A pupil's motivation is influenced greatly by your use of praise. Ask your tutor to observe a lesson and identify your use of praise during the lesson. Discuss with your tutor how effective your use of praise was and what you can do in your next lesson to increase its effectiveness.

The importance of praise to pupils cannot be overestimated (see unit 3.2 in Capel, Leask and Turner (1995) for further reading on praise and motivation).

Motivating pupils to continue to participate in physical activity

It is one thing to motivate pupils to participate in a PE lesson at school but another to motivate pupils so that they continue to participate in physical activity after they leave school. People only continue to participate in physical activity if they are self-motivated; because, for example, they enjoy it, are successful, confident and feel positive about themselves in relation to the activity. Unfortunately, PE teachers have, too often, made pupils feel failures; therefore they lack confidence in their ability. We are sure you know many people who have never undertaken any physical activity since they left school. Do you know why? Ask some of your friends why they do not participate, or why they have never participated. Was their experience of PE at school a major reason for this? Did they feel that they were not successful at PE? If so, why? Continual failure reduces pupils' self-confidence and self-esteem and decreases the probability that they will participate in physical activity after leaving school. To encourage participation in physical activity once pupils leave school you need to use teaching strategies that help to develop a positive climate in your lessons, which enable pupils to achieve success, to feel confident and to enjoy physical activity, therefore encouraging self-motivation.

SELF-ESTEEM

Motivation and self-esteem are closely linked. Lawrence (1988) defined self-esteem as a person's evaluation of the discrepancy between his self-image and his ideal self. The important factor in self-esteem is the extent to which the person cares about the discrepancy. PE teachers can lower pupils' self-esteem. As a teacher you should aim to enhance pupils' self-esteem. A positive climate with good inter-personal relationships, in which specific feedback is provided about pupils' performance on a task, along with information and guidance about how to be more successful, in a way which is encouraging and supportive, is more likely to motivate pupils and enhance self-esteem. Self-esteem is enhanced when pupils achieve success, and success is more likely if progress is measured against a pupil's own previous performance (ipsative) rather than against the performance of pupils who continually perform well (norm-referenced) (see Chapter 11 on assessment).

Mawer indicated that

> effective teachers who seek to raise the self-esteem of their pupils will attempt to communicate with pupils in such a way that:
>
> - they are seen as enthusiastic, relaxed, supportive, encouraging;
> - they show that they value, respect and acknowledge the efforts of their pupils by use of praise and positive specific feedback;
> - their non-verbal behaviour, such as body posture and physical proximity, eye contact, tone of speech, and use of other gestures such as smiling, head nods etc., reflect warmth and a supportive, caring disposition.
>
> Also, pupil self-esteem is enhanced when the teacher:
>
> - knows pupils well and attempts to share pupils' interests and feelings [*this is not the same as being familiar with pupils*];

- is prepared to 'give them time' and is a good 'listener';
- accepts pupil opinions, ideas and lesson contributions, offers pupils opportunities to make contributions to lessons, and attempts to share decision making with pupils; stresses pupil present performance rather than dwelling on past performances;
- has positive expectations of pupils.

(Mawer, 1995, p. 122)

Expectancy theory

In order to enhance pupils' self-esteem you need to know and treat your pupils as individuals (see above). Expectancy theory says that a teacher bases expectations of a pupil on impressions of the pupil. Interactions with the pupil are based on those expectations, which in turn influence the way the pupil responds, the response tending to match the teacher's expectations. The expectation is therefore realised. Thus, expectations are a self-fulfilling prophesy because the teacher communicates to the pupil the expectations through, for example, verbal and non-verbal communication, leading the pupil to fulfil the expectations. If you have high, but obtainable, expectations pupils are likely to perform well, whereas if expectations are low pupils are likely to perform poorly (this can also relate to good and poor behaviour). Sometimes teacher expectations are based on perceptions or stereotypes; for example, that girls cannot do certain activities such as rugby, or that pupils who are overweight cannot make an effective contribution to a game. Think of some perceptions or stereotypes of certain types of pupil which may influence what you expect of pupils in a class so that you can find ways to prevent expectancy theory coming into operation.

In order to prevent expectations influencing pupils' performance you should:

- have realistic yet high expectations of all pupils, and set obtainable, appropriate and challenging objectives and tasks, for them;
- focus on the pupil's current performance rather than previous performance on an activity or task;
- avoid comparing one pupil's performance with that of other pupils;
- use the whole-part-whole method of teaching, i.e. provide an overall picture of what pupils are aiming for, but then break down the activity so that they can practise and be successful on one part at a time before trying the whole activity again;
- work to motivate all pupils;
- provide feedback which helps the pupil to improve; and

- include all pupils equally in the lesson, avoiding concentrating on the good performers.

See unit 3.2 in Capel, Leask and Turner (1995) for more information about teacher expectations.

TASK 7.12 ENHANCING SELF-ESTEEM IN YOUR PUPILS

In one of the next lessons you are planning to teach, write an objective to enhance self-esteem as well as objectives for content knowledge, skills and understanding. Plan teaching strategies to enhance self-esteem (see Chapter 9), ensuring that all pupils can achieve the objectives set and differentiating the work to enable their individual needs to be met. Ask your tutor to observe the lesson, identifying how you enhanced self-esteem and if you did anything to reduce self-esteem. Discuss the lesson with your tutor afterwards and incorporate appropriate techniques to enhance self-esteem into future lessons and avoid those which reduce self-esteem.

SUMMARY

A positive climate in your lessons helps to create an environment in which pupils learn, supporting the other aspects of your teaching. In creating a positive climate you need to consider your self-presentation and the presentation of the working space. In a lesson with a positive climate pupils are actively engaged in learning, motivated by obtainable, appropriate and challenging objectives to enable them to experience success and enhance their self-esteem. Appropriate praise, feedback and guidance provides information and support and enhances further learning. This requires you to differentiate your material to cater for the needs of individual pupils (see Chapter 10), and to treat pupils in a way that shows you are interested in and care about them and their progress. Such lessons are fun for you and your pupils. Now return to Task 7.1 and, in the light of what you have learned in this chapter, suggest if and how the situations identified could be changed to send an appropriate message.

FURTHER READING

Marland, M. (1993) *The Craft of the Classroom*, London: Heinemann Educational.
   A readable book which looks at classroom interaction.

Wheldall, K. and Merrett, F. (1989) *Positive Teaching in the Secondary School*, London: Paul Chapman Publishing.
This book focuses on the teacher developing a positive and effective class environment. Chapter 4 is on 'Enhancing Praise and Reprimands'.

Whitehead, M.E. (1990) 'Teacher/Pupil Interaction in Physical Education – The Key to Success', *The Bulletin of Physical Education* 26, 2, pp. 27–30. This article focuses on failure in PE, which can result in lowered self-esteem. It then goes on to look at lesson climate – in particular teacher/pupil interaction – as one way of avoiding negative perceptions of self.

The books listed below each include one or more chapters about the classroom environment, classroom climate, creating an effective learning environment, and/or strategies for effective teaching and learning, which should provide further underpinning for the aspects of your work introduced in this chapter.

Cohen, L. and Manion, L. (1989) *A Guide to Teaching Practice* (3rd edn), London: Routledge.

Cooper, P. and McIntyre, D. (1996) *Effective Teaching and Learning: Teachers' and Students' Perspectives*, Buckingham: Open University Press.

Kyriacou, C. (1991) *Essential Teaching Skills*, Oxford: Basil Blackwell.

Mawer, M. (1995) *Effective Teaching of Physical Education*, Harlow: Longman.

Rink, J.E. (1985) *Teaching Physical Education for Learning*, St. Louis, Mo.: Times Mirror/Mosby College Publishing.

Siedentop, D. (1991) *Developing Teaching Skills in Physical Education* (3rd edn), Mountain View, Calif.: Mayfield Publishing Co.

8 Safety in PE

INTRODUCTION

Your first priority in any PE lesson is to ensure pupils' safety. In PE, high quality organisation and management skills are crucial in all activities, for example, gymnastics, swimming and athletics, as they influence not only pupils' learning but also their safety in your lessons. You establish rules and routines and shape pupils' behaviour which enhance both learning and safety. Chapter 6 looked at organisation and management skills, this chapter considers safety within PE lessons.

OBJECTIVES

By the end of this chapter you should:

- understand your responsibilities for safety; and
- be able to create a safe environment in your lessons.

UNDERSTANDING YOUR RESPONSIBILITIES FOR SAFETY AND CREATING A SAFE ENVIRONMENT IN YOUR LESSONS

> Teachers, lecturers and others in positions of responsibility, have a duty of care for those in their charge to ensure that planning and implementation include recognition of safety as an important element.
>
> (BAALPE, 1995, p. 5)

Safety is arguably the most important factor in your planning. In all PE lessons the safety of pupils and hence of the environment and equipment must be of paramount importance. All activities taught in PE have their own safety regulations of which pupils must be made aware. The area is vast and the BAALPE (1995) publication *Safe Practice in Physical*

Education is essential reading for all aspiring PE teachers as it covers all aspects of safety. Adams states:

> It is not surprising that the subject leading to most accidents is physical education. Not only may dangerous apparatus be used but the physical effort and bodily contact involved always present dangers. During physical education lessons the teacher must be present throughout.
>
> (Adams, 1983, p. 122)

As a PE teacher you are trusted to teach hundreds of other people's lively children! You do, for example, take them swimming, ask them to throw javelins, do somersaults, archery, rugby, mountaineering, cross main roads to playing fields and go on school skiing trips. All these activities have a risk of accident (an accident is any event which cannot be prevented, or which cannot reasonably be foreseen so that steps can be taken to guard against it), and some, such as a skiing trip, could be viewed as *very high risk* activities.

> In all physical education activities *risk assessment* should be applied wherever foreseeable risks or hazards may occur. A hazard is anything that may cause harm (a busy road or a steep slope) while a risk is the chance that someone may be harmed by a hazard. The role of responsible staff is to decide whether a hazard is significant and, if so, to determine and implement the precautions necessary to eliminate or minimise the risk presented
>
> (BAALPE, 1995, p. 43).

One way of assessing risk is given in Figure 8.1, while Figure 8.2 applies some of these risk categories to examples of activities taught in PE.

Use the information in Figures 8.1 and 8.2 to undertake Task 8.1.

TASK 8.1 AWARENESS OF 'SAFE PRACTICE' IN YOUR SUBJECT

Make a list of all activities you may teach in a PE programme (you may want to refer to the list you made for Task 1.5) and categorise these into: SLIGHT RISK, MODERATE RISK and HIGH RISK. After completing this task refer to Part 2 'Activities' in *Safe Practice in Physical Education* (BAALPE, 1995) and ensure you are aware of the teacher's responsibility for safe practice in these activities.

Risks may be placed on a scale of 1–5 as shown below

5	**Very Likely**
	If the work continues as it is, there is almost a certainty that an accident will happen

4	**Likely**
	An accident is unlikely to happen without an additional factor. This could be the effects of wind, vibration or human carelessness.

3	**Quite Possible**
	An accident may happen if additional factors are present, but is unlikely to happen without them. This additional factor is more than a casual slip or nudge

2	**Possible**
	Probability of accident is low. Other factors must be present for an accident to occur.

1	**Not Likely**
	There is no risk present. Only under freak conditions could there be any possibility of an accident or illness.

Figure 8.1 Risk (likelihood of accident) rating
Source: (European Education Consultants, 1997)

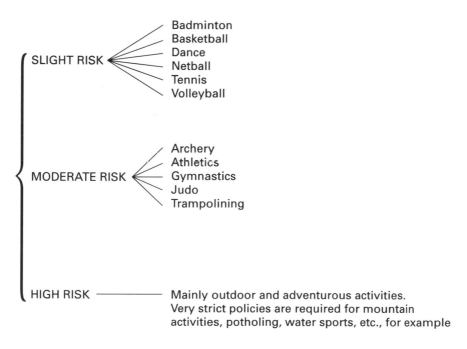

SLIGHT RISK
- Badminton
- Basketball
- Dance
- Netball
- Tennis
- Volleyball

MODERATE RISK
- Archery
- Athletics
- Gymnastics
- Judo
- Trampolining

HIGH RISK — Mainly outdoor and adventurous activities. Very strict policies are required for mountain activities, potholing, water sports, etc., for example

Figure 8.2 Risk categories applied to examples of activities taught in PE

Physical education teachers at primary and secondary levels can greatly improve their policy and safe practice in physical education if they examine very carefully all the working environments in which they place themselves and their pupils. They should remove or significantly reduce the incidence of accidents through effective management of potential hazards.

(BAALPE, 1995, p. 45)

At no time should young people participate in higher risk activities which are not planned, are unsupervised or which the leader has not approved. Cover for all eventualities should be planned for higher risk activities.

(BAALPE, 1995, p. 188)

There is no doubt that activities taught in PE involve risk and that accidents happen. However, this should be put into perspective. You should realise:

- that if safety precautions are taken then accidents are few;
- most accidents occur in the home, not in PE;
- if physical activities are to be exciting, exhilarating, fun, then by their nature they are risky, but this is part of the challenge and fun.

Nowhere in school life is the need for safe practice greater than in physical education. Physical education is by its very nature a challenge to growing children, setting goals which in order to be met demand a mixture of skill, fitness and personal judgement. The risk of accident and injury is ever present, but the ability to anticipate hazards and to minimise them can be developed early on in a physical education teacher's career.

(BAALPE, 1995, p. 9)

THE LAW IN RELATION TO PE TEACHING

As well as knowing any national regulations and specific rules for the activities you teach, you need to know what the law demands of you as a teacher. It has been stated that:

1.2.1.   There are long established and important common law requirements for those acting *in loco parentis*.

1.2.2.   Teachers and others with this legal responsibility must exercise the same *duty of care* as would a reasonable parent.

1.3.1. *In loco parentis* forms the basis for *duty of care* which all teachers must operate when they have children in their care. This applies to all activities within the school curriculum, to extra-curricular activities during or outside normal school hours and whether undertaken on or away from school premises.

1.4.2. Over the years it has been established through the courts that a school teacher should be expected to know a good deal more about the propensities of children than might a prudent parent. Add to this that some aspects of physical education have a high level of risk and required awareness and a *higher duty of care* is now expected of physical education teachers.

(BAALPE, 1995, Chapter 1)

Reporting accidents

If there is an accident in your lesson you need to be aware of the procedures in your particular school for first aid and for writing up an accident report. One example of a school accident form is given in Figure 8.3.

TASK 8.2 REPORTING ACCIDENTS

For each of your school experience schools, find out what you have to do if there is an accident in your PE lesson. What formal procedures are in place? Store this information in your professional portfolio for reference if needed.

Negligence

If there is a very serious accident the law would consider whether there was negligence on the part of the teacher. Negligence is usually considered under the following three factors:

1 The defendant (teacher/LEA) owed a duty of care;
2 The teacher failed in that duty by what he or she did or left undone;
3 The plaintiff (the pupil) must have suffered some damage through that act or omission.

NB. It follows that no claim will succeed in respect of what is strictly an accident.

Where claims have been made for negligence, regulations and books state that the law always considers three vital areas:

SCHOOL ACCIDENT REPORT

Injured or Affected Person

Surname:	Forename(s):
Address:	Age: Gender:
	Status:
	Tutorial if student:

Details of Accident or Incident

Nature (state whether injury, near miss or other):

Location:

Date: Time:

Witnesses:

Details of Injury

Nature (if none write none):

Part of body:

Treatment (tick boxes):

No treatment	☐ First aid		☐ Resumed work/ returned to class	☐	
Sent home	☐ Attended GP		☐ Sent to hospital	☐	
Parent/Carer contact successful/unsuccessful	☐ Time		☐ Detained for___ hours	☐	

Outcome

Not off work or school	☐ Off work or school more than 3 days		☐ Permanent partial disability	☐	
Off work or school less than 3 days	☐ Permanent total disability		☐ Temporary incapacity	☐	

Description of Events Leading up to Accident or Incident

Description of Immediate Actions

```



```

Description of Possible Causes

```



```

Review of Options to Prevent Re-occurence

```



```

Recommendations

```



```

Report Completed by

Name:	Signature:	Date:

Figure 8.3 Example of a school accident report form

1. ENVIRONMENT: facilities and equipment to be safe and appropriate for the activity. (see BAALPE, 1995, p. 45);

2. SUPERVISION: this should be constant. A teacher must never leave pupils unsupervised.

> Student teachers on teaching practice should always be supervised by qualified teachers. Even though they may reasonably assume greater responsibility for classes as their initial training progresses, it is important to realise they cannot assume full *in loco parentis* responsibility until they are finally qualified on satisfactory completion of their courses. The responsibility is retained by the class teachers and cannot be transferred to the students.
>
> (BAALPE, 1995, p. 33)

Your ability to, for example, discipline, organise, observe and position yourself are important in effective supervision. Effective supervision means, for example, that you must keep an accurate register:

> The use of attendance registers at the beginning of lessons, following the movement of pupils, is essential in schools in case of fire. It also further enables the accounting of all pupils and thereby contributes to the *duty of care* required of the teacher . . . The same duty of care by the teacher applies to all pupils in a class whether or not they are able to participate in physical education.
>
> (BAALPE, 1995, p. 34).

3. INSTRUCTION in safety regulations. You must know specific rules for the activity, warn pupils of particular danger, set up safe routines with pupils and use appropriate lesson plans.

In cases of claims these three factors are always examined closely. The environmental factors are very important and you need to establish rules for the pupils you teach to ensure they are safe at all times. Some rules are identified below:

Playing fields

- establish rules for walking to and from playing fields, especially if you have to cross main roads;

- beware of frosty, muddy, slippery surfaces. Make sure pupils wear appropriate footwear;
- if there is no pavilion what is the procedure for accidents? Where is the first aid kit stored?;
- stakes used for goals/markers must be over 5 feet high;
- a whistle is always very useful;
- avoid shelter under trees in a storm;
- if using a car or minibus to take pupils to playing fields (or elsewhere) make sure you have the correct level of insurance cover. Your own personal car insurer may need to be informed that you are transporting pupils and using your car for work purposes.

Tarmac areas

- make sure activities are appropriate for the surface (for example, hockey balls can rise on a hard surface);
- beware of uneven surfaces, frozen surfaces early in the morning, and leaves on the surface, especially after rain;
- have rules (for example, no climbing over fences or railings to retrieve equipment). Establish rules for retrieving balls, especially near roads;
- do not use racing games to touch walls.

Gymnasium/hall

- move out of the way projecting equipment (for example, chairs, piano, mat trolleys);
- activities must be appropriate for the space. Beware of windows;
- beware of slippery and highly polished floors;
- beware of splintered/dirty floors. Shoes may be needed;
- do not allow pupils to work in stocking feet because of the danger of slipping;
- know how the apparatus comes out and fixes;
- do not use racing games to touch walls;
- particular care is needed when 'outdoor' activities come into a confined space (for example, a boy was killed when hit by a golf club being swung by another pupil in a golf lesson in a gymnasium).

There are activities which are notorious for leading to accidents; for example, dive rolls, straddle vaults and leapfrog, using trampettes or when pupils enter the gymnasium before the teacher.

There are ways of protecting yourself against claims for negligence:

- know your subject;
- know the safety rules. Always be seen to carry them out;
- prepare pupils. Warn them of particular dangers;
- have a knowledge of first aid;
- if accidents happen, know the procedures;
- be a member of a union.

You should appreciate how important it is to use all your organisation and management skills to keep pupils 'safe' when in your supervision (see Chapter 6).

TASK 8.3 LEGAL LIABILITY CASES

Look at the following legal liability case studies (Eassom, 1996) and identify the following:

- Is there a 'duty to care'?;
- How has that 'duty to care' been breached (if indeed it has)?;
- In what way(s) has that breach been a causal factor in the injuries sustained?;
- Are those injuries substantial enough to warrant a negligence suit?;
- What factors would influence a court in determining the extent of the 'duty to care'?.

1   In the middle of a Netball lesson, the school secretary arrives to ask the PE teacher if she can spare 5 minutes for an urgent 'word' with the headteacher. The girls are divided up into two teams and left to play unsupervised. During this time, one girl trips and fractures her kneecap. Has the PE teacher been negligent?

2   Whilst trampolining, a fault with the legs of the trampoline causes it to collapse injuring one of the pupils standing by its side. The teacher had not checked the trampoline before its use. However, the trampoline had been serviced the previous week by the manufacturer and it subsequently materialises that it had been repaired with a faulty part. Who, if anybody, is negligent and why?

3   A ball skills lesson is about to begin on the tennis courts when the teacher notices that the end court is unsuitable to play on: it is under the trees and consequently still very wet and slippery after

---

the winter rain. The teacher conducts the lesson, based on a series of relay races, on the adjacent courts and warns the pupils to 'be careful' if they need to go to the end of the courts to retrieve the ball. One pupil invariably runs onto the area, slips, and lands awkwardly on the base of his spine causing serious disability. Would the PE teacher be found negligent?

The outcomes of these specific cases are given at the end of this chapter (see pp. 128–129). Did you answer them correctly?

Rules in PE for safety

As you can see, accidents can happen and as a teacher you need to be aware also of the Health and Safety at Work Regulations (1992) and the need to fill in Risk Assessment forms (an example is given for sports and PE in Figure 8.4).

It would be wise to work to a set of general rules in all your lessons. The following are some things you need to think about in terms of safe practice in PE:

- the teacher must know of any infirmity, physical disability, injury or allergy of any pupil which could affect his performance in the session, as well as being aware of accident-prone pupils;
- the teacher must plan lessons appropriate to the age, sex and experience of the pupils and be aware of limitations brought about by fatigue, fear or recklessness;
- the working space must be made as safe as possible (for example, removal of projecting furniture in halls or not using frozen hockey/football pitches);
- the teacher must know the safety regulations which are specific to activities being taught (this includes rules of the game/sport as these often include safety measures);
- most practical activities require a warm up prior to the session;
- the teacher should make pupils responsible for checking equipment therefore making them 'safety conscious';
- appropriate clothing or footwear must be worn by participants (see rules of the specific game/sport);
- no jewellery should be worn when participating in practical activities. This includes ear-rings, nose-rings and finger-rings. Netball rules (AENA, 1991) state, for example, 'If a wedding ring is worn it shall be taped' and 'Fingernails shall be cut short';

Risk Assessment Data Sheet

Assessment Area: Sport and Physical Education

Hazard Identification Area: _____

Description of Work Area or Activity: _____

Date of This Assessment: _____ Date of Previous Assessment: _____

Name of Person(s) assisting with this Assessment: _____

Name of Competent Person Completing this Assessment:

Identification of Hazard	Hazard Factor	Risk Factor	Risk Rating	Existing Measures Satisfactory	Revised Control Methods
Specific questions listed here depend on the specific activity					
Remarks:					

Signature...
Date:..

Figure 8.4 Risk Assessment form for sports and PE
Source: European Education Consultants (1997)

- long hair must be tied back;
- defective equipment must not be used. Also the teacher must be aware of using improvised equipment;
- if spectacles are worn they must have unbreakable lenses. Wearers of contact lenses should have a spare pair (or pair of spectacles) in case of loss;
- practical activities must be properly supervised and the teacher must be present at all times;
- the teacher should not participate alongside pupils because of the physical mismatch and because it is difficult to join in and supervise at the same time;
- it is essential for the teacher to obtain the headteacher's permission before introducing a new activity, particularly one of a hazardous nature. Also the LEA may require the teacher to have a recognised qualification in the new area;
- any injury must be reported immediately to the teacher in charge;
- the teacher must know the emergency/accident procedure of the school and have a working knowledge of first aid. Some playing fields have no telephone or first aid box on site and acceptable alternative arrangements have to be made.

SUMMARY

Your prime concern must be to ensure your pupils' safety in PE lessons. After reading this chapter you should understand your responsibilities for safety and be able to create a safe environment in your lessons. You should also appreciate how important your choices of teaching methods/strategies are in ensuring that the pupils you teach are safe and unlikely to have any serious accidents in your lessons. In order to ensure safety in your lessons you need to constantly monitor what is happening in your lessons. You must also have effective organisation and management skills (see Chapter 6).

FURTHER READING

Adams, N. (1983) *Law and the Teacher Today*, London: Hutchinson.
Chapters 6 and 7 give some interesting case histories in relation to negligence and supervision.

BAALPE (1995) *Safe Practice in Physical Education*, West Midlands: Dudley LEA.

Chapter 1 'PE and the Law', provides very important information for all teachers. Part 2 on safety procedures for activities is particularly important.

Barrell, G.R. and Partington, J.A. (1985) *Teachers and the Law*, Cambridge: Cambridge University Press.
A comprehensive book examining the law in relation to all aspects of school life.

Stock, B. (1993) *Health and Safety in Schools*, Kingston upon Thames: Croner Publications Ltd.
Chapters 3 ('Health and Safety') and 6 ('Accidents') are particularly informative.

Answers to questions in Task 8.3 (Eassom, 1996)

In all three cases there is an immediate 'duty to care' because the pupils are children and teachers are acting at all times *in loco parentis*. There are further factors determining the extent of the duty to care in each of the three cases.

1   There is no doubt in the netball lesson that the teacher has neglected her duty to care. Pupils must be supervised at all times. This has implications for allowing pupils to get changed for PE without super-vision, perhaps because there is only one member of staff and it is a mixed-sex group. In this case, the potential danger of the activity is not immediately apparent, although it ought to be foreseeable that injury is quite possible when running around on a hard concrete/tar-mac surface. The injury sustained is certainly substantial enough to warrant a liability suit if it is deemed that negligence has occurred. *The deciding factor in this case is whether or not the breach of the duty to care was a causal factor in the injuries sustained.* As it is presented, the facts would suggest otherwise. Children trip and hurt themselves in all sorts of situations. What matters here is whether or not the teacher's presence might have prevented the accident. However, other factors might need to be considered. Was the pupil misbehaving or acting foolishly such that the teacher's presence might have been important in stopping the pupil? Was the injury compounded by the actions of the other pupils trying to help? In other words, did the teacher's absence lead to a worsening of the injury than might have been the case if she had been there? Given that this extra information is not available; judged on the facts as they stand, it is unlikely that the teacher would be found liable. But, she would most definitely come in for harsh criticism over her action in leaving the pupils unattended. It

would have been quite acceptable in this instance to have another adult/teacher supervising the pupils in the teacher's absence, even if that supervisor was not a PE specialist.

Verdict: No negligence.

2   This situation presents something of a red-herring. The teacher clearly neglected his duty to care to quite a large extent. A trampoline is potentially one of the most dangerous pieces of equipment that might be used in a PE lesson. The teacher has an even greater duty to care because of this potential danger, the lack of expertise of the pupils and the foreseeability of accidents occurring. However, what matters here is that prevention of the accident would have required an expertise in trampoline manufacture that a PE teacher cannot possibly be expected to possess. The equipment manufacturer also has a duty to care to its customers. In this case, they are the ones whose breach of their duty to care has been a contributory factor in the accident. The injuries are substantial and the manufacturer is liable for those injuries under the *Consumer Protection Act 1987*. The teacher would have learnt a salutary lesson, but would not find himself in court (at least not as a defendant)!

Verdict: Negligence on the part of the manufacturer.

3   This situation is more clear cut. The facility is unsuitable for the activity to be carried out. Legal precedent was set as long ago as 1938 with the case of *Gillmore v. London County Council* in which the Council were found negligent for allowing a PT class to take place in a hall with a highly polished floor, resulting in injury to Gillmore. In this case, the teacher has attempted to avoid negligence by warning the pupils of the dangers. Nevertheless, it must be foreseeable that children might do just what they are not supposed to do. Here, it is inappropriate to expect pupils in the excitement of the activity to be able to stop and make judgements about the need for care on the slippery surface. The potential danger imposed by the unsuitable playing surface combined with the foreseeability of an accident occurring render a far greater duty to care on the teacher. That duty has been breached; the breach was a contributory factor in the injury; and the injury is substantial enough to warrant compensation.

Verdict: Negligence.

9 Teaching styles and teaching strategies

INTRODUCTION

So far in this book we have looked at the aims of PE and many of the teaching skills you need to achieve these aims. This chapter is designed to help you to see the important **relationship between aims and teaching skills**. It proposes that to achieve any aim, or its constituent objectives (for lessons and units of work), it is essential to use an appropriate combination of teaching skills. Every lesson can be viewed as a challenge to achieve specific objectives with a particular class. In order to meet the challenge you need to decide which cluster of teaching skills or teaching strategy you feel will be most effective. The fundamental role of the teacher is to initiate pupils into new areas of learning. The teacher must help the pupil to 'open the doors' to these new areas. Teaching strategies are the keys that 'open the doors'. **How** you teach is as important as **what** you teach in achieving the aims of PE and objectives for your lessons and units of work.

OBJECTIVES

At the end of this chapter you should:

- understand the concepts of teaching style and teaching strategy;
- understand that teaching strategies are composed of a cluster of teaching skills and approaches;
- appreciate that aims and objectives can be achieved only if the appropriate strategy is used;
- be aware of a range of classifications of teaching strategies;
- appreciate, through an analysis of teacher feedback, that each constituent skill in a strategy needs to be adapted for use in that particular strategy;
- be clear about the importance of using appropriate feedback in PE.

TEACHING STYLE AND TEACHING STRATEGY

An individual's teaching **style** can be defined as the combination of:

1   the strategies most commonly used, together with
2   personal characteristics.

A teaching **strategy** represents the method the teacher has selected in order to achieve a particular objective. For examples of strategies and a useful debate on this aspect of teaching see unit 5.3 in Capel, Leask and Turner (1995).

It is confusing that many writers use the terms 'style' and 'strategy' interchangeably, and that Mosston and Ashworth (1986), who have written a valuable book in this area based on PE teaching, use the term 'style' to label alternative approaches without reference to personal characteristics, although their work is clearly concerned with teaching strategies, as defined above.

That every teacher has an individual style is both to be expected and welcomed as this brings variety and colour into pupils' experience in school. However, it would be unacceptable to applaud difference *per se*. The strategic element of a teacher's style must be selected on a rational basis rather than being a personal preference.

Teaching strategies

Teaching strategies are powerful learning tools that both promote aspects of learning and prohibit others from occurring. A tightly controlled didactic strategy, for example, does not foster creativity in dance, nor does an open ended discovery method result in precision in learning specific techniques such as the discus or javelin. Likewise, the development of co-operative skills in pupils cannot be achieved if they always work alone and self-esteem cannot be developed if pupils are always engaged in competitive situations. A **strategy serves an objective** and should be selected after the lesson objective(s) has been identified. It should be remembered, however, that this **choice of strategy** must also take into account the nature of the class, their previous experience, the teaching environment, the equipment available and the length of the lesson.

The term 'strategy' needs to be understood as including **all the elements** that make up the lesson plan and its implementation; for example:

- the material to be covered (for example, the swimming strokes);
- the sequencing and packaging of this material into (for example, a series of progressive practices);

- the extent of the responsibility devolved to the pupil (for example, to follow instructions exactly or to interpret guidance according to ability or imagination);
- the nature of the communication between the teacher and the pupil (for example, teacher questions, pupil/pupil discussion);
- the focus of teacher feedback (for example, to reward acquisition of physical skill or to promote co-operation and tolerance);
- the form and focus of assessment (for example, against previous personal performance or against national standards);
- the organisation of the pupils and the equipment in the space (for example, highly prescriptive or leaving room for pupil choice).

In considering the notion of a strategy you need to realise that in only very exceptional circumstances do you adopt one strategy for the whole lesson. In most lessons the teacher adopts a series of strategies as the lesson progresses and may even implement more than one strategy simultaneously, if groups of pupils need to work to different objectives. An example of this is shown in Figure 9.1.

In the 1960s and 1970s teaching strategies were the subject of much research and lively debate. Researchers analysed teaching and formulated a variety of classifications of strategies. Some researchers observed teaching and drew up descriptive classifications (for example, Bennett, 1976; Galton, Simon and Croll, 1980), while others carried out a rational analy-

Dance lesson objectives: (a) to perfect an opening unison sequence; (b) to devise a pair sequence for the next section of the dance.		
Objective	**Content/material**	**Strategy**
Body preparation	Warm up	Whole class directed work
Precision in movement	Opening sequence	(a) whole class directed recap (b) peer teaching with work cards to check detail of movement
Imaginative use, in pairs, of opening sequence motif	New sequence	(a) problem set for individuals to enlarge/decrease size of motif (b) in pairs, discussion of each other's ideas

Figure 9.1 Possible pattern of strategies that could be used as part of a lesson

sis and produced prescriptive classifications (for example, Mosston and Ashworth, 1986). Whichever approach was taken each researcher focused on particular variables in the teaching situation and thus arrived at their own classification. Tables 9.1, 9.2 and 9.3 give you a flavour of the work of three researchers. Their proposals do not provide a definitive vocabulary of strategies but a sample of starting points that you may find useful in achieving your objectives with your classes. The further readings at the end of this chapter provide a fascinating insight into this highly complex teaching activity.

TASK 9.1 OBSERVATION OF TEACHING STRATEGIES

Study the work of one of the three researchers referred to below, or one of the others identified in the Further Reading section. Observe two lessons, each taught by a different teacher. Identify the strategies being used as identified by the researcher you studied. Discuss your observations with your tutor, suggesting objectives the strategies were planned to achieve. Use this as the basis for planning your own lessons.

Table 9.1 Teaching strategies identified by Mosston and Ashworth (1986)

Researchers: Mosston and Ashworth (1986).
Mode: Prescriptive.
Variables highlighted: decisions taken by the teacher and decisions taken by the pupils.
Strategies identified: Command, Practice, Reciprocal, Self-check, Inclusion, Guided Discovery, Divergent, Individual Programme Learners' Design, Learner Initiated, Self-teaching.
EXAMPLE OF STRATEGY: Inclusion
Learning objectives: to give pupils responsibility for setting their own goals; acquisition of skill appropriate to each pupil; pupil self-evaluation with reference to their own aspirations and performance.
Constituent teacher and pupil roles: The teacher plans the lesson with a series of simple to complex tasks (often presented on work cards). In an Inclusion episode the pupil decides at what level to enter the task 'ladder'. The pupil assesses own performance and appropriateness of level of work being undertaken. Teacher feedback is concerned with effectiveness of pupil self-assessment and pupil intention related to level of work being attempted.

See Mosston and Ashworth (1986) for details of each strategy, or Table 5.3.4 in Capel, Leask and Turner (1995) for a summary of each strategy. While presenting only one way to conceptualise teaching, the work of Mosston and Ashworth has much to recommend it, not least as it is presented within the PE context.

Table 9.2 Teaching strategies identified by Bennett (1976)

Researcher: Bennett (1976).

Mode: Descriptive.

Variables highlighted: Pupil grouping, arrangement of seating, pupil movement around the room, level of talk allowed, use of homework, types of assessment, whole class/individual teaching, methods of achieving disciplined behaviour, treatment of subject areas.

Strategies identified: 12 types of teacher. Type 1 is typically a 'progressive' teacher. Pupils are allowed considerable choice. An integrated curriculum with intrinsic motivation is favoured. Type 12 is typically a 'traditional', authoritarian teacher. Pupils have little choice in any aspect of the work or its organisation.

EXAMPLE OF STRATEGY: Type 10. 'All these teachers favour separate subject teaching. The teaching mode favoured is teacher talk to whole class, and pupils working in groups determined by the teacher. Most curb movement and talk, and . . . There is regular testing and most give stars for good work' (Bennett, 1976, p. 47).

Table 9.3 Teaching strategies identified by Galton, Simon and Croll (1980)

Researchers: Galton, Simon and Croll (1980).

Mode: Descriptive.

Principal variables identified: Time spent with individuals, groups, whole class. Nature of teacher behaviour in interaction with pupils: types of questions asked, statements given, task supervision and evaluative feedback.

Strategies identified: Individual Monitors, Class Enquirers, Group Instructors, Style Changers (Infrequent Changers, Rotating Changers, Habitual Changers)

EXAMPLE OF STRATEGY: Individual Monitors. Teacher engaged in high levels of giving task instructions and monitoring individual's work. Interaction with individuals is brief, factual and focused a good deal on marking work. Pupils are set individual tasks.

FEEDBACK

The point cannot be made too strongly that unless a strategy contains appropriate teaching skills and approaches, the intended learning will not be achieved. Teacher feedback is a useful example of one of these skills and approaches. Feedback is an essential component of the teaching process as it is a key element in learning. Feedback is essential to learning in that it **focuses pupils' attention** on a particular aspect of the task and provides **knowledge of performance** and **results**.

Benefits of feedback have been identified in terms of knowledge, motivation and reinforcement. Fitts and Posner (1967), for example, indicated that feedback provides information which is processed, which adds to the pupil's understanding of the skill/task/activity and indicates how close the pupil is to achieving a specific goal towards which he is working (for example, how close he is to perfecting a leg kick in breast-stroke). This information can act as a reward which can motivate the pupil to continue the skill/task/activity. This motivation is an important, or even necessary, condition for learning. Feedback also reinforces learning as it provides a stimulus which strengthens the response.

The teacher's knowledge of the skill is important because if the teacher gives incorrect information the feedback can inhibit learning. In your feedback you should aim to identify and reinforce correct pupil responses and to modify incorrect responses. It is important to be clear what you hope to achieve from, for example, a particular practice in hockey. Below is a list of possible objectives:

1 to improve motor skill;
2 to develop co-operative skills such as tolerance, communication, flexibility;
3 to foster creativity/imagination;
4 to reinforce rule adherence;
5 to set personal goals;
6 to support a partner's learning;
7 to improve observation;
8 to encourage evaluative skills.

TASK 9.2 MATCHING FEEDBACK TO OBJECTIVES

Match the following three examples of feedback to the appropriate objective above and devise an example of feedback for those objectives not covered. Compare your answers and ideas with those of another student teacher.

(a) Well done, Mary, you were prepared to try Jane's idea;
(b) Good, Jason, you kept the ball close to your stick throughout the practice;
(c) You are working hard Paul. Which part of the practice do you think you are doing best?

It is clear that if reinforcement of rule adherence was the objective and all the feedback was directed towards motor skill development, there is little possibility of the stated objective being realised. There are valuable references to feedback in literature on the psychology of skill acquisition. These books are well worth studying as they look at the relative benefits of different ways of giving feedback. Alternative ways of giving feedback include feedback to individuals versus groups, positive versus negative, general versus specific, congruent versus incongruent, immediate versus delayed and constant versus intermittent. Some have been found to be more effective than others or more effective in certain circumstances.

Mawer's work on feedback is of value as it includes considerable discussion about types of feedback (see, for example, Mawer and Brown, 1983). He proposes that general feedback such as 'Good' can do little to reinforce learning as pupils do not know what aspect of the task is being referred to. He advocates the use of positive feedback which also identifies that aspect of the work that is being performed well; for example, 'Good work, Peter, you remembered to keep your back rounded as you moved into your forward roll.' As a teacher of PE you should avoid negative critical comments as this can be humiliating to pupils, whose efforts are on show for all to see (see also Chapter 7). Where a pupil is having difficulty, encouraging, informative feedback should be used; for example, 'Well tried Clare, you need to remember to keep your fingers together as you practise your breast-stroke arm action.' From a more general perspective it is always better to draw attention verbally or in a demonstration to what **is** to be done, rather than what **is not** to be done and what **is** correct rather than what **is not** correct (see 'Demonstration' in Chapter 5). A pupil who is not wholly attentive may miss preliminary comments and believe the wrong example is the one to emulate.

Feedback that includes advice on how to improve is most effective if you are able to stay with the pupil to see if she can act on the advice and improve. You can then give wholly positive feedback to the pupil. This is excellent for motivation (see 'Motivation' in Chapter 7). With a large class it is difficult to give constructive feedback to each pupil and you may want to use pupils to provide feedback to each other. This approach is incorporated into the Reciprocal Teaching Style (Mosston and Ashworth, 1986). If you try this approach, which has a great deal to offer, remember that pupils may be unfamiliar with the role of commenting directly on a partner's work. Pupils need to be introduced to peer feedback in a step by step approach, as it demands observational, verbal and social skills. It is not unknown for Reciprocal Teaching to have the opposite effect to that intended. Pupils inexperienced in giving feedback can be negative, critical and dismissive.

The most valuable feedback given to an **individual**, is **encouraging** and **pinpointing aspects of the task** that have been mastered or need more work. The more you know and understand about the task, the better you can identify the aspects of the movement on which you are giving feedback, the better this feedback will be. See 'Subject knowledge' in Chapter 18. Feedback given to a whole class is not without value, but is less effective in the learning process as it is, of necessity, non–specific and seldom directly relevant to every pupil.

TASK 9.3 GIVING FEEDBACK IN LESSONS THAT MATCH OBJECTIVES

In one of your lesson plans indicate clearly your intended objective for each part of the lesson or task. Ask your tutor to observe the lesson, specifically identifying feedback linked to a stated objective with a '3' and feedback not linked to the stated objective with a '1'. Add up your score and discuss your use of feedback with your tutor. Repeat the exercise in another lesson and aim to increase your score.

SUMMARY

As a student teacher you are beginning to develop your own teaching style. This individualises you as a teacher and adds 'colour' to the wide range of strategies you use. Teaching strategies are powerful learning tools and must be selected in line with lesson objectives. The notion that an objective cannot be reached without employing the appropriate strategy is very important for you to understand as a PE teacher. It is very often claimed that purely through taking part in PE pupils acquire personal, social and moral attributes. This view is itself contentious (see also Chapter 2), but there is a very powerful argument that, while benefits other than enhanced physical skill **can** be acquired in PE lessons, this **will not** happen unless the teacher adopts the appropriate strategy. This strategy comprises a cluster of teaching skills, approaches and patterns of teacher–pupil interaction. It is only through the appropriate employment of these building bricks that a strategy can successfully deliver the intended objective.

FURTHER READING

Bennett, B. N. (1976) *Teaching Styles and Pupil Progress*, London: Open Books.

Elliott, J. and Adelman, C. (1975) *The Language and Logic of Informal Teaching*, Cambridge: Cambridge Institute of Education.

Galton, M., Simon, B. and Croll, P. (1980) *Inside the Primary Classroom*, London: Routledge and Kegan Paul.

Mosston, M. and Ashworth, S. (1986) *Teaching Physical Education* (3rd edn), Columbus, OH.: Merrill Publishing.

Oeser, O. (1965) *Teacher, Pupil and Task*, London: Harper and Row.

These books each provide a classification of teaching strategies that you should find useful as a basis for developing your own teaching strategies. We suggest that you consider more than one in order to compare different classifications.

10 Knowing your pupils and planning for different needs

INTRODUCTION

This chapter highlights the central role of teachers in responding to individual pupil needs and creating significant and worthwhile opportunities for all pupils to participate and compete in PE.

Schools comprise communities of pupils with diverse needs, therefore planning for this diversity is of paramount importance. Underpinning the notion of the development of opportunities that cater for individual pupil needs is the principle of equality of opportunity. Such a statement is often raised strategically within school policy documentation. However, if you are to respond to the challenge of providing equality of opportunity for all pupils, whilst catering for diversity of need, you have to plan effectively for differentiated teaching and learning, then regularly review and evaluate how effective this has been.

Many of the points raised in this chapter should be considered as an extension to your mixed ability teaching. However, some of the issues require proactive intervention in order to provide a PE programme that caters for, and includes, all pupils' needs. Although the emphasis in the chapter is on curriculum time, the same principles apply to extra-curricular time, and extra-curricular activities are referred to as appropriate throughout the chapter.

Recent policies and government legislation have elevated the issues of education (in particular PE) and sport to a higher platform. These issues have become even more prominent since the publication of *Sport: Raising the Game* (DNH, 1995). See also Chapters 16 and 17. This document urges schools to review their existing provision, whilst developing further opportunities for participation and performance in PE for all its pupils. The need for planning for diversity is further raised in a number of other recent documents, including equal opportunities legislation (see, for example, *Sex Discrimination Act* (Home Office, 1975); *The Race Relations Act 1976* (Home Office, 1976); *The Public Order Act 1986* (Home Office,

1986); *Education Reform Act* (ERA, 1988); and *Code of Practice on the Identification and Assessment of Special Educational Needs* (DFE, 1994)). These policies complement strategy documents in sport, such as *Building on Ability* (Department of the Environment, 1989) and *Young People and Sport: Policy and Frameworks for Action* (Sports Council, 1993), which also aim to create opportunities for all people to become involved in sport at their chosen level.

OBJECTIVES

By the end of this chapter you should be able to:

- plan inclusive PE programmes that reflect a wide diversity of pupil need and are underpinned by an ethos of equal opportunity for all;
- recognise and interpret the principles of equality of opportunity and develop effective strategies for the practical implementation of these objectives;
- identify a range of networks and partnerships that can offer support, advice and guidance on the provision of accessible, quality PE programmes for all pupils;
- recognise the need for differentiated planning, teaching and learning in order that the PE programme offers pupils appropriate opportunities to develop and flourish individually.

DIVERSITY OF PUPIL NEEDS

When initially considering the issue of planning for diversity a question that is often raised is 'which pupils are likely to require individual help and support in order that their diverse needs can be recognised and accommodated within the PE curriculum?' It could be argued that you should consider all pupils as individuals and plan your programmes accordingly. In PE, as in other subject areas, some pupils, for a variety of reasons, have less opportunity than others to access their full entitlement to the curriculum. Thus, as a PE teacher, you have a responsibility particularly to consider issues pertaining to pupils' gender, disability, racial and cultural backgrounds in order that you are in a position to deliver an effective, pupil-centred, quality teaching and learning environment.

Diversity within school should be promoted as a strength, not a weakness. Pupils should have the opportunity to learn this important principle through the medium of physical activity. PE offers pupils and teachers alike the opportunity to develop their understanding of people's individual needs and diversities within a practical context. Whether the physical activities take place in curriculum or extra-curricular time, they offer opportunities for pupils to come together, share and co-operate with each other. In creating such opportunities pupils and teachers can develop understanding and respect for people's individuals needs. However, this must be specifically incorporated into the curriculum because such opportunities do not occur by chance (see Chapters 2 and 9).

> Good intentions on the part of schools and teachers are not sufficient to ensure that all children are able to participate in and enjoy a wide range of physical activities. There are many issues which need to be addressed to ensure that equal opportunity is provided.
>
> (DES/WO, 1991b, p. 55)

This statement recognises that if pupils' different needs are to be accommodated, then you, as a student teacher, have to spend time assessing and ascertaining the needs of the pupils you work with. It is only then that you can begin to consider how to plan and deliver effective PE programmes that offer opportunity for participation by all.

EQUALITY OF OPPORTUNITY

To this end four key principles related to equality of opportunity, **entitlement, accessibility, integration and integrity**, are fundamental and should be considered in ensuring that all pupils can participate in PE (DES/WO, 1991b, p. 56). Although targeted towards pupils with special educational needs, these principles are also of direct relevance to the broader objective of developing entitlement to PE for all pupils. Thus, when planning and delivering PE programmes you should consider how all pupils' individual and group needs can be met in accordance with these principles.

The first principle is **entitlement**. This states that all pupils have a right to participate in PE. The nature of the activity may require it to be adapted for a pupil with, for example, a special educational need, but this does not lessen the fundamental right of participation within a PE programme. A further example may relate to a pupil from a specific ethnic group whose cultural beliefs and values do not permit her to participate in PE with her legs showing. Thus, you would be required to consider an alternative method of enabling her to participate in that activity (for example, allowing the pupil to wear trousers rather than a gym skirt).

The second principle is **accessibility**. This states that the creation and development of involvement is the teacher's responsibility. Thus, it is your responsibility within schools to adapt and modify activities in order that the needs of pupils are catered for. This may, for example, involve the modification of activities in terms of equipment (for example, larger racquet heads and brighter coloured balls), changes to rules and/or differentiated teaching and learning strategies. Creating access to a particular activity may prove challenging to you as a PE teacher. However, with a commitment to flexible teaching approaches, activities can be modified to accommodate a wide diversity of pupil need. As you plan your next lessons, think how you can modify the activity and tasks for pupils with different individual needs.

A particularly useful way of finding out how you need to adapt activities to accommodate pupils' needs is to consult with the pupils themselves. In many cases they are the experts on their particular needs and you should feel able to use them as a resource to assist with making activities accessible to them.

The third principle is **integration**. This states that whenever and wherever possible, pupils should be included in the PE programme. This is based on the ethos of total integration (disabled and non-disabled participating alongside each other). It is only through the full integration of pupils with special educational needs that non-disabled pupils (and teachers) learn respect for and understanding of the individual's needs. Integration also applies to other needs; for example, those due to different racial and cultural backgrounds, gender and social class. PE affords many opportunities for pupils to work together, solve problems, co-operate and negotiate as a team in order to progress towards a common goal. Thus if there are a range of differing abilities and needs within a group of pupils, by working and learning together they have opportunities to gain mutual understanding and respect for each other (see also Chapter 2).

With particular reference to pupils with special educational needs, in some cases segregated opportunities may be a desirable means of entitlement (the National Curriculum for PE, for example, advocates this). The important point in planning for pupils' differing needs is to initially plan for integration and then, if need be, work backwards towards the substitution and segregation of activities. An example of this would be if you are initially planning for a wheelchair user to participate in football in the PE lesson. However, during the first session you realise that the grass causes mobility challenges to the pupil. Following discussion with the pupil you decide to substitute basketball for football and deliver this within a segregated indoor setting as this is deemed more appropriate.

Thus, substitution involves pupils undertaking a different activity altogether (in England and Wales, the activity should still be part of the National Curriculum for PE). Segregation of pupils may include the splitting of a programme or the replacement of an activity by one that is only followed by a particular under-represented group (for example, disabled pupils).

The fourth principle is **integrity**. This states that if you are going to adapt or modify activities, they should be of equal worth and in no way patronising or tokenistic to the pupil concerned. Thus, if you decide to substitute an activity or segregate a pupil from his peers, the alternatives that you offer should be realistic and equally challenging (and in England and Wales, relate to the requirements of the National Curriculum for PE).

The four principles highlighted above must be seen as central to the planning and delivery of all PE programmes if pupils' diverse range of needs are to be accommodated in a valued manner.

TASK 10.1 PLANNING AND EVALUATING INCLUSION AND DIVERSITY

As you observe and plan PE lessons during your school experiences consider specifically how each of the four principles of **entitlement, accessibility, integration and integrity** is being addressed at three key points in the teaching and learning process:

1　during the initial planning stage. To what extent are the four principles proactively examined in an attempt to reflect the diversity of individual pupils' needs?;
2　during lesson delivery. What mechanisms of ongoing assessment are undertaken whilst the lesson is in progress in order to ascertain the extent of involvement of all pupils?;
3　on completion of the lesson. What methods of evaluation, review and consultation are undertaken in preparation for effective future programming and commitment to the four principles?

In conjunction with your tutor reflect on the extent to which the lessons you observe and deliver encompass the four principles. You may want also to undertake this task for extra-curricular activities.

PLANNING FOR INDIVIDUAL NEEDS

Recent legislation and strategy documents in England and Wales within the fields of education and sport have led to the further recognition of the importance of knowing your pupils and planning to accommodate their individual needs. Developments in both education and sport are important for your work in curriculum and extra-curricular time. The Education Reform Act (ERA, 1988), for example, establishes general principles that should be reflected in the curriculum for all pupils. It recognises that pupils have an entitlement to a broad and balanced curriculum that 'promotes the spiritual, moral, cultural, mental and physical development of pupils at the school and of society' (Chapter 40 1.(2)). In order to offer each and every pupil entitlement to PE you need to consider these principles in relation to the particular circumstances of each pupil so that you can deliver a programme that is planned and organised around the needs of pupils.

The *Code of Practice on the Identification and Assessment of Special Educational Needs* (DFE, 1994) addresses the right to entitlement to an accessible curriculum for pupils with special educational needs. In particular it identifies the processes and methods required to identify and support such pupils. Although the document is of particular importance for identifying and supporting pupils with special educational needs, many of its principles can also be applied to ensure effective delivery for pupils with a range of needs. The *Code of Practice* notes, for example, the importance of early detection and identification of additional support for pupils with specific needs. In PE this may involve a pupil who regularly brings inappropriate and/or dirty kit. If you identify this relatively quickly, discuss it and ascertain reasons, you are in a strong position to try to resolve the issue. In so doing, the pupil is likely to feel less isolated from the group due to perceived clothing differences.

Young People and Sport: Policy and Frameworks for Action (Sports Council, 1993) also identifies the need to create and develop a range of opportunities for young people, with prime consideration being given to diversity. Again, this requires planning for individuals. The document recognises that young people participate in a wide and differing range of activities, but that in order to receive their entitlement they require varying levels of support. Sports clubs, for example, should cater for all levels of involvement within a particular activity. Thus, some young people attend activities for social reasons, fun and enjoyment, whilst others (for example, talented athletes) may demand exit routes to elite clubs, sports medicine and science support to enable them to progress along the road towards excellence.

Sport: Raising the Game (DNH, 1995) identifies many issues of central importance to the development of opportunities for young people's involvement in sport. This document advocates that schools should work in partnership with governing bodies of sport to offer structured opportunities for young people to progress along the sports development continuum from foundation to participation and through to performance and excellence. The sports development continuum identifies stages of development of young people's opportunities in PE and sport. The foundation and participation levels act as a primary focus for developing young people's initial involvement in activities at a formative 'play' and/or participation level.

Performance and excellence address refinement of young people's foundation skills in order that they may perform and achieve high standards of performance, with possible regional, national and international level representation. See Chapter 16 for more information about this continuum.

Sport: Raising the Game encourages you to consider how pupils can be offered exit routes to clubs and governing bodies of sport so that they can develop their abilities further. This may be of increased relevance for some pupils, as the extra-curricular activities you offer provide an opportunity to address very specific individual and/or group needs (for example, wheelchair basketball).

Effective planning is the key to ensuring that you, as a PE teacher, are fully prepared to understand and cater for a wide range of pupils (see 'Planning' in Chapter 3). As you begin to work with pupils during your school experiences you build up a personal record of their individual needs and start to form opinions about their personalities, motivation, attitudes and levels of competence in PE. The information that you start to collate at an early stage enables you to tailor activities and tasks to the needs of your pupils.

The information gathering process takes time and, as you continue to work with particular pupils, wherever possible you should create opportunities for discussion with them. The information you gather from all sources assists you in creating effective needs-led, pupil-centred PE. It is only through your advocation and commitment to this philosophy that you begin to cater for pupils' differing needs.

As well as ongoing assessment of pupils' needs, there is a great deal of information and evidence that can be drawn upon prior to meeting a pupil for the first time. This may include previous teacher reports, form or year tutors' comments and, if pupils are new to the secondary school, primary school reports. The information may be presented in a range of formats which include academic achievement to date (related to National Curriculum attainments in England and Wales), personal qualities, membership of clubs and general attitude and involvement within school. It is important that you find time to read this information. As a student teacher on school experience you will probably find that your tutor gives you a digest of this information after it has been read by members of the PE department and any discussion has taken place with parents, external professional agencies and the like. You may find it helpful to discuss with your tutor how the information about particular pupils was obtained.

However, you must always be selective with the material you feel that you require and always keep an open mind about the needs of pupils. Reports can sometimes colour your view of a particular pupil. Be aware of the potential for bias and stereotyping from written or verbal information given. Use the information selectively to start to identify the individual needs of pupils. If there are specific points you feel need clarification and further investigation follow them up at this stage. These may include queries relating to cultural diversity that may need to be addressed (for example, cultural requirements and values held by particular religious groups with regard to appropriate dress codes for participation in gymnastics). Remember that medical information may be of importance for safety but as a good PE teacher you should be able to adapt to a range of individual needs presented to you.

The most important aspect, however, in finding out about individual needs, is to spend time assessing pupils' needs for yourself. When you initially meet pupils in PE this involves you undertaking skill assessments, considering equipment and resource needs in order that you tailor the activity to encompass as many pupils' needs as possible. An example of a skill assessment may include a pupil's technical ability to execute a forward role appropriately. With regard to equipment needs, you need to consider the size, shape, colour and weight of various items of apparatus (for example, for a visually impaired pupil with limited sight, the edges of benches and vaults need to be clearly marked). You should also consider what resources you require to cater for individual needs (for example, a support teacher).

TASK 10.2 FINDING OUT ABOUT PUPILS' INDIVIDUAL NEEDS

In order to provide an effective PE programme that responds to pupil diversity, as a student teacher you must spend sufficient time at the planning stage ascertaining what pupil needs require supporting. You should gather a range of evidence, in particular focusing on previous levels of attainment, attitude and motivation, commitment to learning and individual personal qualities. Failure to spend time at the initial planning stage may leave some pupils with a lack of opportunity for full participation.

Create a check-list of questions, in a similar format to that in Table 10.1, which help you to consider what you would want to ask your tutor and the pupils (and later when you are qualified, other teachers, parents, external professionals) about individual pupils' needs in an attempt to deliver an accessible and inclusive PE programme. Identify the reason why you want to know something about a particular pupil, then identify from whom and from where you can get that information. In discussion with your tutor, consider what methods of consultation you may use to gather information directly from the pupils themselves.

Table 10.1 Investigating pupil needs

Question	Reason for question justification	Information source
1 What activities has the pupil participated in before?	To plan the level of activity appropriate to a pupil's experiences	School records, previous teachers, pupil
2 Has the pupil any significant medical needs that may need consideration in PE?	To ensure that practical activities are appropriate to a pupil's health and physical needs	School records, parents, medical services
3 Levels of attainment in PE to date?	To note particular achievements and identify specific needs	School records, previous teachers, pupil
4 General attitude and application to PE?	To gain insight into the pupil's commitment to PE	School records, previous teachers, pupil

PLANNING FOR EQUALITY OF OPPORTUNITY

Most teachers would acknowledge an open commitment to, and support for, ensuring equality of opportunity for all pupils. However, if there is

to be genuine equality of inclusion and participation you need to consider
and accommodate pupils' differing needs in your planning and delivery
of lessons. Equality is a concept that is often misunderstood in terms of
its definition, its strategic importance to schools and its practical implications for your teaching.

Many people respond to the question 'what is equality of opportunity?'
by stating that it is about treating all members of society in the same way.
They also advocate that people should focus on the positive aspects of an
individual's ability. This view, although well intentioned, is ill-informed
as it is based on a lack of understanding of the differing needs of pupils.
If all pupils were treated in the same way then pupils' individual identi-
ties would not be recognised. This would increase the potential for
inequality of opportunity.

In contrast, if genuine equality of opportunity is to be provided, you
need to recognise that society does discriminate against individuals and
offers them less access to services such as employment, leisure and
education. As a direct consequence of this, if discrimination is evident at
a societal level, then various forms of discrimination within a school
context are also likely to be evident. You therefore need to recognise that
if the current imbalance of provision is to be redressed, then you need
to treat people differently to meet their individual needs.

On occasions this may involve you undertaking positive action strategies that deliberately target pupils who are under-represented and have
less access to and opportunity in PE, both in curriculum and extra-
curricular provision. This would enable you to tackle, in a proactive manner, the individual or group needs of particular pupils and plan
programmes that offer further opportunities for participation and inclusion. An example of a positive action programme in PE would be where
a teacher has identified few boys participating in a mixed-sex dance session. The teacher therefore attempts to redress the imbalance by deliberately targeting the boys in order to ascertain the reasons for lack of
involvement and then, perhaps, to encourage their participation, offering a dance session only to the boys so that it is non-threatening. This
positive action is justified as it aims to increase the opportunity for a specific under-represented group by creating an environment in which that
group feels comfortable.

The aim of positive action programmes is not to isolate and teach particular groups of pupils in a segregated fashion (for example, those with
special educational needs, boys or girls). It merely allows you the opportunity of looking at ways of tackling their needs and of integrating and
accommodating them within your PE programme.

DISCRIMINATION

Discrimination is principally about the deliberate exclusion of individuals due to perceived differences. Discrimination can take the form of oppressive behaviour by individuals within structural/institutional mechanisms. This includes verbal and physical behaviour which openly and deliberately excludes pupils, with the aim of isolating them, on the grounds of their colour, sex or disability alone. Documented incidences of such open discrimination are limited, but may include pupils being discriminated against purely on the basis that they are perceived as different from their peers. The source of discrimination may come from fellow pupils and, on occasions, teachers.

The type of discrimination which is typically most prominent is subtle and hidden behaviour. In particular the individuals or groups that are isolating people are in many cases responding to stereotypical views and perceptions which they have internalised and reinforced over many years. The way to break this cycle is through education and awareness-raising, both on the part of teachers and pupils. PE offers many opportunities to tackle these issues within a practical context, therefore enabling pupils to learn about each other in a sharing, co-operative and team-orientated context. An example of this could be introducing a new physical activity to pupils that originated from a culture different from the dominant culture (for example, African dance, or the Asian game of kabaddi). Pupils therefore have an opportunity to experience a new activity whilst you have an opportunity to raise and discuss issues of diversity within society.

If there is to be equality of opportunity for all, as a student teacher you also need to stop, consider and question what you are offering pupils and whether the manner in which you teach and support pupils is subject to potentially misconceived and stereotypical beliefs. It can also be argued that if you ignore, and do not challenge, stereotypical opinion and discrimination you are in reality supporting and condoning it. PE offers opportunities to challenge beliefs, opinions and behaviours. By incorporating a range of physical activities from different cultures and proactively encouraging pupils to work together in a variety of settings you can encourage understanding and respect for people's individual values and beliefs through the sharing of experiences.

As well as considering your own behaviour, you also need to consider the impact of structural/institutional discrimination, as it raises issues about how the school and more particularly the PE department, its teachers and pupils respond to issues of equality. If schools are to be proactive in creating choice and diversity, they should adopt a range of flexible strategies for meeting such objectives. A schools equal opportunity policy, for example, needs not only to be implemented but also regularly reviewed in order to monitor its effectiveness in influencing individual teachers to consider their teaching and learning strategies. Although institutions are responsible for establishing their own general guiding principles, they also need to reflect on and question whether their existing structural organisation stifles opportunities for full equality.

TASK 10.3 EQUAL OPPORTUNITY POLICY AND ITS PRACTICAL IMPLEMENTATION WITHIN PE

During your school experiences take the opportunity to look at the whole school and PE department policy commitments relating to equality of opportunity. Read the statements that are made and discuss them with your tutor. From the information you review, consider how effective the policy statements are in offering genuine opportunity to all pupils for full participation in PE. Also find out who has ultimate responsibility for policy implementation, how regularly the policy is monitored and reviewed and by whom. If the policy is, in your opinion, not functioning effectively, record in your professional portfolio why you think this is. You can use this information when you are in a teaching post to help make policy implementation effective.

TASK 10.4 AUDITING EXISTING LEVELS OF PROVISION AND OPPORTUNITY IN PE

Create an audit sheet similar to the one in Table 10.2 to gain knowledge about provision and opportunity in curriculum and extra-curricular PE programmes in your school experience school. This may require you to ascertain pupils' opinions, attitudes and commitment to PE, in which case the best way to obtain information is to consult them directly. How can the information you gather assist you in planning future activities for pupils? Store this information in your professional portfolio for use in your first teaching post to create a realistic action plan with target dates for developing opportunities for all pupils to be involved in PE.

Table 10.2 Audit proforma relating to provision of opportunity in PE

Issue	Strategy process	Action to be taken	Responsibility	Target dates
Under-representation of girls in extra-curricular activities	Consult pupils to determine reasons why	Include a wider range of extra-curricular activities for girls. Run taster sessions with local coaches	PE teacher	6 months
Lack of opportunities for participation for pupils with special educational needs	Consult PE teachers and pupils. Audit current sports equip-ment for suitability for pupils with special educational needs	INSET training on PE for pupils with special educational needs. Contact local authority disability sports development officer	PE teacher PE department	3 months
Lessons do not seem to cater adequately for the needs of all pupils	Review teaching and learning strategies with the aim of accommodating more pupils learning needs. Reflect diversity	Concentrate on teaching and learning strategies in planning lessons in order to cater effectively for the needs of all pupils	PE teacher Head of Department	12 months

DEVELOPING PARTNERSHIPS TO ASSIST PLANNING FOR INDIVIDUAL NEEDS

As school populations become evermore diverse and individual needs of pupils become wider, there is an ever increasing demand on you to respond proactively. You are not expected to be able to respond immediately to all demands. However, if you are to offer an accessible, inclusive and well balanced PE programme that meets the needs of all pupils you need to know where to access information. Some teachers subscribe to various professional journals (see Chapter 18), for example; others write letters to organisations or speak on a personal level with people in order to gain information about pupils' particular needs.

By creating strong, sustainable networks and working in partnership, you are well placed to respond proactively to the needs of your pupils. Networks and partnerships take many forms, some more formalised than others. However, with any networks and partnerships you need to bear in mind the two-way flow of information. You have a unique opportunity both to receive information and to act as a resource yourself. It is important, therefore, that you identify what you can offer colleagues both in terms of practical advice and guidance.

It is also worth considering the potential of a school sports advisory group in which general and/or specific issues of individuals and groups can be addressed. An example would include a disability sports advisory group in which pupils meet with teachers and discuss the appropriateness of activities. In addition, external people may be represented on the forum (for example, representatives of local authority leisure service and physiotherapists).

TASK 10.5 DEVELOPING EFFECTIVE AND SUSTAINABLE NETWORKS AND PARTNERSHIPS

In your initial teacher education course you meet a vast number of potential contacts. During your school experiences review the school's existing external networks and partnerships. Identify the named contacts and what they can offer to the school and, in particular, to pupils. Also identify potential contacts in your work in your higher education institution (HEI) so that you create your own list of contacts in preparation for the day when you have responsibility for individual pupils' learning and need to network and form partnerships to help you with your work. Keep this information in your professional portfolio for future reference. You may want to use Table 10.3 as a model for this.

Table 10.3 Network list

Network contact	*Nature of support*	*Comments*
Sports Council	• funding advice • sports equity information • contact lists • library service	
British Sports Association for the Disabled	• national disability sport organisation • advice and guidance • competition structures (regional and national)	Offer advice particularly relating to physical and sensory impairment
PE adviser	• advice with practical teaching and learning issues • contact base for specific external partners according to need	Assistance with INSET; link to LEA

DIFFERENTIATION

Pupils' individual needs cannot be accommodated if you choose to use only one teaching strategy (see also Chapter 9). In providing equality of opportunity to all pupils you need to ensure that the range of teaching strategies you use accommodates all pupils' learning styles and needs. This process is often referred to as differentiation. Differentiation

> is not a single event it is a process. This process involves recognising the variety of needs within a class, planning to meet needs, providing appropriate delivery and evaluation of the effectiveness of the activities in order to maximise the achievements of individual students.
>
> (NCET, 1993, p. 21)

Differentiation involves focusing on your teaching and the activity in an attempt to identify ways of adapting your delivery and modifying the activity in order that all pupils have an opportunity to learn, develop and progress. This includes considering the varying levels of physical competency and intellectual ability, and the racial, cultural and social backgrounds of pupils.

A range of methods of planning for differentiation in PE are appropriate, for example, those identified in the *Physical Education Non-Statutory Guidance* (NCC, 1992):

- the grouping of pupils in terms of ability, individual and group activity. In some schools pupils are organised into mixed ability groups, whilst in others they may be streamed according to their academic ability (see Task 10.6). Each form of grouping has strengths and weaknesses, both for you as a student teacher and for pupils in terms of their potential to learn and develop. Some teachers argue, for example, that if pupils are streamed according to intellectual ability it offers more opportunities to tailor the lesson content to the academic needs of specific groups. Some teachers also argue that streaming achieves better examination results. In contrast, mixed ability teaching acts as a useful strategy for pupils with a range of differing needs to work and learn together;

TASK 10.6 MIXED ABILITY TEACHING

Discuss with another student teacher the strengths and weaknesses of teaching streamed and mixed ability groups. Record your discussions in your professional portfolio. Try to observe lessons taught to streamed groups and to mixed ability groups, specifically looking at whether the strengths you have identified for each type of teaching are being developed and whether the weaknesses are in evidence. Reflect on how you can maximise the strengths of the relevant type of grouping in your own lessons with either streamed or mixed ability groups.

- the use of appropriate equipment in order to accommodate a range of abilities and to ensure activities are accessible to all pupils. You should consider adapted or modified equipment (for example, larger, brighter coloured balls for pupils with visual impairments, or larger racquet heads for pupils with hand–eye co-ordination difficulties) both in your planning and delivery if you are to create an inclusive curriculum;
- incorporating a range of tasks that vary in difficulty (differentiating by task). You may also offer pupils the opportunity to decide at what level they enter a particular task. An example of this would be where you enable pupils to have different roles and responsibilities according to their needs;

- differentiating tasks by outcome. This is where you determine outcomes of tasks that are appropriate to pupils' individual needs. Williams (1993, p. 30) offers a useful example relating to gymnastics. She states that forward rolls 'can be differentiated by offering a choice of finishing positions which make different demands, for example, ending in a long sitting position, or in a 'V' sit position or in box splits position'.

The key aim in planning and delivering differentiated lessons is to offer opportunities for all pupils to develop and progress in a way that is appropriate and relevant to their individual needs. Differentiated teaching and learning poses many challenges to you in terms of your planning and delivery. However, if you are proactive you are going a long way towards raising the standards and levels of entitlement for all pupils within PE.

TASK 10.7 DIFFERENTIATION IN PE

During your planning of individual lessons and units of work during your school experiences, consider how you are going to differentiate your lessons in order to cater for the needs of as many pupils as possible. Particularly focus on differentiating the learning outcomes and assessment strategies (**differentiating by outcome**) and the tasks (**differentiating by task**). Also consider pupils' methods of learning (see Chapter 17) and the teaching strategies you adopt (see Chapter 9) in order to offer maximum opportunities for all pupils to learn and develop effectively. Evaluate the effectiveness of your planning and use this as the basis for planning future lessons. You may want to ask your tutor to observe the lessons to help you to evaluate their effectiveness.

SUMMARY

It is recognised that schools comprise of a wide range of pupils with a diversity of needs. It is the responsibility of each and every teacher to recognise this diversity and plan accordingly. This is included in the principles of the National Curriculum for PE. A particular strength of planning for a range of differing needs is the concept of making pupils central to all decisions about their future learning. Equality of opportunity is recognised as a basic right within education. In order to include all pupils within PE pupils need to be recognised as individuals.

Differentiation and inclusion should be seen as an extension of your mixed ability teaching. Pupils learn in different ways, therefore you need to adopt a variety of teaching strategies in order to accommodate particular needs and cater for a range of learning styles.

In planning for individual needs, you are posed with many challenges. However, if you are committed to a needs-led, pupil-centred PE programme that nurtures individual achievement and allows opportunities for all pupils to flourish, you are going a long way towards catering for individual needs. In catering for pupils' individual needs you make individual pupils feel valued (see 'Self-esteem' in Chapter 7), but also are contributing to an increasing respect for diversity within schools and wider society. Partnership with a range of agencies and individuals can help to provide equal opportunity for participation for all pupils.

FURTHER READING

BAALPE (1989) *Physical Education for Children with Special Educational Needs in Mainstream Education*, Leeds: White Line Publishing Services.
This book addresses many practical issues of teaching pupils with special educational needs in PE. It highlights issues relating to school policy, safety, assessment and lesson delivery. It provides a useful basis from which to plan effectively for the inclusion of all.

Department for Education (1994) *Code of Practice on the Identification and Assessment of Special Educational Needs*, London: DFE.
The code of practice addresses the needs of pupils with special educational needs, but many of the issues addressed regarding provision can be equally applied to the needs of all pupils. It considers inclusion and entitlement to a broad, balanced and relevant curriculum. It recognises the need for early detection and intervention of support structured around comprehensive, systematic provision. The document is essential reading for all teachers.

Evans, J. (ed.) (1993) *Equality, Education and Physical Education*, London: The Falmer Press.
This book includes a series of articles about concepts, issues and strategies for change in relation to equality in PE.

Lloyd, J. and Fox, K. (1992) 'Achievement goals and motivation to exercise in adolescent girls: a preliminary intervention study', *British Journal of Physical Education Research Supplement* 11, pp. 12–16.

This study was concerned with low activity levels in PE. It investigated the effects of different approaches to the teaching of PE on pupils' achievement and motivation. The results offer an interesting insight on two teaching styles and form a useful basis from which to consider the use of a range of differentiated teaching and learning methodologies.

11 Assessment

INTRODUCTION

As a PE teacher assessment is an essential part of your teaching. You want to find out how much your pupils have learnt. You can only do this by assessing their work. This can range from the very informal comment of 'well done!' as a result of a judgement made about a handstand to the formal assessment involved in the marking of examination work (for example, GCSE or GCE A level work).

You need to understand the basic principles of assessment, but an additional requirement is to refine your skills of observation (see Chapter 4). Most of your assessment will focus on pupils' actions in performance. Actions are often fleeting and PE teachers have to rely on their ability to observe and judge at the time of performance. Teachers of other subjects usually have a permanent record of pupils' achievement in the form of writing or other finished products.

Assessment is an integral part of the National Curriculum in England and Wales. Although PE teachers are only required by law, at the present time, to make judgements against the End of Key Stage Descriptions (EKSD) at KS3, it is good practice for records of assessment to be maintained for all KS. Consequently, schools have had to consider the role of assessment in great depth. This has affected PE departments quite radically. Your school experience schools will be at very different stages in the development of their assessment policies and practices.

This chapter identifies the broad issues and strategies you need to understand if you are to become an effective assessor and recorder of pupils' learning in PE. However, it is important to emphasise that although assessment must be planned for it must be seen as part of the whole teaching and learning process and not as an end in itself.

OBJECTIVES

By the end of this chapter you should be able to:

- understand the role of assessment in improving teaching and learning in PE;
- understand the assessment of National Curriculum PE at KS3;
- carry out assessment in day to day teaching in PE;
- relate assessment in PE to the broad principles and purposes of assessment.

THE ROLE OF ASSESSMENT IN IMPROVING TEACHING AND LEARNING IN PE

Assessment is a vital part of a teacher's work and serves many purposes (see pp. 170–71). As an integral part of teaching and learning it helps to:

- indicate pupils' strengths and weaknesses;
- identify the needs of pupils;
- determine the progress being made by pupils;
- determine the degree to which unit or lesson objectives are being met;
- inform teachers' planning and identify where emphasis should be placed in teaching;
- judge what aspects of teaching have been effective or ineffective.

The National Curriculum for PE (DFE, 1995) requires the PE teacher formally to assess the pupils. This assessment needs to be planned and carried out systematically and the criteria being used need to be very clearly identified. Careful assessments of all pupils must be made and recorded in some way. These assessments, collected at intervals from selected units and lessons over the key stage, provide evidence for the teacher to complete the EKSD for each pupil.

Assessment of pupils on a particular unit of work needs to be carried out against the unit objectives. Assessment of a class, small group or individual in a lesson needs to be carried out against the objectives of that lesson or the particular task set. Assessment skills are needed to judge the quality of the learning outcomes of a lesson and so make an essential contribution to lesson evaluation. Assessment therefore informs the planning of future lessons.

Lesson Objectives to improve front crawl leg kick
to improve front crawl arm action
to co-ordinate breathing with arm and leg action

CONTENT/MATERIAL	ORGANISATION	TEACHING POINTS	EVALUATION
WARM UP/INTRODUCTION a) Swimming front crawl/dog paddle	a) Working widthways individually **or** 1's then 2's	a) Keep head steady Heels to surface	
MAIN THEME/SKILL DEVELOPMENT b) Leg kick at trough add unilateral breathing (trickle)	b) Grip rail or trough with **non** breathing side hand holding trough. Breathing side hand presses further down the wall.	b) Practise head roll i) **Nose in water**. Blow **out** firmly through nose and mouth ii) Rotate head sideways still blow **out** until the mouth clears water. Ear in water. Complete blowing out – breathe in. iii) Shut mouth before returning face to water.	
c) Leg kick holding one float. Include breathing and head roll.	c) Hold float at top end on **non** breathing side, near end on breathing side. Work widthways 1's then 2's	c) i) Smooth roll of head to breathing side ii) Breathing points as for b i) and ii)	
d) Dog paddle Head steady chin on water (pupils show how a dog swims)	d) Working widthways	d) i) Leg kick: swing from hips, legs close together, stretch knees and feet, small splash with heels, depth 1'–18"/30–45 cm ii) Stable head. Eyes look ahead, blow out firmly, hand on breathing side to start pull, breath in as same arm elbow bends, arm action kept under water, hands firm, arm extended in advance of head, pull firmly, fingers together, elbows slightly bent, touch hip, squeeze elbow to side and stretch forward.	
e) Dog paddle Face in water head rolls to side (unilateral) for breathing	e) Working widthways	e) i) Smooth rhythm of head roll ii) breathing points as for b i) and ii) iii) dog paddle and breathing co-ordination as for d ii)	
f) Breathing standing in shallow end	f) Lean forward one foot in advance of other. Hands on knees, face in water. Space pupils. Practise exhaling through nose and mouth with face in water.	f) Concentrate on rolling head sideways. The pupils should practise blowing out through nose and mouth face in water, keep exhaling as head is rolled sideways until mouth clears water, then breath in ('remember to shut your mouth before rolling your head back!') Work for a good breathing rhythm.	

g) Front crawl arm action and breathing standing in shallow end.	g) Lean forward, one foot forward	g) Face in water: As arm on breathing side enters the water blow out and keep looking into water. As arm reaches end of pull i.e. as it passes nose, still exhaling, roll head sideways (ear in water). Begin inhaling as mouth clears water. Complete inhalation during last part of recovery. Close mouth as face enters water and during arm recovery. Repeat.
CLIMAX h) Co-ordinating stroke i) Push and glide. Bring in leg kick and arm action, no breathing for a width. ii) Repeat a) but halfway across width take in one breath iii) Build up to widths breathing every cycle.	h) Swimming widths	h) Check all teaching points. Work for continuity as breath is taken Check continuity and rhythm. Return to earlier stages of progression if necessary.
CONCLUSION/CONTRASTING ACTIVITY i) i) Bounce and submerge to beat of a tambour.	i) Group spaced out standing depth	i) i) Think about breathing!, shut mouth as you submerge, open mouth and smile as you surface ii) sink, rise and smile!

Figure 11.1 Swimming lesson plan

You, as a PE teacher, need to have the following:

- detailed and specific knowledge of your subject area;
- ability to set appropriate criteria;
- ability to observe;
- ability to make judgements about whether what pupils actually do meets the criteria set.

The criteria against which you assess pupils can be related to performance and/or planning and/or evaluating. These criteria need to be clear, **valid** and **reliable**. See also pp. 172–4 and unit 6.2 in Capel, Leask and Turner (1995).

TASK 11.1 IDENTIFYING CRITERIA FOR ASSESSMENT

- Refer to Figure 11.1 (pp. 160–1). Identify the criteria you would use to assess individual pupils on the leg kick as identified for the leg kick teaching points, section d (i).
- How might you record your assessment for each pupil?
- Prepare yourself a check-list/recording chart which you might use.

In your response to the task you have probably realised that there is a strong relationship between teaching points and assessment criteria. One criterion you may have identified for a successful leg kick, for example, is the need for the 'legs to swing from the hips'. This is given as a teaching point. When you set a task you should break down what you expect the pupils to do so that you can identify the constituent parts and know what you hope to see. This process both provides you with teaching points to help pupils in their learning and also with the criteria against which you can assess pupils.

PUPIL NAMES	Criteria for assessment of leg kick				
	swing from hips	legs close together	stretch knees and feet	small splash with heels	depth 30–45 cm
Sam Andrews					
Jo Bailey					
Chris Ball					
etc.					

Figure 11.2 Chart for recording pupil achievement

When you decided on a method for recording assessment you may well have listed the individual pupil names in some way against the criteria for assessing the leg kick. An example is given in Figure 11.2, p. 162.

Assessment of pupils, whether informal (enabling you to make constructive comment to pupils) or formal (perhaps to enable you to report assessments for each pupil), should be focused on the lesson objectives. Only if the improvement of the leg kick was the sole objective of the lesson, in the above example, would it be an appropriate means of assessment for the lesson. However, the content or tasks set for pupils in a lesson should be chosen to enable pupils to meet lesson objectives. It therefore follows that in order to make the assessment of pupils a manageable process you need to be selective in deciding what to assess and in choosing the criteria for assessment.

TASK 11.2 MATCHING ASSESSMENT TO LEARNING OBJECTIVES

Using a lesson plan for a class you are teaching:

- select appropriate criteria for assessment based on your lesson objectives;
- prepare a check-list for recording the assessment of two pupils against these criteria;
- teach the lesson and record the assessment for the two selected pupils;
- consider the extent to which the lesson objectives have been achieved by these two pupils.

As you gain experience, complete this task for all pupils in the class.

In the swimming example given on pp. 160–1, selected criteria based on lesson objectives could be:

- improvement in leg kick;
- improvement in arm action;
- improvement in co-ordination of arm action, leg kick and breathing.

These could be recorded as shown in Figure 11.3 (p. 164). The assessment of the pupils, Sam and Jo, indicates that Jo is not achieving the lesson objectives in two of the criteria. This kind of assessment and recording, if done for the whole class, provides both a record of pupil attainment and also informs your lesson evaluation. Experienced teachers often carry out this kind of assessment informally and keep no written record of it.

PUPIL NAMES	Criteria for assessment		
	improvement in leg kick	improvement in arm action	improvement in co-ordinated arm action, leg kick and breathing
Sam Andrews	✔	✔	✔
Jo Bailey	✔	✘	✘

Figure 11.3 Recording of pupil achievement

However, as a student teacher, practice in assessing and recording your pupils' work helps you to develop the skills you need to carry out good assessment.

In England and Wales the National Curriculum for PE does not require every pupil to be formally assessed in every lesson or even in every unit of work. The following section examines how the process of assessment as required by the National Curriculum for PE may be managed.

ASSESSMENT IN THE NATIONAL CURRICULUM FOR PE

The National Curriculum for PE requires pupils to be assessed and a report for individual pupils to be written at the end of each year and at the end of each key stage. EKSDs set out the standard the majority of pupils are expected to achieve after following the key stage programme of study (DFE, 1995, p. 5) Pupils can be described as 'achieving', 'working towards' or 'working beyond' (SCAA, 1996, p. 2). You, as a PE teacher, are expected to judge the extent to which your pupils' attainments relate to the appropriate EKSD and record your assessment for each pupil. You are also required to produce evidence to support what you have written.

The assessment requirements of the EKSD need to be taken into account when planning a scheme of work for a key stage. These include the planning, performing and evaluating elements of the Attainment Target for PE, including the health related aspects of each key stage (refer to National Curriculum documents). Assessment plans should be included in the scheme of work and consideration given to the most appropriate time for assessments to take place. The ability to co–operate (operate and work as a group), for example, is required as part of the EKSD for KS3. How this ability is assessed depends on the planning undertaken within the PE department. The department may, for example, decide to include all the assessment of this aspect within the outdoor and adventurous activity units or it may be assessed through two units of games.

> ### TASK 11.3 ASSESSMENT OF CO-OPERATIVE TEAMWORK
>
> • Find out when, where and how the PE department in your school experience school assesses and records the co-operative teamwork aspect of the EKSD.

It is not necessary to make a formal assessment of every pupil in every lesson taught, or even to record pupil assessment in all units of work. Units of work that are to be used for formal assessment and recording of pupil achievement need to be identified. In doing this you need to ensure that there is a fair representation of all the areas of activity. The methods of assessment used should allow you to assess pupils' planning and evaluating skills as well as their performance.

In your school experience schools, this quite complex planning task will have already been done by the PE department when drawing up their assessment policy. However, as a student teacher, or as a newly qualified teacher, you are expected to assess pupils and record this assessment in some of the units you are teaching in line with the department assessment policy.

Figure 11.4 shows how you contribute to the accumulation of evidence from different units for use in the end of year reports. The end of year reports from the different years in the key stage can then be combined to give comprehensive details for each area of activity undertaken and enable you to make 'rounded, summative judgements at the end of the key stage about each pupil's attainment' (SCAA, 1996, p. 2).

If you are carrying out a unit assessment, all the pupils in the group need to be assessed against the same criteria. These criteria link directly to the objectives for the unit from which the individual lesson objectives have been derived (see Chapter 3).

The criteria you select should reflect the ages and levels of ability of the pupils. If, for example, a unit objective at Year 7 was 'to improve the tennis serve' then appropriate criteria might be 'to be able to serve the ball overhead and over the net from behind the base line'. Criteria for a similar objective for Year 9 might be the ability to place the ball accurately in the service box and perhaps even the ability to apply spin. This example addresses age difference. However, differences in ability between pupils of similar age also need to be allowed for when you are selecting criteria.

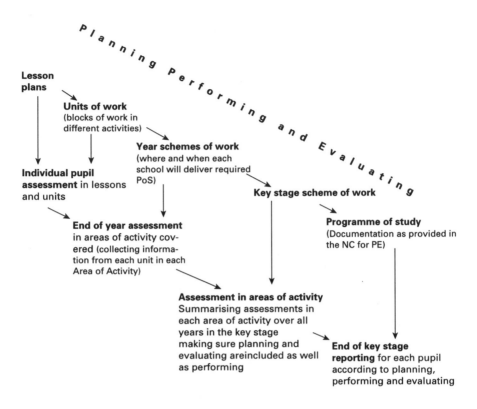

Figure 11.4 Stages in recording assessment information for PE in the National Curriculum

TEACHER ASSESSMENT IN DAY TO DAY TEACHING IN PE

Having worked through the early part of this chapter you should clearly understand that assessment is not a 'bolt on' process but is integral to effective teaching. Given this point it is helpful for you to consider the range of assessment that PE teachers undertake in their day-to-day teaching.

It is hoped that for Task 11.4 you will be able to observe different lessons as well as an extra-curricular activity and that you will see the variety of assessments that the teacher undertakes. In addition to observing examples of assessment (previously discussed) you are likely to see examples of informal assessment. This type of assessment may or may not be recorded. However, the ability to plan and implement informal assessment is an essential part of the PE teacher's role. Some examples of informal assessment you may note from Task 11.4 are discussed on the following pages.

TASK 11.4 OBSERVING ASSESSMENT IN ACTION

Shadow a PE teacher at your school experience school for at least two lessons and one extra-curricular activity. During/after these lessons and extra-curricular activity draw up a list of the following points from your observations:

- examples of **methods** used for assessing pupils. This answers the question of how pupils are assessed (for example, observation of performance, listening to answers to questions, writing down scores/comments, written comments by pupils or assignments);
- examples of **what** the teacher is assessing (for example, attitudes, planning, performance, evaluation, co-operation);
- examples of **who** is doing the assessment. Is it always the teacher?;
- examples of **why** the assessment is being applied. Is it to give feedback to the pupils/parents/governors/others? Is it to motivate? Is it to identify the best performers? Any other reasons?;
- examples of **how** pupils are given the results of assessment. Is it through an informal process such as a brief comment giving positive or negative feedback? Is it through a mark given for a specific performance or evaluation? Any other ways?

Risk assessment

It is assumed that as a PE teacher you have undertaken a risk assessment before every activity, task or lesson, although there may be no tangible evidence that this has taken place (see also Chapter 8). However, there may be clear evidence of risk assessment available. An example could be that the PE teacher transferred the netball practice to the sports hall or cancelled it because the courts were unsafe due to freezing conditions.

Assessment of behaviour

Other incidental but crucial assessments may have been made about the pupils' attitudes and behaviours on arrival at the changing rooms. A boisterous, lively group could indicate to the teacher that he needs to adopt a different approach than that required when a group arrives at the changing room lacking any obvious enthusiasm for the lesson. The assessment of individual pupils' behaviour and attitude is just as important. Failure to recognise a pupil having a negative effect on another pupil or task may lead to major problems in the lesson. In most cases school policy expects evidence of unacceptable behaviour to be recorded. This means that you need to develop confidence in assessing behaviour and attitudes, not only to inform your teaching but to maintain standards of behaviour as written in school and/or department policy documents.

Using assessment for motivation

When discussing individual attitudes, we expect you to have identified the fact that assessment may motivate your pupils (see also 'Motivation' in Chapter 7). It may also act to demotivate them. In the athletics area of activity, for example, to achieve the fastest, highest, furthest can act as very important motivators. However, it is valuable to note that pupils respond differently to such assessment. For motivating pupils it may be better to use informal feedback as a result of assessing certain pupils (such as praising) and to identify the improvement made from their last attempt at the 200 metres, high jump or triple jump. This informal feedback is the means by which pupils are made aware of the continuous process of assessment you, as a PE teacher, carry out in each of your lessons. Your observations of pupil responses to assessment remain a key aspect of your teaching, one which you need to use to maximise pupil learning.

In undertaking Task 11.4 you may have observed the PE teacher carrying out assessment for other purposes, which can be either formal or informal and which may or may not need to be recorded.

Assessment for selection

There are other assessment demands made of PE teachers, including the need to assess to select teams and individuals to represent the school. What process of assessment is required for this type of selection? Clearly PE teachers may use certain criteria for selection, but the selection process could depend on the teacher making judgements about which pupils perform better than others. Team selection criteria may not take account of the really keen rugby player who turns up every week at the beginning of the season but does not make the progress or have the necessary physical attributes required for the team. Thus PE teachers have to be clear about how they justify their criteria for team selection. The keen, but non-selected player may lose self-esteem as a result of the process and you need to consider the effects of such actions. Self-esteem is addressed in Chapter 7.

DEVELOPMENTS IN ASSESSMENT

The assessment practice of PE teachers is no longer confined to the awarding of the traditional effort and achievement grade in the end of year report. A range of assessment and recording methods have to be used if teachers are to provide appropriate comments on pupils' learning. It is becoming quite common to see pupils demonstrate their ability to plan through the use of written work. This may be set as homework and be assessed during the following lesson. Pupils could, for example, be set a task to plan a gymnastics sequence. In the next lesson they could develop and perform the sequence which is assessed by the teacher. The need to record the ability to evaluate has resulted in teachers exploring appropriate but varied means of assessment. Pupils could be asked to complete a chart which provides feedback on another group's or individual's gymnastic performance. This can replace oral feedback and allows work to be collected at the end of the lesson.

The use of videos is another tangible means of recording pupil performance and allows the teacher to grade the performance or the pupils to evaluate their own work after the lesson. Usually PE teachers do not have permanent records of performance except on videotape. However video has limitations and requires considerable skill to be used effectively.

As a PE teacher you must ensure that any assessment you are undertaking, whether formal or informal and for whatever purpose, is based on a good theoretical understanding of the concepts involved. The remainder of this chapter discusses some of the issues you need to consider in relation to any assessment you undertake.

PRINCIPLES AND PURPOSES OF ASSESSMENT

You should now be clear that assessing your pupils plays an important part in your work as a PE teacher. You have been made aware that assessment should be an integral part of teaching and learning. As with every other part of your work it needs to be done well in order to be effective. Pupils and parents, in particular, are concerned that assessment is carried out rigorously and fairly. This is true both of the very informal assessments you make and of the most formal. You should be aware that appeals are made to Examination Boards against the award of GCSE and GCE A level grades. Parents may complain if they feel their child's work is being unfairly judged by a teacher; for example, that he always receives criticism of the work he does, but never receives praise.

Good assessment adheres to certain principles:

- it should achieve a clear purpose and should be fit for that purpose;
- it will be clear what the performance is being measured against;
- it should be valid and reliable.

Purposes of assessing your pupils

A number of reasons for a PE teacher to assess have already been mentioned in this chapter. You want to know what or how much pupils have learned in a lesson so that you can judge to what extent the lesson objectives have been achieved and then plan the next lesson on the basis of this evaluation. In this case you would be assessing for **evaluation**.

It is likely that you want to inform the pupils themselves about your assessment of their performance to help them to understand what you are looking for in their work, to challenge them to greater achievement and to motivate them. Your purpose for the assessment would then be for pupil **guidance** or **feedback**.

When first meeting a group of pupils or when beginning a unit of work on a different area of activity you may wish to make a preliminary assessment of the pupils' strengths and needs, in which case you are assessing for the purpose of **diagnosis**. In each of these three instances the assessment is of direct use to you, the teacher, in your everyday work with pupils.

You may be asked by your head of department or another colleague to conduct trials in order to select pupils for school teams, or to decide which pupils may benefit most from an invitation to take part in an outdoor activity holiday. There may be a school or department policy to group pupils according to their ability in PE. You would need to provide the relevant information for the groups you teach. These assessments are being carried out for **selection** purposes.

You are required to provide grades for the annual reports to parents. You need to grade the work of your examination classes in accordance with the requirements of the Examination Boards. Many of the sixth form pupils you teach will be making applications for university. You need to assess their performance prior to their completing the appropriate forms to provide a predicted grade and to inform the reference about their potential for their chosen course of study. So you are required to assess for the purposes of **grading** and **prediction**.

As you can see, although much of the assessment you do is to fulfil your needs as a teacher, assessment is also carried out for the purpose of providing information about pupils for a variety of other groups interested in the pupils' work (for example, other teachers, parents, higher education institutions, the government).

Measuring pupils' achievement

The purpose for which you are carrying out the assessment should determine the yardstick against which you measure achievement. All assessment involves comparison. There are three types of comparison usually associated with assessment:

- comparison with the performance of others (**norm referenced** assessment);
- comparison with a previous performance in the same activity or task (**ipsative** assessment);
- measurement against predetermined criteria (**criterion referenced** assessment).

Units 6.1 and 6.2 in Capel, Leask and Turner (1995) provide further information.

A race is an obvious example of a **norm referenced** assessment. Each runner's performance is being judged in relation to the performance in the race of the other competitors. Many school examinations and class tests are also norm referenced, the aim being to create a rank order of achievement.

Where a pupil or athlete is judged to have achieved a 'personal best' then the judgement is being made against all previous attempts by that individual to jump, run, swim, etc. This then is an **ipsative** assessment. Much informal assessment carried out by both pupils and teachers in lessons is of this nature – for example, when a teacher praises work which is of a higher standard than in previous lessons. Such assessments are made of any aspect of pupil-activity or behaviour. When a teacher tells a pupil, 'You have behaved better this lesson than ever before', or a pupil reports that, 'It's the first time I've swum a whole length underwater', then ipsative assessments have been made.

In the swimming example given earlier (see Figure 11.1) the teacher is assessing the pupils' swimming, not by who wins the race, nor by whether each individual is swimming more lengths than before, but against some very precise statements of behaviour that, if executed effectively, produce skilful swimming. These statements are the criteria against which the pupils' performances are judged, making the assessment **criterion referenced**. BGA awards, 3-star and 5-star athletic awards are made on the basis of criterion referenced assessments.

If you wish to assess for the purpose of **grading** pupils' achievement, **selecting** pupils or **predicting** their future performance you want to compare their performance with that of their peers. You are most likely, therefore, to carry out a **norm referenced** assessment. In making a **diagnosis** of pupils' needs and strengths you need criteria for determining their level of competence. In this case a **criterion referenced** assessment is most useful. Pupils may well be motivated by the teacher's acknowledgement that their performance is improving. An **ipsative** assessment provides this. However, it could be argued that future improvement of their skill or behaviour would be assisted if you were able to offer **guidance** about what the pupils needed to work on to develop their performance further. A **criterion referenced** assessment like the one illustrated in Figure 11.2 provides the evidence for doing this. Assessments of pupils' achievements against any of the three measures inform lesson evaluation.

VALIDITY AND RELIABILITY

An assessment is of little value if it does not assess what you want it to assess. If you give a group of pupils a written examination which requires them to show their knowledge of the rules and tactics of basketball it only provides you with information about pupil knowledge of rules and tactics. It does not help you to select pupils for the basketball team, as no indication is given of their ability to play the game. If an assessment does not provide you with the information that you want then it is not a **valid** assessment. The assessment may, however, be **reliable**. This means that the written examination would achieve the same range of results if completed by other similar groups of pupils. If you marked the examination scripts on another occasion, or if another teacher marked the scripts, the marks awarded to each pupil would be the same as those you originally gave.

Good assessments should be both valid and reliable. It is possible for an assessment to be reliable and not valid, as in the case of the basketball examination. However, an assessment is not valid if it is not reliable. This point can be shown with reference to archery, as shown in Figure 11.5. If all arrows fall in the same sector of the target (a) then the archer is reliable in her shooting. If the arrows are dotted all around the target (b) then her shooting is neither valid nor reliable. If all the arrows land on the bull

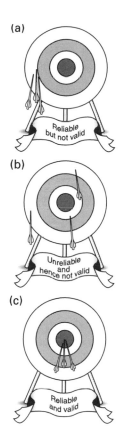

Figure 11.5 Examples of validity and reliability
Source: Open University (1981)

(c) then her shooting is valid and reliable. She has achieved her intention, reliably. In assessment terms it is very difficult to replicate the work of the successful archer.

The need to make assessment integral and closely related to the normal lesson activity has already been addressed. This means that as teacher and assessor you are more likely to use informal methods of assessment which rely on observation and verbal interaction and take place in the usual working space. Such methods are very unreliable. How often have you disagreed with the assessment made by an umpire or referee about whether a shot was good or not? Written tests which include multiple choice items and are carried out in formal examination conditions with the whole cohort of pupils sitting in the same room and being given identical instructions are far more likely to elicit reliable results. But the question is raised about how much of the PE curriculum can be assessed in this way.

The perfect assessment is yet to be developed. Validity may be increased by using a number of different assessment methods. You should try to make your assessments as valid and reliable as possible within the overall aim of ensuring that any assessment you use is fit for the purpose you have in mind.

Work through the following task to find out whether you fully understand and can apply the principles and purposes of assessment discussed in this chapter.

TASK 11.5 PRINCIPLES FOR GOOD ASSESSMENT

Select a unit of work that you are teaching soon. Refer to the learning objectives for the unit. Consider which aspects of the pupils' learning you need to assess. Then:

- list the purposes for assessing this learning;
- decide whether the methods of assessment need to be norm referenced, criterion referenced or ipsative;
- devise two assessments (one norm referenced and one criterion referenced, if appropriate);
- evaluate the two assessments by answering these questions:

1   Which of the two assessments is the more reliable? Note down your reasons for thinking this.
2   Which of the two assessments is the more valid? Note down your reasons for thinking this.
3   Which of the two assessments is more fit for its purpose?:

- in light of the answers to these questions make any necessary modifications to the assessments;
- decide how to record the results of the assessment for all pupils in the group;
- carry out the assessment and evaluate how well it achieved its purpose.

SUMMARY

In completing Task 11.5 you should have shown what you understand about the role assessment plays in improving teaching and learning in PE. You should now be developing competence in assessing pupils.

FURTHER READING

Carroll, B. (1994) *Assessment in Physical Education: A Teacher's Guide to the Issues*, London: The Falmer Press.
Assessment issues in PE are identified and possible approaches to provide solutions in problem areas are discussed.

Gipps, C.V. (1995) *Beyond Testing: Towards a Theory of Educational Assessment*, London: The Falmer Press.
This book provides a theoretical approach to assessment.

School Curriculum and Assessment Authority (SCAA) (1996) *Consistency in Teacher Assessment: Exemplification of Standards in Key Stage 3*, London: SCAA Publications.
A booklet and videotape which help to clarify the expectations in pupil performance at KS3 as written in the EKSD.

School Curriculum and Assessment Authority (SCAA) (1997) *Physical Education at Key Stages 3 and 4. Assessment, Recording and Reporting Guidance for Teachers*, London: SCAA Publications.
This leaflet takes as its starting point the premise that assessment is fundamental to good teaching. It provides practical guidance on ways of assessing and recording achievement in PE that are manageable and effective.

12 Public examinations

INTRODUCTION

Public examinations offer one method of formal assessment. The subject of PE, once seen as purely a physical activity to act as a release for pupils from the 'academic' subjects on the school curriculum, can now be formally examined through all stages in education – from GCSE to degree level. It is for this reason that you need to recognise how schools have developed examination courses and your potential role in the teaching of examination work in PE. This chapter discusses the rapid growth in the development of examinations in PE over the last two decades, the range of examinations available and the implications of this for teachers of PE.

The development of pupils from the age of 14 should be seen as a continuum through to 19 years of age, rather than being confined to KS 4. This has implications for both the way teachers view the options available to pupils from 14 years onwards, and with regard to the possible curriculum in which vocational qualifications can be taken alongside the traditional academic qualifications. It is an interesting time to monitor the development of the vocational and academic routes in the context of examinations as there has been an involved and heartfelt debate for many years as to the value of integrating these two aspects. This debate relates to all subjects or courses taken by pupils, including PE. The potential employment opportunities for school-leavers in the PE, sport and leisure industry are increasing. Examinations in PE are recognised by the industry. This means that, as a teacher of PE, you must remain up to date in this debate, as you will have a responsibility to predict the needs of your pupils. You will also need to be able to guide them on appropriate options throughout their secondary education.

Although limited, the literature on the development of examinations in PE is detailed and helpful. This is noted throughout the chapter and in the further reading section at the end of the chapter. It is not the intention of this chapter to provide in-depth details of every examination but to provide enough background to enable you to research the range of options and courses available.

As a student teacher you may be in a school which offers its pupils opportunity to undertake public examinations in PE. The extent to which you may be able to undertake a role in the teaching of examination courses during your initial teacher education (ITE) course depends on several factors:

- the school's and PE department's policy on the teaching of examinations;
- the timetable of examination classes during the week. They may clash with lessons you should be teaching;
- your specialism(s) and confidence in subject knowledge;
- the staff's confidence in your ability to teach certain units of the syllabus.

It is hoped that you may be able to assist with, or at least observe, the assessment of practical performance and moderation processes involved in the examination of PE at some stage during you ITE course. You may also be able to observe and possibly teach some of the theoretical aspects of the examination course.

OBJECTIVES

At the end of this chapter you should be able to:

- understand the diversity of examinations available in PE;
- research the range of options available to schools, including the 'vocational' and 'academic' routes;
- discuss the issues in examining PE;
- understand the implications of examinations on the curriculum, teaching and assessing of PE.

WHAT PE EXAMINATIONS ARE AVAILABLE FOR PUPILS TODAY?

The growth in the number of education establishments offering examinations in this subject is well documented (for example, Carroll, 1994, p. 80; Francis and Merrick, 1994, pp. 14–15). There has also been a growth in the number of courses relating to PE offered by the awarding bodies.

TASK 12.1 AN INVESTIGATION OF THE WAYS PE IS
EXAMINED

Make a list of every form of public examination or assessment
connected with PE that you undertook when you were at school and
for which you received a nationally recognised certificate. This could
range from BGA awards to GCE A level in Sports Studies.

Now note those available today at your school experience school.
Include the names of the awarding bodies. If your school does not
have a sixth form try to contact your local sixth form or further
education college to find out the examinations and assessments
available within the PE curriculum.

Are there differences between the two lists above? If 'yes', why do
you think this is the case? Discuss this with your tutor or another
student teacher.

Today, the following examinations may be offered:

- GCSE 2 year courses (PE, Games or Dance);
- GCSE short courses (equivalent to half a GCSE);
- GCE A level (PE, Sports Studies or Dance);
- General National Vocational Qualification (GNVQ);
- National Vocational Qualification (NVQ). This could include a range
  of coaching awards;
- Governing Body Award Schemes (for example, AAA 5-star award
  scheme, BGA award scheme, officiating awards);
- Central Council for Physical Recreation (CCPR) Community Sports
  Leadership Award and Junior Sports Leadership Awards.

Table 12.1 shows some of these examinations. It provides an overview of
the way the current examinations fall into a national framework.

The list given in Table 12.1 is not an exhaustive one. It does, however,
indicate some of the common examinations available to pupils today. It
is useful to recognise that although dance is examined as a separate subject by one examination board, it is included within all PE examinations
at GCSE. Dance is also incorporated within the GNVQ Performing
Arts.

It is also important to recognise the distinct 'cut off' between the Intermediate and Foundation Level in GCSE examination grades. A pupil
awarded a grade between A* and C falls into the higher category of an

Table 12.1 Examples of examinations in PE

Level	Name of certificate	Awarding body / Examination Board
Advanced	GCE A level PE	AEB, UCLES
	GCE A level Dance	NEAB (1997)
	GNVQ Advanced Leisure and Tourism	BTEC, C&G, RSA
	GNVQ Advanced Health and Social Care	BTEC, C&G, RSA
	NVQ Level 3 Sport and Recreation (**Outdoor Education)	BTEC, C&G, RSA
Intermediate	GCSE grades A*–C in PE/Games	MEG, NEAB, SEG, ULEAC, WJEC
	GCSE grades A*–C (Short course, equivalent to half a GCSE) in PE/Games	All the Examination Boards offer GCSE short courses, some in PE, some in Games
	GCSE grades A*–C in Dance	NEAB
	GNVQ Intermediate (titles as for Advanced above)	BTEC, C&G, RSA
	NVQ level 2 (titles as above)	BTEC, C&G, RSA
Foundation	GCSE grades D–G in PE/Games	MEG, NEAB, SEG, ULEAC, WJEC
	GCSE grades D–G in Dance	NEAB
	GCSE grades D–G (Short course, equivalent to half a GCSE) in PE/Games	All the Examination Boards offer GCSE short courses, some in PE, some in Games
	GNVQ Foundation (titles as for Advanced above)	BTEC, C&G, RSA
	NVQ level 1 (titles as above)	BTEC, C&G, RSA

Note: **Examples only, more are available – for full listings see British Vocational Qualifications (1995); for a key to abbreviations see the Glossary (p. 306)

Intermediate Level award, whereas a pupil awarded D to G is recognised as having gained a Foundation Level award.

This may be seen as a confusing and bewildering series of different qualifications which are not clearly integrated. Indeed, it is the range of courses and number of awarding bodies that cause confusion to employers, higher education institutions (HEIs), parents and pupils alike. This is why there is a drive to simplify and clarify the issue of qualifications by introducing a single national framework of qualifications. Sir Ron Dearing was given the brief to investigate and report on national qualifications. His review was published in 1996. During this time of change, the job of the PE teacher is to remain up to date with the evolving framework. As a PE teacher you need to analyse the options available and design a curriculum which provides pupils with an accessible, relevant and clear curriculum.

Before embarking on the way examinations affect teaching and learning in school it is useful to highlight some of the most recent changes in examinations and to indicate the potential changes in the future. As noted in unit 6.3 in Capel, Leask and Turner (1995) we are in a state of flux and there are many questions which remain unresolved in the assessment world. Further evidence of this unsettled stage is provided below.

RECENT INNOVATIONS AND CHANGES

NVQs and GNVQs

NVQs and GNVQs are comparatively new. NVQs were introduced in the late 1980s and GNVQs were gradually introduced in the 1990s and are still being introduced.

NVQs

NVQs are strictly vocational awards, solely concerned with providing work related qualifications. They are not normally provided in schools/colleges as they are designed to be assessed in the workplace. The assessment for NVQ is based on competence to perform set skills/tasks rated against agreed national standards of performance. There is no time restriction or limitation on the number of attempts to achieve the required competence. As can be seen in Table 12.1, NVQs can be taken at different levels. This table shows the relationship with other examinations as far as NVQ level 3. It is possible to be assessed up to level 5. Levels 4 and 5 are equivalent to degree and higher degree levels.

The key point to recognise at this stage is that the National Council for Vocational Qualifications (NCVQ) has been charged with acting as the body for quality control for all vocational qualifications. The NCVQ does not have the authority to award NVQs. This authority rests with the examination and awarding bodies (examples of these bodies are provided in Table 12.1). A relevant example is that the governing bodies of sport are expected to convert their awards into the NVQ structure (Levels 1–5). Thus, what was the British Canoe Union (BCU) award of Senior Instructor is now BCU level 3 Coach. If you have any governing body awards you should be aware of the possible changes occurring to the award structures. You should be able to access this information through the relevant governing body.

GNVQs

GNVQs were designed to act as a bridge between the vocational route (NVQs) and the GCSE/GCE A level route. How far this is true remains to be seen. There is a growing opinion that the GNVQ route is being accepted as a route to higher education by providing an acceptable alternative to GCE A level (Highman, Sharp and Yeomans, 1996, p. 113). However, in achieving this, the GNVQ may be moving further away from the vocational route by failing to provide a clear entry into employment.

GNVQs are taught in schools/colleges. They focus on the broad principles and knowledge of the world of work. It is likely that you will be in a school which provides GNVQ courses, as this form of assessment has been well received by schools. Once qualified, you may be asked to deliver units on the GNVQ **Leisure and Tourism** or the GNVQ **Health and Social Care**. It will be in your best interests to find out how your school operates GNVQ courses and assessment.

TASK 12.2 AN INVESTIGATION INTO THE ORGANISATION OF GNVQ COURSES IN SCHOOLS

If your school experience school offers GNVQs to pupils you can complete this task on site. However, you may need to arrange a visit to a local sixth form or further education college to investigate this question.

Find out who is responsible for the development of GNVQs at your school and arrange a meeting or interview with this person.

You should ask structured questions which serve to inform you about the organisation of GNVQs. For instance:

- How are GNVQs timetabled?
- How are GNVQs staffed?
- How are staff trained for working with, and assessing, GNVQ pupils?
- Are pupils able to take GNVQs alongside other courses such as GCSEs or GCE A levels?

- Do parents, pupils, employers and HEIs accept the GNVQ qualification?

Having gained this information consider how this may affect you as a PE teacher. Compare your perceptions of the GNVQ route with those of your tutor and other student teachers. You may be asked your opinion of GNVQs at an interview for your first teaching appointment. We strongly advise you to take advantage of this type of task as it helps you form your views based upon evidence.

As noted above vocational qualifications are an area of rapid growth and demand. Useful texts are listed in the further reading section.

GCSE

During 1995 the Examination Boards were required to seek approval for their revised syllabuses from the School Curriculum and Assessment Authority (SCAA). Until this time the Examination Boards were comparatively free from external constraints. An important criterion was a demand that 'the syllabuses must be consistent with National Curriculum requirements' (SCAA/ACAC, 1995, p. 67). For SCAA's requirements for GCSE PE syllabuses refer to *GCSE Regulations and Criteria* (SCAA/ACAC, 1995).

GCE A level

GCE A levels entitled 'Physical Education' and 'Sports Studies' were introduced in the late 1980s and provided an exciting and new challenge for PE teachers. These two titles were introduced by the Associated Examining Board (AEB). The AEB now provides a single examination, entitled 'Physical Education', which incorporates aspects from both original syllabuses. The University of Cambridge Local Examinations Syndicate (UCLES) also introduced PE at GCE A level in 1996.

The GCE A level in PE is well established and is accepted by HEIs. More educational institutions are placing it as an option for many pupils opting for a GCSE A level route. However, you should recognise that even the GCE A level examination is under review. A comprehensive review of the GCSE and GCE A level examinations is provided by Hodgson (1996). Task 12.3 should help you recognise the syllabus content and the choices available.

TASK 12.3 A COMPARISON OF PE GCSE, GCE A LEVEL
AND GNVQs

Select a GCSE and a GCE A level syllabus of your choice (your
PE department should have copies of syllabuses, even if they do
not offer the examination in the school). Identify the percentage of
final marks given to practical (normally called 'coursework')
assessment and theoretical assessment. How and when is the
practical (coursework) assessed? How is the theoretical knowledge
assessed? List the practical options available. List the theoretical
topics required by both syllabuses. Is there any clear pattern of
development from the GCSE syllabus through to the GCE A level
syllabus? (Can you recognise that a pupil completing a GCSE
course will be able to extend their knowledge and understanding
through undertaking a GCE A level examination in PE or is there
no apparent link between the two?)

You should find Hodgson's (1996) article very helpful in this part
of the task.

Obtain a copy of a GNVQ Leisure and Tourism **Advanced** and
Intermediate syllabus. Identify the award body (BTEC, C & G,
RSA). What are the 'core skills' in every GNVQ? Identify the units
you consider that PE teachers may be asked to deliver. How does the
assessment of coursework differ from the GCSE and GCE A level
syllabuses?

It should be obvious that there is a distinction between the approach
taken by the GCSE/GCE A level route and the GNVQ route. The GCSE
and GCE A level both have a theoretical and practical requirement. The
percentage of practical to theory shifts, with a maximum of 30 per cent
being allowed for practical assessment at GCE A level. There is a clear
intention to relate the GNVQ work to practical projects. Pupils are
encouraged to work in close liaison with local firms/organisations. An
example of this could be an investigation of the leisure needs of the local
aged population. The assessment takes account of the pupil's ability to
work as an individual as well as a member of a group. It also recognises the
pupil's ability to apply knowledge in a practical, work related
environment. A key aspect of GNVQ work is the expertise of the teacher
being able to guide and act as a facilitator for this type of applied learning.
As a PE teacher you need to recognise the strategies you can use to allow

pupils to investigate and develop their knowledge of working and learning in this different environment.

In all examinations there is an element of teacher assessment and normally a clear process of local/regional or national moderation of the practical coursework. With the exception of some aspects of GNVQs the written examinations/assessments are externally assessed (see unit 6.3 in Capel, Leask and Turner (1995) for further information).

This section has focused on the GCSE, GCE A level and GNVQ awards, as they have a major influence on teaching and learning in schools. However, your school experience school may not offer any examination

---

TASK 12.4 WHY AND HOW SCHOOLS DECIDE TO INCLUDE PE EXAMINATIONS

The purpose of this task is to establish an understanding of the views and factors that influence a school's decision to include examinations in PE in the curriculum.

Find out the reasons why PE is, or is not, offered for examination at GCSE, GCE A level or GNVQ at your school experience school (remember there is not a GNVQ entitled PE, but there are PE related GNVQs). To do this you need to question the head of the PE department and the school's curriculum co-ordinator. Your initial questions may raise many further points which are important for you to note, so be prepared to allow some time for this task. It is important to seek permission from the person you want to question, clarify what you are seeking information on and the possible length of interview so that an appropriate time can be arranged. It is also helpful to provide a list of questions before you meet to allow the person to prepare for the interview. You need to take care in the manner and tone that you adopt when asking questions about this aspect of the curriculum as you may touch on some contentious issues.

Follow up questions for this task could include:

- What are the advantages/disadvantages of examinations in PE for pupils?
- What are the advantages/disadvantages of examinations in PE for teachers?
- Are there sufficient resources (time, staff expertise, funding)?
- What process of evaluation is undertaken to establish the value of such courses?

courses, as noted above. You may feel that this is right or that all schools should offer some examination in PE. It is important to recognise the underlying views that have led to decisions being made about examinations in this subject at your school.

In relation to Task 12.4 the following comments can be made.

A view that PE can be formally examined is becoming more common; however, the decision is not one made by the PE department in isolation but one that has to be agreed by all staff involved with making curriculum judgements. The curriculum co-ordinator and other senior management staff may need to justify the inclusion of PE as an examined subject to the school governors.

Part of the debate will include other subject leaders who need to be persuaded to give up some of their curriculum time if PE is to be included as an examination option. This is a particularly problematical and contentious issue as the KS4 curriculum is very crowded and all subject areas claim priority for additional time in the curriculum. The view that pupils do not need to be formally examined in PE is therefore a key debate with other subject specialists and outside agencies. It is important for you to be familiar with this debate so that you can formulate your arguments (see Task 12.5) if the need arises.

Other considerations of time and staff expertise must be taken into account. For example, if a GNVQ is offered as an option this normally requires blocks of time such as half a day per week per GNVQ. This could be an expensive use of staff time. The cost of training staff to undertake new examination courses may influence decisions. Available facilities, including use of a classroom base and video facilities, also need to be secured. These are only a few examples of the debate. You should understand that it is not a simple decision to examine or not in PE.

TASK 12.5 MAKING A CASE FOR INCLUDING PE AS AN EXAMINATION SUBJECT

With another student teacher develop a case for including PE as an examination subject. Try to look at the 'whole' issue and present your case in a way which takes account of possible objections from different interest groups.

Discuss with other student teachers to see if there are other issues you could include.

THE INFLUENCE OF EXAMINATIONS ON THE CURRICULUM, TEACHING AND ASSESSING OF PE

We have touched briefly on some of the debate about examinations. It is helpful also to look at the influence that these may have on the PE curriculum in terms of teaching and assessing. Some of these influences are considered below. Task 12.6 is designed to help with each of these.

Timing

Any examination course is expected to be given time **additional** to the normal National Curriculum entitlement for PE. A pupil opting for GCSE PE would be expected to follow the normal KS4 PE curriculum as well as undertake the examination work concurrently. Does your school provide an appropriate timetable with sufficient hours for both aspects?

When are the practical and theoretical activities examined? It is important to recognise that any summer practical activity being examined in a two year course may need to be formally assessed (and moderated) by the end of the first year. This could be because the activity is not revisited or that the necessary facilities are unavailable the following year.

Planning

Planning for the examination course is crucial. How the syllabus 'fits' with the National Curriculum for PE programmes of study and units of work is important. Departments need to plan a programme which meets the needs of their pupils and is not repetitive or disjointed. Also, pupils on examination courses may need time in a classroom or laboratory as well as practical lessons. The decisions about the timetable for all these sessions cannot be taken in isolation from decisions about National Curriculum PE.

Are pupils following the GCSE course introduced to activities that are not taught within the National Curriculum for PE framework? Can some of the theoretical work be covered in National Curriculum PE time? These are just two of the questions PE teachers must answer in planning the examination curriculum.

Facilities

The activities offered to the examination pupils are also influenced by the facilities available. The school may have a swimming pool, so can offer Swimming as one of the practical options. However, it may not have easy access to canoeing or sailing facilities so these would not be offered by the school even if the Examination Board offers these practical options. The facilities also dictate the timing of teaching certain activities. If there is only one indoor space available for the whole PE department, planning to maximise this facility is crucial.

Staff expertise

You may feel very confident about teaching and assessing some of the theoretical and practical aspects of an examination course. However, this is not the case for many student teachers or qualified teachers who have not taught the work before, particularly in terms of theoretical content. This is quite understandable, and provides a strong case that whilst you are a student teacher you should gain every opportunity to observe, team-teach, take small groups, and discuss with your tutor and other PE teachers in your school experience school any work involved with examinations.

Some of the aspects which teachers are concerned about are:

- having sufficient knowledge of specific aspects of the course (for example, the anatomy and physiology units);
- time for preparation of the theory and practical aspects of the course;
- the ability to make the links between the theory and practical aspects of the course;
- teaching theoretical principles through practical application (more of a concern at GCE A level, which should be taught through an integrated approach);
- the actual teaching of non-practical lessons (not all PE teachers are familiar with classroom based teaching and learning);
- the setting and marking of homework;
- teaching and assessing mixed ability groups in examination work;
- the use of information technology (an integral aspect of any GNVQ work);
- availability of resources (textbooks, journal articles, videos);
- keeping up to date with changes to the content of syllabuses.

There is a view that PE specialists have to 'earn' the opportunity to gain experience in the teaching of examination courses. It is still a comparatively recent innovation, but this should not deter you from gaining whatever experience you can.

Coursework assessment

Although you have dealt with this aspect of examination work through working through the tasks in this chapter it is helpful to focus upon the practical requirements for the GCSE syllabuses. The practical nature of PE makes it particularly important to accumulate evidence of attainment in all aspects of practical work. Other subject areas such as drama have similar demands in the need to 'capture' the performance for assessment. As no two performances are the same it is hoped that your pupils will develop and refine their performance, whether it be in the demonstration of a better sprint technique or a clear ability to work as a team in tennis doubles. Not only is the performance assessed, but the pupils' ability to plan, evaluate and analyse is also assessed. This may mean that you have to plan a formal assessment programme after each unit of work. You should also try to include an internal standardisation procedure which involves working with other PE staff in agreeing the marks given for each activity. Internal standardisation normally entails all PE staff working on the GCSE PE course meeting together to jointly assess the pupils in the practical aspects of the examination. There are many different means of trying to standardise the grades across the range of activities within the department, but all of them require additional time and care to ensure that there is a parity of assessment across the activities. All Examination Boards provide clear criteria for assessment and practical assessment sheets for recording pupils' marks. Examination Boards also give clear guidance on the timing of such assessments.

Examination Boards include interim assessment sheets for use by schools. Interim assessments should be undertaken at the end of the practical teaching unit or as near as possible to it. Most boards stipulate that every pupil must have an interim assessment part way through their examination course. These assessments have two very clear purposes: to recognise the standards that the pupils have achieved to date and to act as formative guidance for the rest of the examination course (see also Chapter 11). It is helpful to refer to the interim assessment sheets before guiding pupils as to which are their best options for the final examination. What should start to become clear is that although pupils are taught some practical activities as part of the examination syllabus, they may not need to be summatively assessed in all of these. As an example, an Examination Board offers up to ten different games on a syllabus. A school may decide to teach football, basketball, netball, squash and badminton as part of the examination course. Not all pupils achieve their best grades in these activities so should be guided to opt for the practical coursework that can serve them best. The practical coursework assessment needs to be timed so that the pupils have an opportunity to improve on their previous interim (normally first) assessment in preparation for the final assessment. These final sets of practical coursework provide the basis for moderation.

Moderation

Moderation is a process which Examination Boards use to check that all examination centres (for example, schools and colleges) are working to the same expectations and standards of performance and understanding. In PE this normally involves a day on which a school or group of schools bring all their examination pupils together to show a range of practical work. This provides the opportunity for external moderators (from the Examination Board or other experienced teachers) to gauge the standards of assessment in each school. There is a chance that some schools might have been too generous or too harsh in their assessment and decisions from the day(s) of moderation are important to all concerned. Each Examination Board provides details of its requirements and objectives for the moderation process. The organisation of the moderation day needs to be effective and efficient. The PE staff need to plan a programme for the day which meets the demands of the Examination Board.

TASK 12.6 A REVIEW OF THE INFLUENCE OF EXAMINATIONS ON THE CURRICULUM, TEACHING AND ASSESSING IN YOUR SCHOOL EXPERIENCE SCHOOL

This task can only be completed if your school experience school offers examinations in PE. As with other tasks in this chapter, try to arrange a visit to another school if yours does not offer examinations in PE. Investigate the following:

- What time allowances are given to examinations in PE?
- When are the practical activities examined in your school and why?
- Where and when do pupils have theoretical lessons?
- How are examination and National Curriculum PE classes at KS4 planned?
- Do the facilities impose any constraints on examination activities?
- Ask the PE staff about their initial and present concerns when teaching examinations in PE (refer to 'Staff expertise', p. 187).

- Discuss with the PE staff how they organise the coursework assessment. Try to get practical experience in this through sharing the assessment procedures with the staff responsible for this aspect of the course.
- Read the section above about moderation in GCSE and/or GCE A level work. Discuss requirements and objectives with PE staff. Ask to observe or assist with a moderation day.

This task should give you a realistic insight into the planning and implementation of examinations in PE in one school. Other schools have different methods and strategies for implementing examination syllabuses. Share your findings with other student teachers completing the same task to gain a wider perspective of this important area of work.

SUMMARY

Examinations in PE are well established, but the national picture is still subject to considerable change. PE teachers need to see the potential of linking different courses together. This could mean pupils undertaking some GNVQs, GCSEs and GCE A level concurrently. The hope remains that in unifying the qualifications we will be able to provide our pupils with appropriate and relevant qualifications for the twenty-first century.

FURTHER READING

Capel, S., Leask, M. and Turner, T. (1995) *Learning to Teach in the Secondary School: A Companion to School Experience*, London: Routledge.
This book is particularly helpful when looking at how to teach and set appropriate assignments for GNVQs, GCSE, and GCE A level theoretical work.

Carroll, B. (1994) *Assessment in Physical Education: A Teacher's Guide to the Issues*, London: The Falmer Press.
This book provides some very informative background on the broad issues of assessment and the growth of examinations in PE. Unfortunately, as with all issues on examinations, this is not completely up to date.

Dearing, R. (1996) *Review of Qualifications for 16–19 Year Olds: Summary Report*, London: SCAA Publications.
A useful and readable review of the national framework proposals.

Higham, J., Sharp, P. and Yeomans, D. (1996) *The Emerging 16–19 Curriculum*, London: David Fulton Publishers.
This book provides a wealth of general information about vocational and academic routes being offered to this age group.

Hodgson, B. (1996) 'Which exam?', *British Journal of Physical Education*, 27, 2, pp. 23–6.
This article provides a synopsis of GCSE and GCE A level syllabuses available in PE.

McConachie-Smith, J. (1996) 'PE at Key Stage 4', in N. Armstrong (ed.) *New Directions in Physical Education: Changes and Innovation*, London: Cassell Education, pp. 82–93.
This is an interesting and readable chapter which provides a clear and optimistic view of the way ahead for KS4. It also provides a curriculum overview which looks at the integration of vocational and academic routes.

13 Extending your expertise as a teacher

INTRODUCTION

Central to the process of developing your ability as a teacher are the numerous opportunities and experiences you get in schools. Whenever you enter a new situation you accumulate a vast amount of information very quickly. Early in your school experiences, much of your time is spent collecting general information about the PE department and work of PE teachers. These aspects are considered in Chapter 1. At this stage you are shifting from viewing teaching from a pupil perspective to a teacher perspective. The intention of these early school experiences is for you to challenge the views you hold about PE and to consider your own preferred approaches to teaching.

As your initial teacher education (ITE) course progresses and you begin to concentrate on developing your own teaching ability, the focus of the information collecting process changes. The intention of observation by you of experienced teachers at work, and working with them and other student teachers in team teaching situations, is not for you to copy the practice of others by reproducing what you observe but to get some idea of the ways in which teachers vary in their approaches and how pupils differ across age ranges. You begin to analyse what is happening in the lesson and to make decisions about your own teaching.

Gradually you are given more and more opportunity to take control of teaching and learning, first by planning and implementing tasks in a variety of activities, then planning and implementing complete lessons and units of work. As you begin to take on the full role of the teacher, you are observed by your tutor teaching short episodes then whole lessons. You may also have the opportunity to use a video to watch yourself teaching. Central to your development as a teacher is your ability to observe and analyse what is happening in your own lessons and to use your professional judgement to reflect and act on those observations and analyses in order to improve your teaching. At this stage you should be reflecting on your own teaching and beginning to make judgements about its quality and effectiveness.

In this process you may identify issues/problems in aspects of your teaching or pupils' learning. You can use action research to help identify and address such issues/problems in your day-to-day teaching.

In this chapter we consider how you can make the most of the observation opportunities and experiences incorporated into your course. These are likely to include **observation by you** of your tutor, other experienced teachers and other student teachers, and **observation of your teaching** by your tutor, other experienced teachers, another student teacher or by video. We also introduce you to other information gathering techniques, moving from simple to more complex techniques. The chapter also introduces you to action research.

OBJECTIVES

By the end of this chapter you should have:

- some knowledge of techniques available for gathering information about PE lessons and teaching;
- some insight into the range of questions which can be addressed through lesson observation;
- an understanding of the role of reflective teaching and action research in developing your expertise as a teacher;
- a framework to help you to research teaching and learning issues throughout your professional life.

TYPES OF INFORMATION GATHERING TECHNIQUES

The information you gather by observation or by using other information gathering techniques are of two types:

- **quantitative** techniques: any method that produces data which can be reduced to a numerical form and can be analysed statistically (for example, a record of the number of times an event occurs). Some rating scales collect quantitative data – for example, those recording **duration** (a record of when an event starts and when it finishes, usually by using a stop watch, e.g. pupils' time on-task (see Chapter 6)); **interval** (a record of what event occurs in a set period of time, e.g. non-verbal behaviour); or an **event** (a record of the number of times an event occurs in a lesson, e.g. a demonstration). 'Closed' questions on questionnaires can also be quantitative;

- **qualitative** techniques: any method used to gain insight rather than statistical analysis; for example, unstructured observations, anecdotal records of observations, diaries, some rating scales, documents, interviews, and 'open ended' questions on questionnaires.

In Chapter 1 we identified some of the information you need to collect on your preliminary visit prior to each school experience. In this chapter we consider other information you should collect in lessons about teaching and the means of collecting that information.

OBSERVATION

Effective observation is important to you as a PE teacher. Chapter 4 focused on observation of pupils. You also spend a great deal of time, particularly early in your school experiences, observing experienced teachers teach – but why? By observing experienced teachers you can gain insights into the teaching and learning process. You can see how to translate into practice the knowledge and information you gain about teaching in other parts of your ITE course. You are also observed teaching your own lessons, which should provide valuable feedback on your teaching. Observation **by you** of experienced teachers and **of your teaching** by experienced teachers should encourage the development of self-awareness so that you can be a self-monitoring teacher as you start your first teaching post.

The popularly held view of observation is that it is simply a matter of using your eyes. This implies that two people observing the same event (for example, a PE lesson) would make similar comments on what they see. This is certainly not the case when student teachers observe the same lesson (see Task 13.1) and the difference is even more pronounced when the notes of experienced and student teachers are compared. It is evident that our interpretations of events are influenced by our unique backgrounds, our own experiences as pupils and as student teachers and by the teachers and lecturers we encounter (see Chapter 1). We must be aware of the fact that our view of the world influences what we 'see' in a teaching situation, and that we need to find **systematic, objective** ways of observing classrooms and analysing what we observe which allow us to make informed interpretations and rational decisions, based on objective information.

Background information for undertaking an observation

Background information about the class and lesson is important in undertaking any lesson observation. This can be collected from the teacher using a sheet such as that shown in Figure 13.1.

Procedures for observation

Whatever the observation and by whom, it is important that a **specific procedure** is adopted. The procedure in Figure 13.2, which is described in terms of you observing an experienced teacher, should also be used if your teaching is being observed.

Some of these points are considered in more detail below.

Observation focus

It is important that there is a **focus** for any observation in order to obtain maximum information. The focus of observation should change over time. When you first go into a school experience school you observe various aspects of work in the school and PE department (see Chapter 1). In the early stages of observing lessons taught by experienced teachers and

---

Observer... Date......................................
Class................................ Class size........................ Boys/girls/mixed......................
Year/Key Stage................ Time................................ Room...................................

What are the objectives of this lesson?

1.

2.

3.

What is the focus of the observation?

You may want to add other information appropriate to the observation.

Figure 13.1 Background information for lesson observation

- Agree with your tutor (and the teacher, if different) the intentions of your observation, its exact purpose and precise focus. The focus may come from, for example, the content of your course at a particular moment, an issue discussed at a previous observation or, later, from your own lesson evaluations. You may want to talk through with your tutor/the teacher the intentions of the lesson before determining the focus of the observation.
- Find an observation technique which allows information to be gathered on the area of focus. Agree this with your tutor/the teacher.
- If appropriate, practice using this technique before undertaking a specific observation.
- Have a clear idea about what is likely to be seen in the lesson. Discussion with your tutor should help you with this.
- Undertake the observation.
- As soon as possible after the observation discuss, analyse and interpret the observation with your tutor/the teacher.

Figure 13.2 A procedure for effective observation

observation of your own teaching, the focus is likely to be on immediate, practical issues of subject-specific teaching, i.e. on basic teaching skills and techniques. Your tutor can focus observation of you on a weak area or persistent problem, or on a new area to challenge you to develop a new teaching skill. Later, observation may focus on how effectively these teaching skills are combined.

Any observation of a PE lesson could have many different foci. The focus could be on, for example:

- the lesson plan and the stages of the lesson from the moment the pupils arrive to their dismissal from the changing rooms at the end;
- the teacher's use of skills such as verbal and non–verbal interaction, positioning, use of praise and reprimand; or
- the pupils and their response to the tasks set by the teacher and the types of problems they encounter.

These issues, and others which may form the focus of an observation are addressed in earlier chapters in this book. Several observation tasks are identified in those chapters.

In your early school experiences your tutor helps you to decide the focus for observations. Later in your development you select the focus of your observation on the basis of lesson evaluations, using your developing professional knowledge and judgement to select aspects of your teaching you need to improve.

How an observation takes place in a lesson depends on the focus of the observation. If, for example, you are observing a specific management activity you need to scan the whole environment rather than concentrate on the activity in which pupils are participating. You therefore need to be alert to the whole class rather than a few pupils; to be able to observe pupils furthest from you as well as those closest to you. In some situations you may need to focus on one or a few pupils (for example, if a pupil is not on-task and beginning to misbehave). If you are monitoring pupils' skill development you focus on the activity in which the pupils are participating. You need to be alert to the whole class, but also need to be able to see what individual pupils are doing.

Examples of techniques for observing teaching and learning in lessons

Lesson observations can use quantitative or qualitative techniques for recording information (see pp. 193–4). The same event may be observed using different techniques, each providing different amounts of information and detail. Likewise, similar information can be collected in different ways. The particular technique chosen depends on, for example, the observation focus, the specific reasons for collecting the information, the type of information needed, and the type of investigation (whether wide or narrow, long or short term). The most appropriate technique must be selected for the purpose and the information needed. Different techniques may be used at different times or a mixture of techniques used for any one investigation. Qualitative techniques may be less formal and less systematic, therefore allowing for observation of a broader range of behaviours and for unanticipated events which can then be interpreted. Such observations may help to identify a focus for further observation/investigation. A second, more focused, observation may use a quantitative technique.

Observation schedules

These are useful, structured frameworks for recording lesson observation. The advantage is that they can be constructed to focus the observation on a particular issue and can be used to provide either quantitative or qualitative information.

There are many observation schedules – for example, Academic Learning Time – Physical Education (ALT–PE), (Siedentop, Tousignant and Parker, 1982) (see Task 6.3 and Appendix 1) and the Cheffers Adaptation of the Flanders Interaction Analysis System (CAFIAS) (Cheffers, Amidon and Rogers, 1974) (see Task 7.9). Hopkins (1993) provides examples of observation schedules and check-lists developed by teachers who were concerned with gathering information on a variety of issues. Underwood (1988) includes schedules for analysing such aspects in the PE context. You can, of course, develop your own for a specific purpose. Examples of observation schedules for a range of teaching skills are given in Appendix 1. One example is given in Task 13.1.

TASK 13.1 AN OBSERVATION SCHEDULE FOR LOOKING AT THE PURPOSE OF TASKS SET BY THE TEACHER

Observe a lesson taught by your tutor, using the observation schedule in Figure 13.3. Identify the lesson objectives with the teacher before the lesson. During the lesson listen carefully to the teacher and make a decision as to whether or not each task set is related to the development of the pupils' ability to **plan, perform** or **evaluate** movement (since these processes are inter-related any one task often appears in more than one column). Also note those tasks which encourage pupils to work co-operatively with others, apply safety principles or promote the learning of health and fitness principles. An example is provided (Figure 13.4) to show what a completed schedule might look like for a gymnastics lesson. Discuss the lesson with your tutor afterwards to check your interpretation of events in the lesson.

Observation by you of experienced teachers

Observation is not easy. There is a tendency to watch the lesson and hence not 'see' the key aspects of the lesson. In order to observe rather than watch, you need to practice. To make best use of the opportunities for **observation by you** of experienced teachers on your school experiences you should adopt a systematic procedure (see Figure 13.2).

Participant observation

In most observation situations the observer plays no part in the lesson other than as an observer from the outside. In such observations the

Part of lesson*	Planning	Performing	Evaluating	Working with others	Safety	Health and Fitness

Figure 13.3 Observation schedule: identifying the purpose of tasks
*Refer to Chapter 3 for identification of parts of a lesson. You may want to include the time in minutes for each part of the lesson

---

TASK 13.2 DEVELOPING AN OBSERVATION SCHEDULE

Select a teaching skill on which you need to work to develop your ability. Using the information in this chapter, devise an observation schedule to focus on your use of this teaching skill. You may use the observation schedules in Appendix 1 to help you start on this. Ask your tutor to observe your use of this teaching skill in a lesson using the observation schedule. Explain how the observation schedule should be used. Discuss the effectiveness of the observation schedule after the lesson and adapt if necessary. Also discuss the outcomes of the observation. Work to develop your competence in using the teaching skill, then repeat the observation using the same (or revised) observation schedule. You can repeat the task focusing on different teaching skills.

---

observer should sit out of the way in the lesson so as not to disrupt the lesson. The focus is the participants' behaviour, the lesson plan, the teacher or the pupils. A **participant observer** is normally a member of the group and participates in its activities. You may find it valuable occasionally to look at the lesson from the pupil's perspective by being a

Parts of lesson	Planning	Performing	Evaluating	Working with others	Safety	Health and fitness
Introduction and warm-up	Pupils asked to plan their own stretches	teacher reinforces quality in running actions				Questions and answers on how to stretch safely
Development of skill or topic *Floor work*		Pupils all perform same rolling movements		pupils share mats	Lifting techniques reinforced	
	Pupils plan sequence to include three rolls	Pupils choose starting and fin-ishing positions from work cards	Pupils asked to watch one another's sequence and give feedback			
Climax *Apparatus*		Pupils practise transition from jump on bench to roll on floor		Pupils co-operate in placement of apparatus	Safe lifting and placement of benches taught	
	Pupils plan sequence. Weight on hands movement added			Pupils teach sequence to partner		
Conclusion		Pupils practise weight on hands movements after apparatus put away	Questions/ answers on quality in rolling	Pupils work together in putting apparatus away	Correct lifting reinforced	

Figure 13.4 Example of completed observation schedule used in a gymnastics lesson

'pupil', i.e. participating in the tasks presented by the teacher. More often though you undertake the role of participant observer by helping the teacher and/or another student teacher by 'team teaching' the lesson. This often occurs after an initial period of observation of experienced teachers and before taking full lessons yourself.

A situation preferred on many ITE courses is 'paired' teaching. Here the lesson is planned jointly with the teacher or another student teacher. The pair then negotiate who is to deliver the various parts of the lesson, paying particular attention to both the 'lead' and 'support' roles. The role of the person in the support role can vary from being available, to providing pupils with feedback, to helping differentiate tasks for low and high ability pupils.

Working in this manner can have advantages for the teacher, pupils and the student teacher, providing all are aware of the others' roles and careful planning has taken place.

Observation of your teaching

Observation by your tutor

As a student teacher you should not be left alone in sole charge of a lesson, particularly in a potentially hazardous subject such as PE. Therefore there are many occasions when **you are observed** by your tutor taking all or part of a lesson. You may also be observed by another student teacher on some occasions. In order to gain the most from these observations you should prepare carefully with your tutor; the procedure shown in Figure 13.2 should help you.

Using video

In a practical subject such as PE the **use of video** provides a valuable tool for observation of your teaching. It can also be used to assist observation of pupils (see Chapter 4 for observation of pupils). It has the advantage of allowing you to focus on any number of aspects of the teaching and learning process. The main problem with using this technique is the disruptive influence it has on the pupils. For this reason it is better to video over a period of time to allow pupils to become accustomed to it. It is also difficult to record dialogue, particularly outside on a windy day. Wet weather can also cause problems. Task 13.3 is an example of a use to which video may be put. The purpose of this task is for you to compare your perspectives of a lesson with those of another student teacher.

TASK 13.3 ANALYSING A TEACHING EPISODE USING VIDEO

Arrange for one of your lessons to be videotaped. After the lesson watch the video and record what was happening during the lesson. Ask another student teacher to do the same. Compare the similarities and differences between your two records. Try to find out why the differences have occurred. Do the same task for a videotaped lesson taught by the other student teacher.

This task should make you aware that different people see the same lesson differently, depending on the perspective being taken. If you leave the observation open (as above) the differences may be more marked than if you focus the observation in the lesson. You may want to observe the two videotapes again with a specific observation focus in mind, for example, where was the student teacher positioned during the lesson?, what time did pupils spend on-task? In so doing, you may want to use an observation schedule (see examples in Appendix 1).

Taking action as the result of observation

The section above should enable you to use effectively the opportunities for observation built into your ITE course. In order to maximise the opportunities, you need to be able to use the information collected effectively. The conduct of an observation and post-lesson debrief is crucial to developing your ability to reflect on your lesson. After any observation the observer should discuss with you the outcome of the observation to help you reflect on, analyse and evaluate your lesson and your teaching and to examine the professional judgements you made. You then need to act on the outcomes to make changes to improve your teaching and to monitor the outcomes to see that they are effective. Make sure you use this process to gain as much information, help and advice as possible about your teaching.

REFLECTION

Reflection enables you to reconsider what is worth doing and alternative approaches to what you are doing in your lessons, thus developing sensitivity to what you are doing and how. Here we concentrate on reflecting on what happens in your lessons, but you should also reflect on the values, attitudes and beliefs you hold about PE and about teaching (see Chapter 1) as well as larger social, political and ethical issues of teaching (see, for example, Hellison and Templin, 1991). A further approach to the process of reflection is offered by McNiff (1993, p. 80).

The basis for reflecting on what happens in your lessons is your knowledge about and understanding of, for example, the content, your teaching skills and how pupils learn. Spending a couple of minutes at the end of a lesson reflecting on what you did, what worked, what did not work, what might have worked better and what you might do next time enables you to gain insight and learn from your mistakes. This relies on your observation in the lesson and your powers of recall of the lesson. To enhance the effectiveness of your lesson reflection you need to develop techniques to help you recall events. As soon as possible after the lesson, 're-live' the events which took place, before you forget what you saw. Jot down the main events of the lesson, particularly if there was any deviation from the lesson plan or if there were any 'critical' incidents which occurred, or take more extensive notes. You should draw on your experience of similar situations in the past and observation and feedback by your tutor. Your tutor can encourage reflection by taking an enquiring approach and asking questions such as 'why did you do that?' This reflection forms the basis of your lesson evaluation (see also Chapter 3).

You then need to monitor whether any changes made as a result of observation and reflection are effective. A follow-up observation should be undertaken after implementing any change to determine if any change has actually occurred. This is the beginning of undertaking action research.

ACTION RESEARCH

The term 'action research' refers to a process that teachers use to investigate their own practice and answer questions about the quality of teaching and learning. Action research involves systematically looking at your own practice to:

- identify a specific issue which is causing you some concern;
- collect information to enable you to identify whether the perceived issue/problem is real, or to define the issue/problem further so that you can systematically investigate it (i.e., collect information about the identified issue, interpret the information and monitor the change).

This relies on skills of observation/information gathering, reflection and evaluation. It also requires you to explore what others have written about a particular topic.

Very often action research starts by identifying a perceived issue/problem in a lesson. This may be identified through your lesson observations/information gathering, reflections and evaluations. Common foci for action research in PE include:

- solving a particular issue or problem related to pupil learning (for example, improving social cohesion in a class, improving your mixed ability teaching, finding different ways of achieving differentiation in your lesson;
- monitoring your own performance in an area of weakness (for example, not praising pupils enough, not using demonstrations effectively, having a monotonous voice);
- achieving a particular goal – for example, promoting creativity, getting boys and girls to work together more effectively, using particular learning resources (for example, teaching cards for use in reciprocal teaching) or teaching strategies (see also Chapter 9).

Before undertaking action research you need to understand fully the ethical implications and implement these throughout; for example, you should tell your tutor what you intend to do and the sort of information you are going to collect, and check that your tutor is in full agreement with all aspects of your investigation. If collecting information from other people you must be sure that they know why you are collecting it and that you have their full agreement and permission to collect the information. You must also maintain confidentiality. For further details about these and other ethical considerations refer to the guidelines in Capel, Leask and Turner (1995, unit 5.4).

Collecting information by observation of your teaching can be undertaken by, for example, your tutor, another student teacher or by video, or by pupils or other teachers completing a questionnaire or interview. Observation techniques have been described above. Some other techniques for gathering information are outlined below.

Information gathering techniques

Field notes and diaries

Very often field notes are used as a first step prior to narrowing down the focus of an investigation. They are particularly relevant for observations designed to allow you to describe events in a lesson, either considering the whole range of events that occur (for example, recording your general impressions of a teaching environment), or describing all events in a broadly defined area of concern (for example, pupil behaviour). Such observations are designed to enable you to identify any issues/problems and to determine what you want to look at in more detail. You can then collect information systematically to focus further investigation on the issue/problem. Field notes are particularly useful if you wish to undertake a case study of an individual pupil or group of pupils (for example, if you are involved in a 'shadowing' exercise). In such instances observations and field notes are made over a long period of time and can then be collected into a diary. This can then be used to reflect on and analyse patterns over a period of time. It is important to maintain confidentiality and avoid direct reference to individuals in your field notes (see ethical issues in research in unit 5.4 in Capel, Leask and Turner, 1995).

Questionnaires

These can be a useful means of acquiring information about teaching and learning from the perspective of the teacher and/or the pupils. By asking pupils specific questions about the lesson, for example, you can gather valuable information about the impact of your teaching on the pupils. Questionnaires can provide quantitative and/or qualitative data. Open-ended questions can elicit a phrase or comment and may be more illuminating, but rely on the language ability of the pupil. Bell (1993) provides detailed guidance on designing and administering questionnaires.

The questionnaire in Table 13.1 would be quick to administer and provide you with quantitative and qualitative data about a lesson. It includes both closed and open-ended questions.

Table 13.1 An example of a simple questionnaire

Do you enjoy PE lessons?	Usually/sometimes/never
How much of this lesson did you enjoy?	All of it/some of it/none of it
How successful do you think you were in what you were asked to do?	Very successful/quite successful/not at all successful
How much did you learn in this lesson?	Very much/something/not much
How active do you feel you were in this lesson?	Very active/quite active/not active enough
How much equipment did you have?	Enough/not enough
How much help did you get from the teacher?	Enough/not enough
Write down anything you particularly enjoyed about this lesson	
Write down anything you feel could make this lesson better	

If care is taken in their construction questionnaires can be easy to administer and provide a large amount of information. One problem is that in a normal teaching situation questionnaires take time to give out, complete and return. Another problem is that they depend on whether or not the pupils have the ability to understand the questions. When constructing a questionnaire or selecting one already developed, ensure that the language is at the right level for the pupils and is jargon free so that they understand exactly what you are asking. There is also a danger that pupils may not be truthful but try to please the teacher by writing the type of answer they think that the teacher wishes to hear.

Using information gathered

An important point to note is that the information collected is only the starting point for your investigations. It should be used to inform your reflections, evaluations, discussions with your tutor and other student teachers, and to determine any action to be taken (for example, developing, implementing, monitoring and evaluating a solution).

By conducting research in this way you are testing education theory. Definitions of good practice emerge as you draw theory from practice. You apply the outcomes to your own teaching in order to address an issue, to solve a problem or to achieve a particular goal. You may then look at the same issue, problem or goal in more depth or from a different perspective, or move onto another focus. You can also share your findings with others, for example, you could write an article for a journal or present a paper at a conference applying what you learnt to teaching more generally, where relevant (see also Chapter 18).

Task 13.4 gives you guidance in conducting a mini action research project of your own.

TASK 13.4 AN ACTION RESEARCH PROJECT

An action research project may be part of your coursework. If not, undertake this task.

Identify an issue you want to address, a problem you want to solve, an aspect of your performance you want to monitor or a particular goal you want to achieve, with a view to improving your own practice. Investigate what others have found out about the issue in question. Decide the best methods of collecting information (if necessary

---

enlist the support of your tutor or another student teacher; it is often helpful to undertake action research in pairs). Arrange appropriate lesson(s) for the information to be collected. Analyse the information and try to come to some conclusions. In the light of your results consider how you might modify your practice. Try to change your practice as appropriate and monitor the changes made. Repeat the information collecting at a later date to determine how successfully you have modified your practice.

SUMMARY

In this chapter we have tried to help you to 'see' what is happening in order to 'read' the complex situations you encounter. It is widely acknowledged that observing experienced teachers teach is one of the best methods of gaining insights into the teaching and learning process. The problem is that time spent in school, and in lesson observation, can be wasted if there is not a clear focus. In this chapter some techniques for focusing your observations and obtaining relevant information have been identified. The examples of observation schedules in Appendix 1 should help you. The chapter has also introduced you to the need to reflect on your observations and critically analyse what you are doing. Only by adopting a critical stance are you able to respond in a rational, reflective and professional way to the many factors which will no doubt impinge upon the teaching of PE throughout your professional life. Undertaking action research should help you to identify issues and address problems identified through, for example, observation, reflection and evaluation. This means thinking critically about what you are doing, finding ways of systematically investigating it, and making sense of your investigations. As an action researcher you create your own education theory from professional judgement. We hope you find this chapter of help in improving your teaching and extending your expertise as a teacher.

FURTHER READINGS

Bell, J. (1987) *Doing your Research Project: A Guide for First-Time Researchers in Education and Social Science*, Milton Keynes: Open University Press.
This book is designed for people who are undertaking small-scale research projects. Part 2, 'Selecting methods of information collection', provides examples of information collecting techniques.

Capel, S., Leask, M. and Turner, T. (1995) *Learning to Teach in the Secondary School: A Companion to School Experience*, London: Routledge.
Unit 5.4 offers further advice on the conduct of an action research project.

Darst, P., Zakrajsek, D. and Mancini, V. (eds) (1989) *Analyzing Physical Education and Sport Instruction*, Champaign, Ill.: Human Kinetics.
This book contains a variety of observation schedules specific to PE.

Hellison, D.R. and Templin, T.J. (1991) *A Reflective Approach to Teaching Physical Education*, Champaign, Ill.: Human Kinetics.
This book sets out in some detail the principles and practice of reflective teaching.

Hopkins, D. (1993) *A Teacher's Guide to Classroom Research* (2nd edn), Buckingham: Open University Press.
This book is a good starting point for anyone wishing to research their own practice. It contains practical ideas and examples of a variety of information collection techniques.

Randall, L.E. (1992) *The Students Teacher's Handbook for PE*, Champaign, Ill.: Human Kinetics.
This includes many systematic observation schedules.

Underwood, G.L. (1988) *Teaching and Learning in Physical Education: A Social Psychological Perspective*, London: The Falmer Press.
In this study, 2,000 pupils in 14 schools were observed to investigate teaching and learning in PE.

Wragg, E.C. (1994) *An Introduction to Classroom Observation*, London: Routledge.
Wragg records and analyses different perspectives on life in the classroom.

14 The role of technology in PE teaching

INTRODUCTION

This chapter looks at some of the ways in which you, as a PE teacher, can use technology to improve your method of working.

Many technological devices have been used in the past by PE teachers to improve the quality of their work. An early example is when loud hailers were replaced in the early 1930s by amplifiers to announce results at school sports days. Other useful innovations over the years have been the slide projector, the film projector, the record player, the film loop, television and the overhead projector. More recently we have had the cassette, compact disc and video players and, of course, computer technology. Undoubtedly the future will bring further advances.

Audio-visual aids have become an increasingly important part of the work of the PE department. They are a valuable aid in the teaching and learning process, and you need to be able to operate the equipment and access these resources in your school with confidence.

Computers are available in every school. Computer skills are as relevant in PE as in any other subject. Increasingly in schools computer technology is being used to link departments and co-ordinate the work of the school by providing access to central administrative processes. They are also used to enhance pupils' learning. As a PE teacher you need to have a working knowledge of computers and how they may help you and your pupils. This part of the chapter is a reminder for those of you who have good computer skills and provides an introduction to becoming computer literate for those of you lacking knowledge. In either case, you should set time aside to improve existing skills and learn new skills so that you can use computer programs with confidence.

OBJECTIVES

By the end of this chapter you should:

- have developed an understanding of the need for careful planning when using audio–visual aids;
- appreciate the role of technology in your work as a PE teacher;
- be aware of the skills needed to access this technology.

AUDIO-VISUAL AIDS

Why you should use audio–visual aids in your teaching:

- to **extend the scope of what you can provide** in your classroom, gymnasium or outside. You can, for example, show demonstrations of world class performances in different physical activities. This is especially useful in an area where you may lack the expertise to demonstrate yourself;
- to **enable pupils to see outstanding sporting events**. You can show events not normally accessible to pupils because, for example, they are too expensive or occur in another country;
- to **enable pupils to better understand the content**. There is truth in the saying 'one picture is worth a thousand words'. Visual materials such as video, film, wall charts or pictures can be used to give a clearer idea of what is being taught, whether it is how muscles function or how to do a forward roll in gymnastics;
- to **add variation to presentation in your teaching**. You can increase pupil motivation, prolong their attention span and make the topic more exciting by including audio–visual aids in your teaching.

TASK 14.1 CHECKING YOUR KNOWLEDGE OF AUDIO-VISUAL AIDS

In your school experience school check which of the following are available and where they are located. Make sure you know how to book equipment in advance and what you need to do to check that it is where you want it to be at the appropriate time. Ensure that you can, if and where appropriate, use the resources in you work with pupils.

- Reading materials: books, magazines, other library resources.
- Chalk boards/whiteboards.

- Wall charts/pictures/maps/photographs/worksheets/reciprocal teaching cards.
- Models (including skeletons, hearts, etc).
- Overhead projector.
- Slides.
- Film strips, loop films.
- Television/video.
- Radio.
- Cassette/compact disc.

Before using any audio–visual aids with pupils, always check that they are appropriate to the age of the pupils and match their level of ability. You must ensure also that they are contributing to the achievement of your learning objectives. Make sure, for example, that you watch a video yourself before showing it to pupils. It is also essential that you have the technical skills needed to use the audio–visual aid effectively. Skills that you need to use in your teaching at some time, include:

- finding the starting point on a cassette or videotape easily;
- using the slow motion or stop–action facility on a film;
- preparing transparencies that are clear and large enough for the pupils to read easily; and even
- writing legibly in a straight line on a whiteboard.

If you are not sure, seek help from the technician at your higher education institution (HEI), then practise before you use each piece of equipment in a lesson.

TASK 14.2 USING AUDIO-VISUAL AIDS

With reference to an activity that you are teaching currently:

- prepare a report of various types of audio–visual aids that could be used effectively in your teaching;
- identify the resources available in the school.

Is it appropriate to amend some of your units of work to include additional use of audio–visual aids? If so, make the necessary amendments and evaluate their effectiveness.

THE ROLE OF THE COMPUTER IN PE

A computer can be used to help with the many **administrative** and **organisational** activities you have to carry out in your day-to-day work as a PE teacher (for example, recording and processing information). You can also use a computer to help in the **teaching and learning** process. For these activities and processes you need to know what hardware and software is available to you and have the skills to use it. Below are some of the skills you need and some possible sources of information.

Word processing

You can store information and retrieve it electronically on a computer. This is particularly useful if the information is going to be used again, as it can be updated readily without the need to re-enter identical material. Using a computer to produce written material such as letters and notices, or to revise curriculum documents or PE handbooks, is efficient and effective. Information sheets look much more professional when word processed, as do tests, worksheets, and materials prepared for non-participants or for wet weather sessions.

In order to undertake such tasks effectively and efficiently you need to have basic word-processing skills. Task 14.3 is designed to help you to decide, if you are unsure, whether or not you have these skills. If you have difficulty in completing any part of the task you are advised to seek help from the computer centre at your HEI.

TASK 14.3 BASIC WORD-PROCESSING SKILLS

Check that you are able to format a disk, copy a disk, access a word-processing package, access and save a file, copy a file, type adequately (not necessarily touch type), use different functions such as font size, bold, italics.

Prepare a notice to inform pupils of the start date and time of a new lunchtime club. Print and save this notice.

Retrieve the notice. Change the activity, date and time. Save and print as before.

Databases

A database is an information retrieval program. You can use the computer to store information, manipulate and sort data according to certain requirements and then print out the results in the form required. Computers do not make mistakes, so provided you put the information into the system accurately the computer can perform operations very quickly and so save you a considerable amount of time.

There are many ways you can use a database to assist with the administrative and organisational activities of a PE department. It is possible that information stored in the school's central computer system can be accessed by the PE department. This is obviously extremely useful in preparing class lists, for example. However, even if this is not the case and the PE department needs to create its own databases, these can be updated and information transferred relatively easily, as required. At the start of a new academic year, it is a simple task to change Year 7 to Year 8 and amend the names of pupils in classes, for example. The database can then be used for sorting pupils into 'option groups', for grading and record keeping. You could also use a database program to keep the records for the annual swimming gala or other event, or to catalogue the equipment in the PE department. Additionally you could use database programs to statistically analyse numerical data (for example, to analyse the results of fitness tests or sports day records). There are many database programs that are available and it is advisable to become familiar and skilful with one of them to discover its capabilities and uses.

TASK 14.4 DATABASE PROGRAMS

- Familiarise yourself with the database program being used by the PE department in your school experience school.
- Is it compatible with the school's main administrative program?
- Make a list of the ways the PE department is using the database program.
- Look at the database programs available in the computer centre at your HEI. Select one of these and make a list of the ways you think it might be used in your work as a PE teacher.

Schools are increasingly using computer technology to help with the assessment, recording and reporting of pupil acheivement. You may have found, when looking at the databases used by the PE department and the school, that 'statement banks' are being used in writing pupils' reports. One of the ways in which you could contribute to the development of pupil information technology (IT) skills is by involving them in the process of PE assessment. This could be through self-assessment and the recording of this assessment using the computer. See Chapter 11 on assessment.

Electronic mail (e-mail) and information superhighways

Computers are able to send information to other computers through the use of a modem and existing telephone lines. Most schools and HEIs have access to the narrowband technology needed to use e-mail for communication and to access the Internet (the Net) and World Wide Web (the Web) as sources of information. You can therefore send information to and receive information from anyone else with compatible equipment. This is referred to as networking and has obvious advantages for the PE teacher. Setting up fixtures between a group of schools, for example, could be made much easier using e-mail.

Changes in the way information can be compressed by using digitalisation means that even narrowband networks can carry an increasing range of functions. Access to the most up to date information has obvious advantages to you as a PE teacher. You can, for example, access information relevant to your GCSE and GCE A level teaching, such as up to date library resources and the latest information in the sports world. You can also enable pupils to gain access to the information services themselves, particularly to assist research in their project work.

You should ensure that you set time aside to use the computer centre in your HEI and/or school to familiarise yourself with gaining access to the information systems available to you. There are search programs and indices such as GOPHER, LYCOS and YAHOO (see Capel, Leask and Turner, 1996, Chapter 10), and others that are specific to areas such as sport psychology and exercise science which can be accessed. As you move around the Web you can identify the 'addresses' most relevant to your needs. Another source of 'addresses' is the increasing number of colleagues who share your interests and are Net users. Time you spend now learning about Internet and the World Wide Web should be time well spent as access to broadband networks, and the increase in quality and quantity of information that this means, is in the government's plans for all schools and HEIs. You need to be able to access JANET (Joint Academic Network) now so that you might more easily access SUPERJANET (Super Joint Academic Network), a broadband application, in the future.

Practice in using the Internet will enable you to access information to use in your teaching. Additionally you will be able to assist pupils in accessing information for themselves and so help with the development of their IT skills.

TASK 14.5 ACCESSING THE NET/WEB

When accessing the Net/Web it is important to read and carry out instructions carefully and accurately.

- Log onto the system and access the Internet (you may need help to do this the first time).
- Using the search tools indicated, find out the following information:

Lycos	http://lycos.cs.cmu.edu	'volleyball'
Yahoo	http://www.yahoo.com/	'an activity of your own choice'
Alta Vista	http://www.altavista.digital.com/	'women in the Olympic Games'

- Find out information about a topic that interests you. Write down what the topic is and how you intend to search for the information. Note each step of the search. Print out relevant information.

USING COMPUTERS IN TEACHING AND LEARNING

The simplest use of a computer as a teaching aid is as a somewhat sophisticated audio-visual aid in which information can be displayed using graphics, sound and text. Additionally, you can utilise a number of systems that have been developed linking computers with video, particularly with laser videodiscs, to teach practical activities. Access time to any frame of information on the disc is very quick, with the computer being able to find and play any part of the disc. Interactive video lessons allow you to show demonstrations of performance from many different angles and to focus on specific parts of the body depending on the information recorded on the disc. If you are fortunate enough to have access to interactive video you should find it an invaluable teaching aid in areas such as dance composition or where the analysis of a specific technique is required such as in a golf swing.

With the growth of health related fitness there have been a number of software programs developed to report on physical fitness testing. There are many commercial software packages available. If you decide to use one of these in delivering the health related aspects of the PE curriculum you must take care that you use it and that it does not dictate what you do.

If you have developed sufficient skill you can also use software packages to help you teach theory aspects of PE at GCSE or GCE A level such as exercise physiology, biomechanics and sports psychology, particularly in relation to practical laboratory work. Exercise physiology software packages are available which enable pupils to be actively engaged in collecting and processing data relating to physiological processes such as 'determination of oxygen consumption', 'body composition', and 'dietary analysis'. Examples of packages for biomechanics include 'force measurement', 'film analysis' and 'motion sensing', and for sports psychology include 'motor control applications', 'measurement of motivation/anxiety levels through measurement of physiological changes', and the 'recording and processing of answers to questionnaires'.

You can access information from CD-ROM applications to inform your teaching in PE generally but more specifically in the delivery of theory courses. These can be generic resources such as ERIC or SPORT DISCUS or discipline-specific such as Psychlit or BASES.

Pupils in examination classes can be set work to find information using the INTERNET or CD-ROM applications. When using such technology as a teaching strategy you need to make sure that the pupils know how to use it. If necessary you need to develop their skill level as an integral part of your lesson planning. As with all lesson content you must justify its inclusion and evaluate its use in relation to the achievement of lesson and unit objectives (see Chapter 3). Pupil technological skills should be developed to enable them to access information relating to their work in PE. The development of these skills should not be seen as an end in itself.

TASK 14.6 USING CD-ROMs

Check the CD-ROMS available in the library in:

- your school experience school;
- your HEI.

Note those relevant to your work. Access one that interests you (if necessary ask the librarian for assistance).

Find out if any teachers at your school experience school or elsewhere use such resources. If yes, determine for what purpose it has been used and its value. Discuss this with another student teacher.

There are too many videos, software packages, CD-ROMs and other technological aids on the market to identify. Three suppliers of these materials are given at the end of the chapter. If you decide to use some of these aids in your teaching you should contact them to see what is available and relevant to you. Sometimes it is possible to preview materials before purchase. Additionally, you can consult with PE teachers and other student teachers to identify other sources. You should then consider carefully how useful these materials might be in helping you to achieve your objectives. Remember that IT should be used to help you in your role as a teacher, it should not determine what that role should be.

SUMMARY

Technology is the methods, theory and practices governing the application of practical or mechanical sciences. Specific skills are needed if you are to use technology effectively. This chapter has aimed to help you extend your expertise as a teacher by introducing you to the skills you need to enable you to use technology; specifically audio-visual aids, computer technology and IT. Efficiency can obviously be increased by using IT in administrative and organisational activities, but using computer technology in the teaching situation does not ensure that more effective learning takes place. You must evaluate using technology as you would any other teaching strategy and judge its worth in relation to the aims and objectives you are trying to achieve (see also Chapter 9).

FURTHER READING

National Council for Educational Technology (NCET) (1995) *Highways for Learning*, Coventry: NCET.
A basic text providing information on various aspects of IT. It includes an introduction to using the Internet and useful addresses.

Underwood, J. and Underwood, G. (1990) *Computers and Learning: Helping Children Acquire Thinking Skills*, Oxford: Basil Blackwell.
This book looks at issues raised when using computers in teaching and learning. Principles can be related to PE.

Some adddresses for technological resources for teaching:
Boulton-Hawker Films Ltd, 28 George Street, Hadleigh, Ipswich IP7 5BG.
COACHWISE, 114 Cardigan Road, Headingley, Leeds LS6 3BJ.
Jan Roscoe Publications, 23 Stockwell Road, Widnes, Cheshire 4PJ WAS.

15 Your wider role as a PE teacher

INTRODUCTION

A PE teacher's responsibilities and areas of expertise extend beyond those related directly to delivering the PE curriculum. A PE teacher is required to do more than just meet the aims and objectives of the PE curriculum. This chapter looks at aspects of work that enhance PE in school and the role PE can play in the wider curriculum.

PE is often seen as a discrete subject, separated from the rest of the curriculum because of its particular focus on physical skills. The outcome of this is that PE teachers may distance themselves from some whole school aims/policies, such as aims for spiritual development or whole school assessment policy, and other teachers can overlook the contribution PE can make to such aims/policies. The first part of the chapter looks at the role of PE in achieving broader educational aims and hence contributing to whole curriculum delivery. It uses cross-curricular dimensions, skills and themes within the National Curriculum in England and Wales as examples of how PE can contribute to broader educational aims in the school. The chapter then looks at the relationship of the PE department and the PE teacher to other organisations, both for work in curriculum time and in extra-curricular time. It then considers extra-curricular activities, day visits and residential fieldwork in relation to PE.

OBJECTIVES

By the end of this chapter you should understand:

- your role and the role of PE in achieving broader educational aims, particularly in relation to cross-curricular dimensions, skills and themes;
- the relationship of the PE department and PE teacher to other organisations;

- the role of extra-curricular activities;
- the role of visits and residential fieldwork in pupils' education.

YOUR ROLE AND THE ROLE OF PE IN BROADER EDUCATIONAL AIMS

You have two roles in your future career: your role as a teacher and your role as a teacher of PE (see Chapter 1).

There is some truth in the argument that you are a teacher first and a PE teacher second. This is because there are certain expectations that all teachers have a responsibility to live up to. These expectations are closely tied to the purpose of schooling and the government's investment of millions of pounds into schools, some of which comes to you as your salary. In a society schooling is principally designed to pass on to pupils that which is seen as desirable, in, for example, knowledge, practices and morals. Teachers are expected to be role models of acceptable citizens and to do all in their power to promote the development of desirable qualities in their pupils. It goes without saying, therefore, that we are concerned with, for example, the moral, social and emotional development of pupils. These concerns are ours **not because we are PE teachers, but because we are teachers.** If we did not contribute to the all round development of the pupil we would not deserve our title as teachers (see also Chapters 1 and 2).

There are at least two ways of meeting your wider responsibilities as a teacher. One is in subject neutral situations such as in being punctual, well organised, fair and unprejudiced, in all your dealings with pupils. The other way is subject-specific, to look carefully at ways in which, by being engaged in learning in PE lessons, pupils can also be challenged to achieve broader educational outcomes such as developing social skills. The point was made in Chapter 9 that teaching strategies are capable of achieving a wide variety of outcomes, both broad educational aims and PE-specific objectives. It is very difficult for a teacher to be serving too many masters in a lesson and it is usually essential to decide which outcome is to predominate in a unit of work or lesson. The point to realise here is that while PE can most certainly make a valuable contribution to broad educational aims, it may only do so if the teacher spends less time on developing such objectives as psycho-motor skills and tactics in games. It is for the teacher to decide where the focus should be, when it should be on broader outcomes and when on specific PE objectives. See also Chapter 2.

PE and cross-curricular dimensions, skills and themes

In plans for the National Curriculum in England and Wales in the late 1980s and early 1990s, attention was drawn to the responsibility of schools to look beyond the named subjects and to ensure coverage of broader educational aims, which were named cross-curricular dimensions, skills and themes. In brief, these were listed as:

Dimensions

- providing equal opportunities for all pupils, for example, *challenging myths, stereotypes and misconceptions*;
- educating pupils for life in a multi-cultural society, for example, *extending pupils' knowledge and understanding of different cultures, faiths*.

Skills

- communication;
- numeracy;
- study;
- problem solving;
- personal and social;
- information technology (IT).

Themes

- careers education and guidance;
- economic and industrial understanding;
- environmental education;
- health education;
- education for citizenship.

(from NCC, 1990a, pp. 2–6)

Every curriculum subject was expected to play its part in meeting these broad cross-curricular aims and it is obvious from the lists above that some subjects would make a direct contribution in certain areas.

There is little doubt that PE can and should contribute to all of these cross-curricular dimensions, skills and themes. We can, for example, play a part in the **dimension** of 'educating pupils for life in a multi-cultural society' by our interest in, and possible use of, physical activities from other cultures. At different key stages we can help to consolidate work on all the **skills**; for example, possibly numeracy at KS1, communications and problem solving at all KS and study skills and IT skills at key stage (KS4). As far as the **themes** are concerned we have potential to contribute to them all, although our subject received very little mention in the booklet published on each theme (see NCC, 1990b, c, d, e, f). For a broad coverage of cross-curricular issues see unit 7.2 in Capel, Leask and Turner (1995).

While the dimensions, skills and themes were dropped from the National Curriculum after the Dearing review (Dearing 1994), they encompass a range of most valuable educational skills/topics, any of which, in our role as a teacher, it would be valuable for us to promote. Below, we provide some examples of how we could be involved in work on the themes, either on our own initiative or in conjunction with whole school cross-curriculum projects. Although the ideas below are linked to specific examples in National Curriculum documents, they are examples only and PE could play a significant part in work on all the themes.

Careers education and guidance

At KS3, task 3D (NCC, 1990d, p. 3) is concerned 'to identify local employment opportunities'. A valuable focus here would be to look at sports/leisure facilities and survey the range of jobs available in both public and private facilities.

At KS4, task 4A (NCC, 1990d, p. 35) aims 'to strengthen understanding of the qualities required for team work'. In PE a useful exercise would be to gather information on the 'team' involved in supporting, for example, a rugby XV. The workings of such a 'team' could be a fascinating study.

Education for economic and industrial understanding

At KS3, task 15 (NCC, 1990b, p. 33) proposes a focus on 'how design of goods and services, including packages and advertising, affects consumer choice'. Pupils could look at the way sports shoes are advertised and marketed, particularly in relation to the sports personalities involved.

At KS4, task 1 (NCC, 1990b, p. 40) proposes a focus on 'scarcity of resources [which] means that carefully considered choices have to be made between alternative uses'. Pupils could find out how a sports/ leisure facility manager decides to allocate her space and how she evaluates the effect of this decision.

Environmental education

At KS3 (NCC, 1990e, p. 6) the topic of 'taking individual and group responsibility for the environment' is identified. In the context of an outdoor activity pupils could pay particular attention to threats posed to the environment, by over-use, for active leisure pursuits. This could be followed up by a meeting with local planners and conservationists to find out what steps they are taking to minimise these threats.

At KS4 (NCC, 1990e, p. 33) studying 'the Green Belt Issue' could include an investigation into ways in which land is used to cater for active leisure and recreation.

Health education

This booklet (NCC, 1990c) spends little time on the physical aspects of health, maybe leaving this to PE. However, it is crucial that we are centrally involved in any whole school policy or programme on the promotion of health education.

At KS3 (NCC, 1990c, p. 17) the topic of 'psychological aspects of health education' is identified. This could be an opening for pupils to look at the all round benefit of exercise, particularly as a deterrent to stress. Pupils could perhaps survey reasons for adults being involved in physical activity and share their findings.

At KS4 (NCC, 1990c, p. 19) it is suggested that pupils should 'understand the relationships between food, body image and self-esteem'. This topic could provide an ideal opportunity to take time to discuss the fallacy of 'the ideal body' and to arrive at some sensible views on body shape and health.

Education for citizenship

At KS3 (NCC, 1990f, p. 25), under the heading of 'work, employment and leisure', it is suggested that pupils could 'investigate the importance of health and safety in workplaces'. This could provide an interesting opening for an inquiry into health and safety in sports facilities, with pupils carrying out simple risk assessments for sports activities in school (see Chapter 8).

At KS4 (NCC, 1990f, p. 26), under the heading of 'being a citizen', pupils could debate and then research the extent of voluntary work in providing physical activity opportunities for the community. A class or group of pupils might consider setting up a club in school to experience first hand all that is involved in running such an organisation.

TASK 15.1 INCLUDING WORK FROM THEMES IN PE

With respect to at least one theme, study the appropriate DES book-let and identify four further ways (two at KS3 and two at KS4) in which PE could be used as a medium to achieve its goals.

Discuss with your tutor if it would be possible to implement at least one of your ideas during your time in your school experience school.

Moral and social dimensions of teaching PE

Aspects of dimensions, skills and themes are focused on the moral and social dimensions of education. Although referred to above, this section highlights these separately.

Moral education promotes behaviour that is fair and honest; behaviour that is the outcome of pupils having formulated acceptable ethical principles or moral rules. Social education promotes the development of skills/attributes such as tolerance, co-operation, adaptability and communication. PE is often identified as an ideal medium for developing desirable moral and social behaviour (see also Chapter 2). Among the many perspectives on this issue is the view that through playing games pupils learn to be honest, unselfish and co-operative. An alternative view is that unless a person is honest, unselfish and co-operative that person cannot be satisfactorily involved in playing a game. Whichever view you hold, the same point as made in Chapter 2 arises: it is unlikely that pupils will become 'more morally and socially aware' simply by playing games or being involved in PE. As a teacher you must take steps to highlight whatever attribute you want to promote and tailor the lesson and the teacher/pupil interaction accordingly. Feedback is very important here. If you want to promote co-operation, you need to use teaching strategies that require pupils to co-operate, being sure that you identify and praise good examples and provide guidance where skills are lacking. See also Chapter 9.

In working to achieve moral and social aims and objectives in PE, you are helped and hindered by situations the pupils encounter elsewhere. You are, for example, helped by the code of practice that is expressed in the school aims/rules and is hopefully evident in every aspect of school life. You are not helped by the examples of undesirable behaviour displayed by sports people in the media. It is no easy job to prevail upon youngsters to follow **your** code of practice and **not** that exhibited by a sporting hero.

Thus, you have a role in supporting the broader aims of the school, whether cross-curricular or the broader aims of the National Curriculum. Likewise, others have an interest in, and influence on, aims of PE in the school. These are considered below.

TASK 15.2 PROMOTING DESIRABLE MORAL AND SOCIAL BEHAVIOUR IN PE

Using the completed sections as examples, identify approaches you can use in PE to develop the other attributes identified.

Attribute	*Approach*
Rule adherence	Discuss with pupils why a rule is necessary. Praise pupils following rules.
Losing gracefully	Ask each member of a losing team to speak to a member of the winning team to congratulate them on being successful and say what they did particularly well
Winning modestly	
Being fair in using time, space and equipment	
Showing tolerance of others' ideas	
Add other attributes and approaches you can identify	

Implement at least one of these approaches as appropriate, in a lesson

---

THE RELATIONSHIP OF THE PE TEACHER TO OTHER ORGANISATIONS

The PE department is not a self-contained and self-sufficient entity as it may have been in some schools ten years ago. The responsibility for defining the aims of the PE curriculum no longer lies solely in the hands of the PE department. In very few situations does the PE department have staff and facilities to achieve its aims solely from its own resources. Thus, PE teachers are required to work closely with a number of other groups. This means that you need skills beyond those related directly to teaching, including **political** skills such as tact, diplomacy and astute observation, powers of articulacy and persuasion and networking skills. The circumstances that have brought this about include:

- the introduction of the National Curriculum in England and Wales;
- the increased power of school governors including parents;
- the shortage of time for PE in schools;
- the shortage of money for schools;
- the introduction of OFSTED inspections;
- the requirement that the school produces a prospectus, setting out, for example, how all areas of the National Curriculum are covered, and how their delivery, including that of PE, is in line with school aims;
- the use of school league tables with reference to sports opportunities;
- the use of PE/sport in marketing schools;
- the proactive role of governing bodies of sport in promoting their sport;
- the involvement of the Sports Council in developing programmes to encourage young people to take part in sport;
- the power of the media.

The outcome of the developments listed above is, first, that there are a number of groups who have an interest in influencing the direction PE should take in a school and, second, that a wide range of personnel outside the school have an interest in playing a part in delivering the curriculum.

In response to the first point, you as a teacher must ensure that the curriculum is designed in a way to cater for every pupil and to fulfil the broad requirements of the National Curriculum. It would be unacceptable if a strong local personality or a generous sponsorship offer resulted in a narrowing of the activities delivered or a disproportionate amount of extra-curricular time being devoted to elite performers. The curriculum must also reflect school aims and may well incorporate PE teachers' own standpoint on the role of PE.

In meeting the second point, you as a teacher need to look to the whole community of pupils and to the breadth of their PE experience. Outside support is invaluable but should promote school curriculum policy rather than direct it. Offers of support should be carefully considered and only accepted if the planned curriculum is enriched rather than narrowed.

Organisations and groups who would like to influence the nature of PE in school

While the aims of the National Curriculum for PE are spelled out clearly (see Chapter 2), as are the areas of activity to be covered, there is still considerable leeway for the precise focus of the work. Many groups are proactive in defining what they feel should be in the curriculum. These include:

- the Sports Council;
- governing bodies of sport;
- the medical profession;
- Her Majesty's Inspectors (HMI);
- the local authority;
- school governors; and
- parents.

It is as well to remember that their proposals have an underlying motive – that is, they wish to achieve certain goals. The medical profession, for example, would wish to see a preponderance of activities that challenge the physical fitness of pupils. This is because they would see health promotion as the key aim of PE. Government may argue for more time for high profile sports because they want PE to play a central part in producing olympic gold medallists and winning sports teams. A school parent–teacher association might argue for the broadest possible curriculum and open access to extra-curricular activities, because it holds a 'Sport for All' philosophy. In any debate about the nature of PE in schools, you must be mindful of what lies behind proposals from others. Considerable tact and diplomacy are needed in such debates. You, as a PE teacher, must direct the debate back to first principles and share with interested parties the breadth of the role PE is expected to play in the education of every pupil. Relevant here too is the need for PE to be working in concert with whole school aims (see Chapter 2).

Neither groups having an interest in influencing the direction of PE nor personnel with an interest in playing a part in the delivery of the curriculum need necessarily be a threat; both can offer opportunities. See also Chapters 16 and 17. Seldom before has there been such widespread interest in school PE, nor have there been so many willing, capable hands available to help. Keeping in mind the cautionary advice given so far about keeping control over the PE curriculum, it is essential that you do not isolate yourself in the PE department from the rest of the school and from other organisations. You need to be acutely aware of opportunities and threats, and be ready to take appropriate, quick action. This could, for example, involve your putting in a claim for involvement in an exciting project or alternatively lobbying for support to oppose a development disadvantageous to PE in your school.

TASK 15.3 PRINCIPAL INFLUENCES ON THE PE CURRICULUM

Using the aims of the PE department in your school experience school, consider who might have influenced their identification. How many reflect aims of the National Curriculum for PE? How many pick up whole school aims? Compare your school's PE aims with those from another school identified by another student teacher and the list of aims for PE you ranked in Task 2.2. Discuss why there are similarities and differences. Keep this in your professional portfolio for later reference.

Organisations and groups which may be able to play a part in providing a quality PE experience for all pupils

As indicated above, as a PE teacher you need to consider carefully the way in which outside agencies can contribute to the curriculum. Retaining an objective perspective can be difficult when teaching – equipment and facilities are offered free, from, for example, a sports governing body. It is the case however, that such are the pressures on staff time and financial resources that it would be short-sighted not to look for and use local expertise. This must always be done in the context of a balanced curriculum that caters for the needs of all pupils. It is for you to determine the PE curriculum, within National Curriculum guidelines, and to use outside groups and organisations to support your programme.

Expertise that may be called on can be found in local authorities, among personnel involved in the Sports Council National Junior Sports Programme, from governing bodies who employ sports development officers and from qualified coaches in local clubs. Individuals from these agencies bring with them specific sport/activity expertise together with the most up-to-date knowledge of every aspect of the activity. They also provide invaluable links between physical activity in school and that in the local community. Among the contributions they can make are the provision of high level work for able pupils and ensuring that a broader curriculum is available for all. These contributions, which could be in curriculum or extra-curricular time, can be arranged as one-off taster sessions or on a regular basis over a number of weeks. Chapter 16 addresses school-community links (see especially Task 16.1).

We now consider two aspects of your work that may or may not involve other organisations or groups, but which are integral to your wider role as a PE teacher.

EXTRA-CURRICULAR ACTIVITIES

Extra-curricular activities are designed to extend the curriculum of schools and have always been a particularly important part of PE programmes. You only have to look at the history of PE in the United Kingdom to understand their importance. PE teachers have played a central role in the provision of school extra-curricular programmes, particularly promoting physical activity and sport beyond that provided in the curriculum.

As a student teacher you will probably be asked to help with extra-curricular activities in your school experience schools. This is an opportunity you should take. We encourage you to ask if you can help with extra-curricular activities whilst you are in the school. Your role will change according to your expertise in the activity in which you are helping. If the activity is a particular strength of yours you might want to undertake some coaching, whereas if it is an area in which you need to learn you are likely to undertake a support role. We advise, however, that whatever your experience you only help with extra-curricular activities and do not take responsibility for any activities yourself whilst in the school because you need to be careful with the amount you take on. You are going to be tired at the end of a school day and are going to have lesson evaluation and preparation to do for your classes next day. Do not take on too many extra-curricular activities which leave you so tired or without enough time to prepare adequately for your lessons.

As well as helping with the activity, take the opportunity to think about the role of extra-curricular activities in schools in preparation for your first teaching post. This will help you in preparing for an interview and selecting a school suitable for your first post (see Chapter 18) as well as in taking extra-curricular activities in your first post.

TASK 15.4 EXTRA-CURRICULAR ACTIVITIES IN YOUR SCHOOL EXPERIENCE SCHOOL

Write a list of all extra-curricular activities in your school experience school. How many of these are physical activity and sports? When are these offered? What is the purpose of each of these – for participation by all or for competition? Who they are open to (for example, to all or to team members)? Now find out who takes each of these.

Compare your findings with those of another student teacher who has undertaken the same task. Record these in your professional portfolio to reflect on as you develop as a teacher.

There are many factors which influence what is offered within an extra-curricular programme. These include the PE teacher's own interests and strengths. Practice varies greatly but PE teachers may have coached one or more school teams and/or offered one or more activities open to all pupils, possibly in activities taught within the curriculum and/or in which they are interested.

In many schools PE teachers have taken account of pupils' needs and interests in determining what to offer. They have, for example, recognised that:

- it may be difficult for pupils to participate in extra-curricular activities after school because they have to catch a school bus home, or on Saturdays because they have to work; therefore they offer activities in the lunch time or before school in the mornings;
- pupils studying for GCSE may want to participate in activities in which they do not have a commitment to team-mates every week, so that if the demands of GCSEs are too great at any one time they can take a week off;
- pupils like individual activities in which they can come and go as they want;
- interests of pupils change over time. It may be of interest to note that the most popular leisure activities after pupils leave school have been identified as football for boys and swimming for girls, followed by racket sports and athletics for both boys and girls, therefore team games are not very important in later years;
- skilled pupils who play in school teams have plenty of opportunity to participate as they may also play for clubs, the county or at higher levels outside school. However, for less skilled performers the

opportunities for participation outside school are much more limited. Some PE teachers therefore focus on providing extra-curricular activities for the latter group.

TASK 15.5 PUPILS' PARTICIPATION IN EXTRA-CURRICULAR ACTIVITIES

Using the information you collected in Task 15.4 above, select two or three extra-curricular activities offered by PE teachers in your school experience school, at least one of which is open to all and one of which is a competitive activity. Ask the teacher if you can go along to the activity. When you are there, ask some of the pupils why they go to the activity, what they like about it, what other activities they go to and why. Consider these responses in the light of what you consider to be the purposes of an extra-curricular programme.

However, it is important for you to recognise that what is offered in extra-curricular time is also influenced by the current context in which schools are working and hence by school management. In a climate of market-led education policies, with open competition by schools for pupils, one marketing strategy can be to publicise the success of school teams. Further, government initiatives to increase the performance of

---

TASK 15.6 ROLE AND FOCUS OF EXTRA-CURRICULAR ACTIVITIES

There is continuing discussion about the role and focus of extra-curricular provision in schools. What are your views on the role of extra-curricular activities in schools?

What answers would you give to the following questions?:

- What should extra-curricular provision provide: competition for some or involvement for as many pupils as possible?
- Should the promotion of teams and the winning of trophies predominate or should activities be provided to promote opportunity and activity for all with a view to promoting life-long participation in physical activity?

Take the time to reflect on these questions and discuss these and other issues with other student teachers to help you clarify what the role of extra-curricular activities should be.

elite sports people in order to improve the performance of our national teams has led to a focus on participation and opportunities for elite performers and consequently to a focus, in at least some schools, on sports teams and their performance (see, for example, DNH, 1995).

One type of extra-curricular activity designed to extend pupils' experience is day visits and residential fieldwork. This is considered in the next part of the chapter.

DAY VISITS AND RESIDENTIAL FIELDWORK

School visits take place beyond the classroom for a wide variety of reasons. Many such visits involve members of the PE department and they may even involve student teachers as temporary members of the department whilst on school experience! A visit to an international sporting event, an outdoor education residential or a sports exchange/tour can all take you outside the confines of the school grounds, perhaps to another part of the county or country, or maybe even abroad. As a student teacher, or newly qualified teacher (NQT), you are not expected to lead such a visit, but the experience that you gain from assisting is widely recognised as being of substantial benefit. However, before committing yourself to help to run a visit you should ensure that you feel confident that you can carry out the responsibility that is placed on you. In order to do this it is obviously important to clarify at the outset what exactly your role will be with whoever is organising the trip.

One word of caution; you should carefully examine your own motives for wishing to involve yourself in the trip. If you are attracted solely by the chance to see a big match, have always fancied a go at rock climbing, or perhaps would like a 'free' ski trip, then you should probably think again. The level of commitment required on all such visits is high, as is the level of responsibility on the staff team. The amount of supervision that is required probably means that you will have little opportunity to pursue the activities for yourself. Be under no illusion, such trips are hard work and demanding, but of course they can also be particularly rewarding. Many teachers have found that taking their pupils beyond the classroom enhances their working relationships with them a good deal. This is, in turn, of benefit to relationships on return to school, not only with those particular pupils who attended the trip but also often with other pupils.

Like so many other teaching situations it is neither feasible nor desirable to lay down prescriptive legislation to cover all eventualities in planning and delivering educational visits. What follows could be considered as a set of guidelines that should be of use during your school experience as well as later in your teaching career. Your school experience school has guidelines governing field trips, as has the Local Education Authority (LEA), and it is obviously important that you follow these procedures when planning and delivering such events. The guidelines below should help you to maximise what you learn by helping in any such event as a student teacher or NQT and so should better prepare you for running such a trip on your own.

Why are we going?

Whilst a great deal of important planning needs to be undertaken, much of which focuses on the practical issues concerned with the health and safety of pupils and the smooth running of the trip, it is very important to be clear at the outset of the aims of the event. Indeed, the 'Why?' is of fundamental importance and informs almost every aspect of the organisation and delivery of the trip. It may be that the visit is part of a unit of work from the PE curriculum or forms part of some cross-curricular theme. It may be targeting a particular group of pupils with special educational needs or is an element of a personal and social education (PSE) programme. Whatever the aims, everyone involved should be clear about what the trip is for. If the pupils think they have signed up for a holiday they may get a rude awakening, which in turn presents staff with untold problems.

It is not uncommon to involve the pupils in the setting of objectives for such events and indeed to involve them in planning also. Such involvement can increase the potential for achieving the learning outcomes.

What next?

Once the aims are clear some more decisions can be made: who is going, when and where are they going and what are they going to do when they get there. Some of these issues are obviously linked, but once agreed it is possible to move sensibly to the practical issues of how all this is to be organised.

In the limited space in this book not all issues can be addressed, but below are some points that you need to consider in relation to the identified aims.

Who is going?
- year group?
- tutor group?

- target group?
- open to any pupils?
- pupils and/or staff from other schools?
- which staff will go?
- will there be any other adult helpers?

When will you go?

- term time?
- holiday?
- weekend?
- early, middle or late in the programme?
- what is your work load at the proposed time?
- do you have other commitments at that time?

Where will you go?

- is the venue suitable in order to achieve objectives?
- what is its proximity, journey time/cost?
- do you have previous experience of the area?
- is there relevant information available regarding the area?
- if residential, what sort of accommodation?

What will you do when you get there?

- are the planned activities suitable in order to achieve objectives?
- can you manage such activities?
- is there possibility for differentiation?
- are there environmental considerations?

Other factors
All the above are influenced by the costs involved and your pupils' ability to meet them.
What is the school's policy on charging?

Providers

Schools often make use of day and residential centres as part of their educational visits programme. Such contracting out may range from the employment of individual specialist staff on an *ad hoc* basis to the use of a large commercial activity centre or a tour company. Choosing the right provider is an issue that requires considerable enquiry. You certainly have to go beyond the glossy brochure. Clearly the quality of the provision and the price are key issues, but as a starting point it should be clear that the course offered fits the aims of your programme. Do they, for example, offer an off the peg package or are they prepared to work with you to tailor a course to suit your needs? Being able to talk to another teacher who has already made use of the centre could be particularly informative.

Recent legislation has introduced a licensing scheme for providers of adventure activities. Schools offering adventure activities to their own pupils do not need to be licensed, but from October 1997 all other providers need to be. In order to obtain a licence all areas of their operation are inspected, including management systems, staff expertise, suitability of equipment, safety procedures and many other health and safety arrangements.

TASK 15.7 CHOOSING A PROVIDER

Obtain details of the LEA's residential centres, along with details of a commercial centre that offers courses suitable for your pupils. For a suitable hypothetical course of your own choosing, devise criteria to judge what is on offer, and then evaluate the centres in the light of your criteria.

How will you make it all happen?

Once decisions have been made on the above then the detailed planning can begin. Much of the practical organising of visits relies on the application of common sense. This is reflected in school and LEA guidelines, which you must follow. As a professional educator you are, or are becoming, an effective organiser, but it is worth remembering that the consequences of getting it wrong away from school are generally higher than when you deliver a poorly planned school-based lesson. You should not underestimate the level of responsibility that you are taking on. The next section, which makes no claim to be definitive, outlines a number of important things that need to be undertaken.

Approval

Before signing up pupils for the 'big event' or sending off any deposits, clearly approval needs to be sought from the head teacher, and in some cases the governing body and the LEA. Who gives approval depends on the nature of the planned trip; generally if adventurous activities are involved, the LEA needs to be consulted as well. If your school is Grant Maintained, however, the decision lies with the head teacher and governing body alone. Refer to your school guidelines for the correct procedure.

TASK 15.8 SCHOOL PROCEDURES FOR EDUCATIONAL VISITS

Obtain a copy of your school's policy document on educational visits, and the LEA guidelines if appropriate, and from them find out the following:

- What are the procedures for gaining approval for a visit that includes adventurous activities?
- What is the school's policy on charging for educational visits? Is there any facility for offering assistance towards the cost of a visit in the case of hardship?
- What insurance cover does the school and/or LEA have in place for educational visits? Do either recommend additional cover for visits abroad or for visits concerned with adventurous activities?

What are the insurance implications for staff of using their own cars to transport pupils on educational visits? Do staff have to obtain a minibus licence to drive school vehicles?

Parental consent

Consent in writing needs to be sought from the pupils' parents for any visit or journey that is not part of the everyday routine of the school. In order for them to give their consent they want to know what is planned. The information that they require might include:

- dates and times of departure and return;
- destination, with address and contact telephone number if possible;
- the objectives of the visit;
- details of activities to be undertaken;
- names of group leader and accompanying staff;
- method of travel;
- code of conduct relating to expected standards of behaviour;
- financial arrangements, to include charges/voluntary contributions, methods of payment, cancellation arrangements and advice on pocket money;

- insurance, what cover has been arranged;
- clothing/footwear/equipment requirements;
- prohibited items.

The above list identifies a good deal of the practical planning that has to be completed. For some visits such planning can prove complex and time consuming. There is a need to be realistic in the time allowed for such planning. Some events need to be arranged over a year ahead of the date of departure! This also allows pupils to spread payment, which may enable some pupils with less ability to pay to participate.

Pupil information

Along with the parental consent form for the pupils, there is also a need to collect specific information about each member of the party, including staff. Such information might include:

- personal details, full name, address, date of birth, etc.;
- next of kin contacts, work and home;
- medical details (for example, current medication, allergies, potential ailments, doctor's name and address);
- special dietary needs on moral, health or religious grounds.

Pre-visit preparation

There is always a need for some preparation with the pupils prior to departure, if only to establish where they need to be and what they need to bring. Codes of behaviour, group organisation, objective setting, skill acquisition, menu planning are just some of the issues that may also need addressing and may involve preparation sessions spread over some weeks or even months. Passports may be needed. Pupils with non-European passports may need visas.

Post-visit reflection

A review of the pupils' experiences of the visit is essential if the learning outcomes are to be realised and maximised. The review starts by reflecting on what was done, and goes on to look at what was learnt and finally to transfer the learning. Finding time for reflection is often difficult, so planning a review session into the programme is important. There is sometimes a temptation to set it aside for more pressing matters. This, however, undermines all the hard work of organising and delivering.

Some form of evaluation of the visit itself and the effectiveness of the planning is also clearly of benefit, particularly if there is an intention to repeat the visit. It may be appropriate to provide a report to the head teacher.

Before you go!

Away from your normal teaching environment it may be appropriate to adopt a more relaxed style, but don't forget that you are still the teacher and your interactions with pupils and colleagues are watched and talked about. You should always remember the responsibilities that come with being a teacher.

It should be clear from this section that being involved in educational visits involves a high level of commitment and responsibility, as well as a good deal of hard work. However, do not be daunted, the benefits for your pupils and your own professional development are many. Teaching beyond the classroom can be a most rewarding experience!

SUMMARY

This chapter has looked at aspects of your work which extend beyond that related directly to delivering the PE curriculum. Four specific aspects of that work have been considered: the role of PE in achieving broader educational aims and hence in whole curriculum delivery, particularly in relation to cross-curricular dimensions, skills and themes; the relationship of the PE department and the PE teacher to other organisations, both for work in curriculum and in extra-curricular time; the role of extra-curricular activities; and finally day visits and residential fieldwork in relation to PE. This should enable you to see beyond your immediate work in developing your teaching skills to become an effective teacher, to the broader skills you need as a PE teacher.

FURTHER READING

Hunt, J. and Hitchin, P. (1988) *The Residential Course Planner*, Kendal: Groundwork Group Development.
   In loose leaf format, this book contains much detailed practical advice on undertaking a residential trip. It also has photocopiable materials that can be used to involve the group in all aspects of the trip, from setting the objectives to reviewing the event. Written from experience, it is a useful text to help novice and experienced planners alike.

Smart, J. and Wilton, G. (1995) *Educational Visits*, Leamington Spa: Campion Communications Ltd.
This is a readable and well presented summary of everything a teacher must do to put an educational visit together. Photocopiable materials include sheets to help with administrative tasks as well as pro formas. Thorough and accurate.

16 From school to community: PE beyond the classroom

INTRODUCTION

One of the key aims of PE is to 'teach pupils, through experience, to know about and value the benefits of participation in physical activity while at school and throughout life' (NCC, 1992, Section B1.1.1). To achieve this aim, PE teachers must be aware of the rapid changes taking place, and the reality of the external forces that are influencing what we can offer young people.

> The range of physical activities in which young people can partici-
> pate is growing wider. Many opportunities to participate fall outside
> the physical education curriculum and many are provided outside
> the school. The range of agencies involved in providing such oppor-
> tunities is expanding, including local leisure centres, sports and
> dance clubs, the youth service, outdoor pursuits centres and organ-
> isations, special needs groups and many others. There is undoubt-
> edly a need for much better co-ordination of all these activities
> between the different bodies involved. This is essential to ensure
> that young people are made aware of all the opportunities available
> and how to gain access to them. The development of partnerships
> can also ensure that the best use is made of all the available
> resources. This includes physical resources both in and out of
> school, as well as the human resources of teachers, parents, coaches,
> youth workers, and many others involved in providing young people
> with opportunities for physical activity.
>
> (DES/WO, 1991a, p. 49)

It is essential that as you prepare for the teaching profession you understand the context of PE as it affects young people's lives in the school and
in the community and that you are prepared to respond to the initiatives
made by different education, sports and dance institutions and organisations since 1988. See, for example, *School Sport Forum* (Sports Council,

1988), *Active Life Styles: School to Community* (Sports Council, 1991), *Physical Education for Ages 5 to 16* (DES/WO, 1991), *Champion Coaching: The Power of Partnership* (NCF, 1993), *Physical Education in the National Curriculum* (DES/WO, 1992), *Young People and Sport: Policy and Frameworks for Action* (Sports Council, 1993), *Why Physical Education?* (BCPE/Sports Council, 1994), *Sport: Raising the Game* (Department of National Heritage, 1995), *Setting the Scene* (Department of National Heritage, 1996).

The challenge for the PE profession now is to create a system that guarantees co-ordinated progress of each young person's PE experience through their own school and into the local community. It should be the PE teacher working in partnership with sport and dance personnel who manages and co-ordinates that system through school and community cluster networks.

OBJECTIVES

At the end of this chapter you should:

- understand the context of PE embracing both school and community;
- be aware of the additional role of a PE teacher as manager and co-ordinator of PE, sport and dance opportunities;
- know about a partnership in action model that could provide an integrated, progressive and continuous strategy for implementing lifelong participation in physical activity.

PE, SCHOOL AND COMMUNITY

No longer is PE confined to a school day. School provides the foundation for sport and dance development experiences that go beyond the school premises. Partnerships between school and community provide the opportunity for a co-ordinated programme of physical activities that meets the needs of young people.

Teachers of PE need to understand the similarities and differences between PE, sport and dance development if they are going to manage effectively **continuous pathways of opportunity** for the benefit of all young people involved in physical activity, whatever their age or ability.

To create 'continuous pathways of opportunity', teachers must follow a logical sequence of development as they draw up action plans for young people in their school based careers.

First, teachers must understand the nature of PE as a foundation subject in the National Curriculum and its statutory entitlement for pupils aged 5–16. The head teacher and governors are the custodians of the curriculum and PE teachers are responsible for delivering all aspects of the Programme of Study. This is the core experience from which other forms of physical activity can develop. (Chapter 17 includes more detailed discussion of PE in the National Curriculum.)

Second, teachers should explore PE as part of the whole school curriculum. PE provides an excellent context for a range of cross-curricular themes and dimensions such as health and safety, personal and social education, socio-cultural, environmental and aesthetic developments (see also Chapter 15).

Third, each school should provide an extra-curricular programme which gives pupils the opportunity to focus on new sport and dance activities or to develop interests that began in the school day (see 'Extra-curricular activities' in Chapter 15). The extra-curricular programme is where partners from the community (for example, youth sport managers, coaches, dance development officers and parents) can make significant contributions and support development in the next two stages.

> Limitations on curriculum time and lack of appropriate facilities usually make it impossible for pupils to participate in a full range of team or individual sports during normal school hours. Consequently, the provision of extra curricular sporting activities provided either by staff in the school or other agencies, significantly increases the opportunities of both general participation in sport and the development of excellence.
>
> (NCC, 1992, Section H1.1.3)

The **fourth stage** involves the recognition of each young person's individual potential by providing appropriate competitive experiences and performance related activities. They may choose to concentrate on a specific activity or to take part at a more intense level of performance. In any case

> only a clearer local and regional mapping of what is on offer, and a better co-ordination of both information and provision will allow young people to find their way through the maze. Good schools make an effort to guide the pupils into further opportunity at their level of experience but not all schools feel that is their prime function. If talent is to be nurtured and developed as fully as young

athletes deserve, ways must be found to ensure that the transition is smooth and the path open.
(Office of HM Chief Inspectors of Schools, 1995, Paragraph 80, p.35)

The significance of the PE teacher's developing role emerges at the **fifth stage**. Schools which value the importance of sport and dance can build vital links with the community, thus opening up a whole spectrum of opportunities based on the foundation, participation, performance and excellence of activities in the sports development continuum (see Figure 16.1).

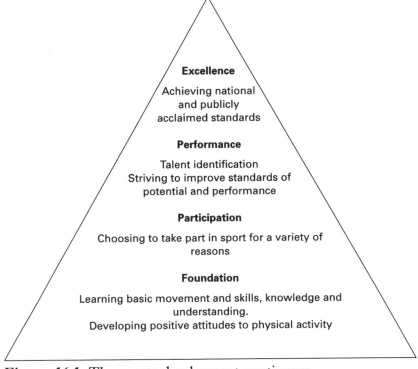

Figure 16.1 The sports development continuum.
Source: Adapted from Sports Council (1993, p. 8)

CHANGING ROLE OF THE PE TEACHER

Each stage is critical to the goal of providing opportunities for young people. Through quality controlled partnerships the 'seamless web and continuous opportunities' mechanism that the PE profession has been searching for during the last decade may be created.

Effective partnerships are dependent on good organisation and management. Where partnerships occur in the curriculum, the school should take the responsibility for ensuring that all those involved in teaching are aware of their different roles. While it may be beneficial for sport's leaders, coaches and dancers to assist during curriculum time, their role should be one of support not substitution for the teacher. The teacher must retain overall responsibility for planning, organisation and monitoring to ensure that pupils' physical activity is coherent, consistent, progressive and controlled.

(NCC, 1992, Section H1.2)

The role of PE teachers must therefore widen. They must consider not just how they manage but who and what they are managing. They must analyse not only the nature of the task but the nature of themselves as human beings in an active environment; not just what they know but how they transmit that knowledge to young people.

Headteachers and governors may wish to nominate a teacher to be responsible for all aspects of co-ordination. This approach helps to encourage:

- development of a full and varied extra-curricular programme;
- provision of an environment for the development of excellence;
- use of the school's physical education facilities by the local community;
- opportunities to generate income through the community use of school facilities.

(NCC, 1992, Section H1.2.3)

Teachers therefore need to be able to:

 (i) audit and utilise the support and ever growing expertise of a range of partners in delivering to young people the breadth and depth of opportunity that the National Curriculum demands (particularly the challenge and opportunities offered by key stage 4 (KS4) in the National Curriculum);

 (ii) co-ordinate and manage partnership in order to ensure a rich and varied diet of experiences for all young people whatever their ability;

(iii) control the planning and delivery of the PE, sport and dance development programmes within the context of the school and its community cluster.

The time seems right therefore to introduce a new kind of 'PE teacher' into the PE department, who might be called 'a Youth Sport/Dance Co-ordinator'. Such teachers would ensure that maximum use is made of all available physical and human resources, both in and out of school, so that young people, whatever their age or ability, can follow the right pathways and exit routes in foundation, participation, performance and excellence activities (see p. 242). It is likely that their specific role would be to contribute to the interpretation and delivery of the National Curriculum alongside after-school sport and dance development for 5 to 16/19 year olds. However, as part of a team of staff they would use designated time to:

(i)   establish a coherent and unified partnership action plan to manage school and community resources effectively so that they can network sport and dance programmes;

(ii) provide leadership and become proactive sports and dance development managers of opportunity and facilitators for young people at all levels of ability;

(iii) focus upon performance development and talent identification by contributing to the coach education programme;

(iv) provide opportunities for young people to fulfil their creative and expressive needs through community dance development.

Wherever possible in your own initial teacher education course you should seek opportunities to work alongside sport and dance personnel in the community. This experience would put you in touch with young people with a diversity of needs, including the disabled, the talented and economically and socially deprived individuals and whole communities.

In the early years of your teaching career you should see the development of your professional competence as embracing a wider portfolio, to include a role in the school and community. The need to be versatile and responsive to current and future trends in the social and political climate, which offers PE for young people, is crucial to your professional success.

An awareness of cross-curricular dimensions, themes and skills (see Chapter 15), as well as continuity and progression between the primary and secondary phases of education, will be part of your overall continuing professional development (see Chapter 18).

TASK 16.1 FROM SCHOOL TO COMMUNITY

If possible, on your next school experience (or induction year in your first teaching post) carry out an audit of the school and its community and identify gaps in provision. The audit focus should be based upon pupils' needs. It should include the following:

Pupils
What is available to pupils in terms of:

- the level of access, i.e. at foundation, participation, performance or excellence?
- the range of sports, games and dance activities?
- gender differences in accessibility?
- opportunities for the disabled?

School
What is available at the school in terms of:

- equipment?
- facilities?
- teaching and coaching expertise?
- training in coaching for teachers?
- links already established with primary feeder schools, clubs, leisure and sports centres?

Community
What agencies exist within reach of the school's community?

- local authorities and leisure services?
- leisure/sports centres?
- sports clubs?
- dance organisations?
- governing bodies of sport?

What personnel are available?

- sport development officers?
- youth sport managers?
- dance workers/entrepreneurs?
- coaches?

What are their roles and responsibilities? How can they help?

- How can they support teachers in delivering continuous, progressive quality experiences and opportunities in PE, sport and dance development?
- Are they available to work in the school?
- Do they provide equipment support services?
- What level of opportunity can they provide – performance and excellence?
- Is there a **Champion Coaching*** scheme, **Top Programme**[†] or **Sports Fair**[††] scheme in the area?
- What competitive systems/tournaments are available?

Do the local sports clubs have a:

- school link officer?
- junior division?

- coaching programme?
- system for access by disabled young people?

Does the local leisure/sports centre:

- encourage juniors to attend?
- provide concessionary rates?
- provide extra facilities for the school?

Store this information in your professional portfolio for reference when needed.

* **Champion Coaching** emerged from the National Coaching Foundation in 1991 and is a development programme that concentrates on the delivery of quality after-school coaching for young people aged 11–14 who are reaching or have reached performance level. It is a national scheme delivered at local level through partnerships of schools, their local authorities, and governing bodies of sport. It is also linked to the Youth Sport Trust Development Programme (see, for example, NCF, 1993).

† The **Youth Sport Trust Top Programme** began its full training initiative in April 1996. As part of the Sports Council's National Junior Sports Programme, the Top Programme offers opportunities to young people aged 4–18. The Trust's ambition is that by the year 2000 every young person in the United Kingdom, whatever their ability, will have the opportunity to take part in a number of linked programmes which include:
Top Play: Aimed at introducing sport to 4–9 year olds. It focuses on core games and skills.
BT Top Sport: Aimed at 7–11 year olds. It focuses on specific sports. During the latter part of the 1990s there will be an extension of the Top Sport programme to include gymnastics, athletics and swimming.
Top Club: Aimed at helping sports clubs to establish quality improved provision for young people 11 to 18. Other initiatives targeted at pre-school children (Top Tots) and key stage 2/3 pupils (Top Link) will be launched during 1997. See, for example, Haskins (1997), Shenton (1996) and Youth Sport Trust (1996a, 1996b).
   Since its launch in June 1996 the Youth Sport Trust has been working with the Department for Education and Employment (DFEE) and acting as the central co-ordinating body for the development of specialist Sport Colleges.

†† **Sports Fair** emerged in 1996. It is supported financially by the Sports Council and delivered through Youth Clubs UK. It has links with the Youth Sport Trust Top Programme, but its main focus is on providing worthwhile sporting experiences in a youth club setting. Supporting its development is a training scheme under the heading of Sports Train. See, for example, Edwards (1996).

PRIMARY AND SECONDARY PARTNERSHIPS IN ACTION

Figure 16.2 sets out the networking process that can emerge over a period of time as more and more teachers develop the expertise and skills in Sport and Dance development with the support of local, regional and national partners. It is a partnership in action model that could provide an integrated, progressive and continuous strategy for implementing lifelong participation in physical activity.

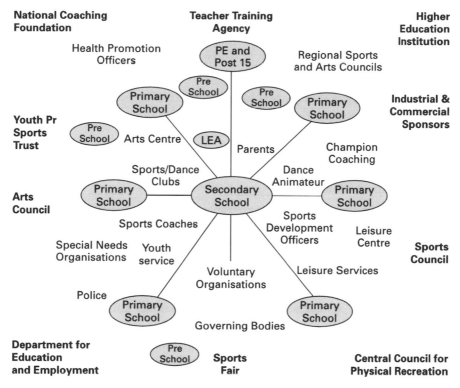

Figure 16.2 Primary–secondary cluster development model (Shenton, 1997)

> PARTNERSHIP IN ACTION is about co-operation, mutual respect, understanding of each other's skills/expertise and enterprise to create structured pathways of opportunity for pupils through curriculum time, extra and extended curriculum.
>
> (Shenton, 1994, p. 17)

It is based on the belief that continuity and progression between the key stages of the curriculum and consequently much stronger links between primary and secondary schools will be of significant importance for the development of appropriate experiences for young people's quality of learning and quality of life. Each secondary school, along with its main primary feeder schools, defines their own geographical community boundary according to their needs.

At the centre of this networking process is the PE teacher in the secondary school who can initiate and manage change and the transition process. The PE teacher can implement the five stages of access and opportunity that were identified earlier in this chapter (see pp. 241–2), using other teachers and expert providers from the community.

In this way the teacher can co-ordinate the many initiatives and action plans that are currently in circulation, and which are emerging from a range of national organisations in sport and dance, and turn them into workable partnership ventures. For example:

- Central Council for Physical Recreation;
- National Coaching Foundation;
- Sports Council;
- Arts Council;
- Sports Fair UK;
- Youth Sport Trust.

TASK 16.2 INFLUENCE OF NATIONAL ORGANISATIONS ON SCHOOL AND COMMUNITY DEVELOPMENTS

Make time to discover the roles and responsibilities of the national organisations listed above. Identify their main initiatives and development programmes and analyse their significance and impact upon young people as we move into the twenty-first century. Use the literature in your library, the further reading at the end of this chapter, and the list of addresses at the end of the book to aid you. Store this information in your professional portfolio.

By the time you have completed Task 16.2 and created a detailed file of national organisations and agencies in the community who are willing and able to support PE, sport and dance development for young people of school age, you should be aware of the scope of the PE teacher's task in co-ordinating and managing partners in extra- and extended-curricular and community based activities.

One of the initiatives you may have identified in this process is Sportsmark (English Sports Council, 1996). By the end of 1997, a substantial number of schools across the country will have submitted evidence and consequently received Sportsmark and/or Sportsmark II Gold Awards, one of the latest initiatives from the National Junior Sports Programme.

TASK 16.3 SPORTSMARK AND SPORTSMARK II GOLD AWARDS

Read the sections below about Sportsmark and Sportsmark II Gold Awards and consider what might be the potential significance and impact of this

---

initiative on the progress of the PE and Sport in the school and its community.

PE in the curriculum
Schools should provide a minimum of two hours of timetabled PE lessons each week for every pupil across KS3 and KS4.

Games in the PE Curriculum
Schools must prove that they are devoting at least half the time spent in PE lessons to games, as defined in the National Curriculum.

Extra-curricular activities
Schools should provide a minimum of four hours each week of organised sport outside timetabled lessons to all interested pupils. At least 50 per cent of pupils should take part regularly. There should be a minimum of six different activities (covering at least four areas of activity in the National Curriculum to achieve Sportsmark Gold).

Competitive activities
Schools should provide a wide range of competitive opportunities for all pupils throughout the year to achieve Sportsmark Gold (minimum of six sports).

Teachers' qualifications
Teachers should be encouraged to gain coaching qualifications or leadership/officiating awards. All potential Sportsmark Gold schools need to provide evidence that teachers hold a specialist PE qualification and/or a currently valid governing body award for the sport with which they are involved.

Links with sports clubs
Schools should have developed links with a number of local sports clubs as a way of providing pupils with further sporting activities. To achieve a Sportsmark Gold there must be evidence of formal agreements with clearly identified roles and responsibilities of a liaison tutor in each club.

Governing body/Community award schemes
Schools should make sports governing body awards and leadership awards to their pupils available, either alongside or through GCSE Physical Education or as an extra-curricular activity.

Additional supporting information
All schools wishing to qualify for Sportsmark or Sportsmark Gold Awards must show evidence of a quality PE programme being delivered in PE lessons. A copy of the latest OFSTED report is required as part of the submission process.

The support of the local PE adviser/inspector and chair of governors to the school in question is also requested.

Source: Adapted from English Sports Council (1996)

SUMMARY

It should be clear from what you have read so far that amidst the many national and regional initiatives currently taking place that teachers and their partners in the community hold the key to unlocking progressive and co-ordinated opportunities for all young people to realise their full potential in PE, sport and dance as we move into the twenty-first century.

In your first appointment school you may need to work hard with other members of the department to persuade your head teacher and the school governors that the following ingredients are an absolute minimum if quality provision is to be achieved:

- a minimum of 10 per cent curriculum time for PE;
- qualified PE staff and partners who will be supporting the overall PE, sport and dance development programme in the school and community;
- time during the school day for the implementation of links and networks with primary feeder schools and community partners;
- an appropriate budget for transport, equipment, and the use of facilities on the school site;
- health and safety policy guidelines to support all the activities pursued by pupils and their teachers in the different activity environments in the school and the community.

FURTHER READING

The following publications provide further reading on working in partnership:

British Association of Advisers and Lecturers in Physical Education Areas 3 and 4 (BAALPE) (1992) 'The Development of Effective Partnerships between Schools and Outside Agencies', *Bulletin of Physical Education*, 28, 1, Spring pp. 29–31.

Campbell, S. (1995) 'Coordination of Effective Partnerships for the Benefit of School Aged Pupils', *British Journal of Physical Education*, 26, 2, pp. 10–12.

Department for Education and Employment (DFEE) (1995) *Our School – Your School*, London: DFEE.

Department for Education and Employment (DFEE) (1996) *Sports Colleges – A Guide for Schools*, London: DFEE.

Department of Education and Science and the Welsh Office (DES/WO) (1991) *National Curriculum for Ages 5–16*, London: HMSO. See particularly Chapter 12 and Appendix C, pp. 49, 67–74.

Department of National Heritage (DNH) (1995) *Sport: Raising the Game*, London: DNH.

Edwards, P. (1996) 'Getting Active – Sports Fair', *Magazine of Youth Clubs UK*, Summer, pp. 20–1.
This provides information about the Sports Fair UK initiative.

English Sports Council (1996) *National Junior Sport Programme*, London: Sports Council.
This document includes information about Sportsmark.

Haskins, D. (1997) 'From school to community: The Next Step with Top Play and BT Top Sport', *Primary Focus: The British Journal of Physical Education*, 28, 1, Spring, pp. 11–14.

Laventure, B. (1992) 'School to Community: Progress and Partnership', in N. Armstrong (ed.) *New Directions in Physical Education, Volume. 2: Towards a National Curriculum*, Champaign, Ill.: Human Kinetics, pp. 169–97.

National Coaching Foundation (NCF) (1993) *Champion Coaching: The Power of Partnership*, Leeds: White Line Publishing Services.

National Curriculum Council (NCC) (1992) *Physical Education: Non-Statutory Guidance*, York: NCC.
See section H: 'Partnerships, Physical Education and Sport'.

North West Sports Council (1993) *Going for Gold: A Regional Strategy Study on Performance and Excellence in the North West*, Manchester: North West Sports Council.

Office of HM Chief Inspector of Schools (1995) *Physical Education and Sport in Schools: A Survey of Good Practice*, London: HMSO.

Shenton, P. (1996) 'Physical Education and Sport in Partnership! Is the Youth Sport Trust Realising a National Vision Through a Local Recipe of Good Practice?', *British Journal of Physical Education* 27, 2, pp. 17–19

Sports Council (1993) *Young People and Sport: Policy and Frameworks for Action*, London: Sports Council.

Youth Sport Trust (1996) *Annual Report 1995/96*, Loughborough: Youth Sport Trust.
This provides information about Top Play, BT Top Sport and Top Club.

17 The background to, and developments from, the National Curriculum for PE

INTRODUCTION

> Together I want us to bring about a sea change in the prospects of British sport – from the very first steps in primary school right through to the breaking of the tape in the Olympic final . . . My ambition is simply stated. It is to put sport back at the heart of weekly life in *every* school. To re-establish sport as one of the great pillars of education alongside the academic, the vocational and the moral.
>
> (Prime Minister's letter, DNH, 1995)

Why does a chapter on PE begin with a statement on sport? Because this statement made history. Never before has a Prime Minister made such a personal, direct and unequivocal statement about sport and about sport in schools. He has set us a challenge.

The effects of government policy are being felt throughout sport. The policy is also having, and will continue to have, a profound influence on the teaching of PE and the provision for sport in schools. You will be aware by now, and particularly after reading Chapter 16, that the role of the PE teacher is changing as a result of the increase in numbers of people who can contribute to provision for sport in schools and also as a result of the significant increase in resources now available through the National Lottery. For further discussion about how PE and sport are different and how they complement one another see Murdoch (1990).

The process leading up to the publication of *Sport: Raising the Game* (DNH, 1995) makes interesting reading and forms the first part of this chapter. It is appropriate, also, to chart in more detail the evolution of the National Curriculum from the first progress reports to the current implementation of the Statutory Orders; to trace the issues that have become significant; to evaluate how far what was originally intended is being achieved; to pose the questions: 'What now is PE in the light of developments in sport?', and 'Does PE need to change or rethink its emphasis and if so in what way?'

OBJECTIVES

At the end of this chapter you should feel more confident in making a response to the following critical questions that arise from this challenge:

- What led up to the publication of *Sport: Raising the Game?*
- Where does PE fit into this development?
- What effect does this emphasis on sport have on PE in the National Curriculum?
- Does PE have a unique role in the school and, if so, what might this role be?
- In what ways do PE and sport differ and in what ways do they complement each other?

Your responses to these questions should assist you at an interview for a teaching post (see Chapter 18) and help you to make reasoned and convincing statements about PE and sport to key people – for example, school governors, head teacher, parents, sports personnel and the pupils themselves.

WHAT HAPPENED BEFORE *SPORT: RAISING THE GAME?*

Chapter 16 has already alerted you to the fact that the last decade has seen many significant influences on both PE and sport. It has been a period of hitherto unknown central government interest, involvement and influence. This period of quite remarkable change nevertheless reveals some consistent trends in thinking and in the progression of ideas.

The Desk Study: Sport in Schools

The beginning of this period of change can be traced back to the mid 1980s when there was quite unprecedented media interest in the state of sport in schools. The extensive media interest in sport in schools during this period focused on, and in many instances, exaggerated, two current prevalent perceptions that, first, sport was in a decline both within the school context and in the winning of international honours and, second, that the former was responsible in a direct way for the latter. There was an urgent need for evidence, relating to both the incidence and the state of sport in schools, that would serve to refute many of the misconceptions and ill-founded allegations that were being levelled directly at schools, school sport and PE and also indirectly at the different sports bodies that were in any way involved with schools. There was also a need for a the production of a defined policy for sport in schools based on this evidence.

This led to the commissioning, and writing, of what came to be known as *The Desk Study: Sport in Schools* (Murdoch, 1987). While this document had limited and controlled circulation, it did nevertheless signal the beginning of a period of considerable impact on developments in PE and sport in the ensuing ten years.

Parry (1988), in reflecting on the study soon after its publication, voiced regret that, with the brief to consider 'the place of sport in the PE curriculum', the study focused only on the descriptive answers to factual questions when there was such an obvious opportunity to ask significant questions relating to the *justification* of sport within the curriculum.

> This sort of question is conspicuous by its absence from many PE and sport documents, and I believe it to be a very serious weakness which has contributed significantly to present-day difficulties.
>
> (Parry, 1988, p. 106)

This may well be the case, but the purpose behind commissioning *The Desk Study* was not to seek justification for sport but rather to provide more specific and detailed evidence of the state of sport in schools, to recognise significant issues and to suggest which of these issues might provide a suitable basis for advice on a policy for sport in schools. The study deliberately confined itself to the decade from the late 1970s to late 1980s. The completed study presented the Department of Education and Science (DES) and the Department of Employment (DoE) with five key recommendations that were to form the basis of joint action by both government departments (DES and DoE). These recommendations were to:

- improve provision for, and place more emphasis on, PE and sport in the primary school;
- implement corporate strategies and action for PE and sport involving all appropriate agencies;
- make clear statements of policy for both PE and sport;
- consider education and training for providers in schools and other agencies;
- provide adequate resources including finance.

(adapted from Murdoch, 1987, pp. 50–3)

School Sport Forum

To approach the defining of a policy, as identified above, the two government departments (DES and DoE, as they were in 1986), through the Sports Council, set up a working group known as the School Sport Forum. The remit of the forum was to address the recommendations from *The Desk Study*. The subsequent report of this group (*Sport and Young People: Partnership in Action*, Sports Council, 1988) raised a number of significant issues. These are summarised below:

- the Sports Council (through DoE) was taking an influential lead in the future of sport in schools;
- this focus on sport in schools would have inevitable implications for PE in general and for the curriculum in particular;
- similar political interest and involvement was not being shown by DES in the impact that this could have on education;
- there was actual and potential funding being released by the above initiatives in sport that could not be matched by education;
- time allocation for PE in the curriculum in schools was inadequate to provide the underpinning for sport in schools that was being demanded;
- primary ITE was inadequate to equip teachers to deliver an appropriate curriculum in the critical years of a child's development;
- education and training was being seen by the Sports Council as being critical to the future of sport for young people.

National Curriculum and the School Sport Forum

It was a fortuitous coincidence that at the same time as the setting up of the School Sport Forum in 1986, the Secretary of State for Education was launching detailed plans for the subsequent Education Reform Act (ERA, 1988) that gave rise to the National Curriculum in England and Wales. The juxtaposition of these two significant and separate developments, one in sport and the other in education, meant that the opportunity was there to address both PE and sport in some detail from different viewpoints but at the same time and at the same level of significance within government policy. Had it not been that PE was included within the ten subjects of the National Curriculum, the future of PE could have had a very different history, and the impact of the strong initiatives within sport could have threatened PE very profoundly. As it was, PE had the opportunity to establish itself firmly within the Statutory Orders of the National Curriculum and to meet developments in sport with dialogue rather than the aggression of survival. The challenge to the PE profession in preparing the National Curriculum was to present a clear rationale for the subject that would be nationally recognised. The potential for coherence that this offered to the teaching of PE was something that the profession had been calling for for some time. For the first time a single voice may speak and be heard.

The School Sport Forum report (Sports Council, 1988) was published in advance of the report of the National Curriculum Subject Working Group in PE (SWGPE) (DES/WO, 1991b). These intervening years allowed the recommendations of the School Sport Forum to be absorbed by the specific groups to which they were targeted. This report undoubtedly had an influence on the general thinking of the SWGPE and laid a foundation for the approach that was adopted towards sport in the curriculum and its context within the school. Ultimately both reports carried some very similar messages and these have formed the basis for policy development and implementation both in education and in sport.

The broad assumptions acknowledged by both reports were that:

- PE and sport are not the same but have a very significant working relationship for mutual benefit where 'sport, including competitive games, is an essential part of PE' (DES/WO, 1991b, Chapter 4, see 4.1, p. 7). (An early chapter in the proposals to The Secretary of State, 1991, was entitled 'PE and sport'.);
- the models adopted for both coaching in sport and teaching in the PE curriculum should be as compatible as possible;
- the critical years for both PE and sport are the primary years;
- the preparation of teachers for this age group is inadequate in terms of time allocation;
- PE and sport should be accessible to all young people;
- partnerships are essential if the young people are to benefit, as no one agency can deliver what is required on its own;
- the local community in which the young people live should be the place in which these partnerships are worked out and implemented.

You will see that these were serious assumptions as the developments arising from them are considered in some detail in the later chapters of this book, and the innovations and examples of good practice that have resulted are explained and discussed (see, for example, Chapter 16).

PE AND THE NATIONAL CURRICULUM

But what of PE? What has emerged from these debates, proposals and reports that has served to define the subject in a way that has shaped curriculum policy and implementation in schools? How much of the rhetoric contained in the various documents has been retained as workable practice and what has been lost and why?

The first attempt to produce a National Curriculum for PE was made by an informal working group set up by the British Council of PE (BCPE) in 1990. This was the Interim Working Group–PE in the National Curriculum. This arose as a result of the decision of the Secretaries of State to introduce the subjects of the National Curriculum in sequence. That PE came in the last group with Art and Music was no surprise. The delay, while regretted, gave BCPE the opportunity to use the time positively and have a first stab at what the profession considered a National Curriculum in PE might be. This procedure was unique to PE and a request to DES secured support in principle for the group to begin its work. The absence of a guarantee that the results would be used, and also the absence of any direct financial support, only strengthened the resolve of the group to succeed. The production of a report from the group in July 1990 was received well by DES which, as a result, financed a seminar for dissemination and consultation within the profession. This served to confirm the status of the document to professional colleagues and to DES. This was reinforced when the SWGPE under the Chairmanship of Ian Beer, Head of Harrow School, decided to use this slim document as the basis of its early discussion.

Some of the key principles that were central to this report survived the later rigorous process of the SWGPE. This strengthened considerably the confidence within the profession that we could actually influence such major changes and that the 'people' had been consulted. This was an interesting and welcome reinforcement of one of the critical principles of good innovation.

The principles for the PE curriculum contained in the BCPE report were that:

- the model (*or the PE curriculum*) should be developmental;
- the model should show clear progression;
- initiation into culturally valued activities is important;
- these activities are both vehicles and contexts of learning;
- the isolation of school from community should be reduced;
- the model should progress from a broad general base to specialism;

- there should be increasing responsibility for self-directed learning;
- personal and social education should be provided for;
- the concept of safety should be addressed in all its forms.

(BCPE, 1990)

You will recognise that all these principles have survived the lengthy process of the production of the National Curriculum documents in the various staged reports, subsequent reduction as a result of Ron Dearing's review (Dearing, 1994) and finally Schools Curriculum and Assessment Authority's interpretation of the statutory orders.

What is important now is that you, as you implement the now much reduced curriculum, should be aware of how much importance you should still place on these original, critical principles. The implication of each of these principles for good practice in PE is profound. Each is worthy of considerable investigation that is not possible within this chapter (although most of these principles are incorporated in other chapters of this book – for example, progression is considered in Chapter 3, safety in Chapter 8 and school–community links in Chapter 16). You are urged to consider each in depth and to realise the importance of each to their professional delivery of the National Curriculum.

TASK 17.1 PRINCIPLES FOR THE PE CURRICULUM

When you are on school experience find out by discussion with your tutor, reading of school documents and observation how many of these principles are in operation in the school. Compare your findings with those of another student teacher in another school experience school. Record this information in your professional portfolio for reference later.

Subject Working Group for PE (SWGPE)

The next stage in the process of producing a National Curriculum for PE was for the SWGPE to translate these principles into a workable structure for the subject that would reflect clearly what the subject was within the total educational process. This would be in the form of **Attainment Targets (AT)**, **Programmes of Study (PoS)** and **End of Key Stage Statements (EKSS)** in line with the structure of the ten subjects of the National Curriculum as a whole.

Key fundamentals to be absorbed into the curriculum were that the pupils had to 'know', 'understand', and be able to 'do'. This was a common theme across all subjects in the National Curriculum and suited the needs of PE particularly well. One of the major considerations in how to provide for this was to clarify what is meant by the **learning process** in PE. Much of the current literature on the learning process, and there is much of it available in recent publications, emphasises the need to concentrate on the competences required by young people to continue to learn after leaving the formal institutions of learning; that is, school and higher education. This means that there must be an emphasis on the **process of learning** rather than on the **end product and outcome of the learning**.

It was from this that the SWGPE formed **Attainment Targets (AT)**. Initially there were three: planning and composing, participating and performing, evaluating and appraising.

TASK 17.2 THE DEVELOPMENT OF ATTAINMENT TARGETS IN PE

Procure a copy of the SWGPE's Interim Report of December 1990 (DES/WO, 1990), in which the three ATs are explained in some detail. From these you can trace the evolution of the ATs through the development of the curriculum for PE. Reflect on these in relation to PE in your school experience school.

Programmes of Study (PoS) designed to meet these ATs were proposed as the six Areas of Activity with which you are familiar: athletic activities, dance, games, gymnastic activities, outdoor and adventurous activities, and swimming. This aspect of the SWGPE's work gave rise to considerable discussion. Some members proposed that the PoS should be devised within a framework that addressed the continuity and progression of learning within our subject rather than being directly related to discrete activity areas. Thus the PoS would be more readily compatible with the learning process. This 'continuity and progression' model was proposed as having three phases (see Figure 17.1). This was not adopted as a framework for PoS, but should not be abandoned, as it still may serve to provide a very useful progressive and continuous learning context to inform the way in which you should approach the teaching of the areas of activity. This model is compatible with much of the understanding of how children develop in this area of study.

FIRST PHASE
INTEGRATED PLAY
OPTIMISING MOTOR CONTROL IN A VARIETY OF
ACTIVITIES
MOVEMENT EDUCATION

SECOND PHASE
DISCIPLINED FORMS OF PHYSICAL ACTIVITY
DEVELOPMENT OF SKILL UNDERSTANDING AND
APPRECIATION
'PHYSICAL EDUCATION'

THIRD PHASE
EDUCATION FOR RECREATION • HEALTHY
LIFESTYLE ENHANCEMENT
EDUCATION FOR LEISURE/VOCATION

Figure 17.1 Three phases proposed for the continuity and development model
Source: Murdoch (1990)

End of Key Stage Statements (EKSS) began as a statement of ten levels in the way that other subjects have retained them. Simplification of the curriculum by the Secretary of State reduced the EKSS for PE to one statement at the end of each key stage. While this can be seen to reduce the burden on assessment recording and reporting, it did remove a very powerful and useful teaching/observation tool (see Chapter 4). These levels are given in detail in the Interim Report of December 1990 (DES/WO, 1990) and you are advised to refer to these as support for the planning of progressive learning experiences for your pupils. Much of the detailed thinking on progression is clearly set out for you in this document. The progression is logical and compatible with the natural flow of children's learning and development.

You should appreciate by now that the National Curriculum for PE is but 'a shadow of its former self'. That the Statutory requirements are considerably reduced does not mean that you, as a good teacher, do not use the information that was generated in the earlier stages of the process to the benefit of your learners in PE.

At this point we again assume that you are familiar with the structure of the National Curriculum for PE as it is currently delivered (if not,

TASK 17.3 ATTAINMENT IN PE

This task requires that you have access to:

(i)   the SWGPE's Interim Report, December 1990 (DES/WO, 1990); and
(ii) the SWGPE's PE 5–16 Proposals of the Secretary of State, August 1991 (DES/WO, 1991b).

In the August 1991 document, read sections 8.8 to 8.17, pp. 26–7. Consider the detailed levels of attainment given in the December 1990 Interim Report, pp. 33–59, and also in a shortened version in August 1991, pp. 20–3.

Can you appreciate the principles of progression that underpin the level of attainment? Can you trace them through these levels?

This understanding should be of considerable help to you as a tool for your observation of pupils working within the Attainment Target of PE towards EKSS.

re-read the documents now). The remainder of this chapter raises some underlying issues that should inform the teaching of the curriculum, and also the extra-curriculum, and give you support for decisions about how the PoS link with pupils' learning.

THE UNIQUE ROLE OF PE IN SCHOOLS

The inclusion of PE in the school curriculum for pupils aged 5–16 was assured by its inclusion as one of the ten subjects of the National Curriculum. But what of practice? Does the subject receive adequate attention in what is always seen as a busy, full curriculum? Do you know what to say when you have to defend PE in terms of its value to the growing and learning child? The range of values for each individual that can realistically be attributed to a good PE programme is impressive and perhaps not articulated often enough.

Values can be defended as:

- physical development;
- motor development;
- fitness and health;
- aesthetic awareness and expression;
- social development, communication, competition;
- cognitive development;

- self–esteem, self–concept with related self–confidence;
- significant intrinsic meanings in being active.

It is not possible to expand here on any of these but see Task 17.4.

TASK 17.4 EXPLAINING VALUES OF PE

Using each of the headings above, write a short paragraph that would explain each of the values to at least one of the following:

- chair of governors;
- head teacher;
- parent who believes in an 'academic' education;
- staff colleague;
- pupil.

  Discuss your explanation with another student teacher and with your tutor so that you can formulate your arguments for future use.

The unique role of PE *vis-à-vis* sport

With the dramatic increase in the potential for sport in schools (see also (Chapter 16), PE must look to clarify its role and if possible to declare what it offers young people that none of the other providers in sport can do as well or better.

  Both government reports cited earlier, i.e. Schools Sport Forum and the National Curriculum, made a very clear and unambiguous statement that where sport was being provided for pupils in school that this would be planned and managed by the teacher of PE. This challenge has already been set before you in Chapter 16 (see particularly, NCC, 1992, Section H1.2). It is very important that you respond positively to this challenge. What does this mean for you, and how do you do it? You hold key and critical knowledge and understanding about what is offered to young people in the name of PE, when, how and why. Your guidance for this resides in your awareness and understanding of critical underpinning aspects of the National Curriculum referred to above; namely, it could be expected that you:

- understand the learning process;
- know about progression;

- appreciate what is meant by continuity;
- can implement differentiation in respect of all pupils.

You should be in the most advantageous position to provide what is referred to above because you are the only person within the PE/sport delivery team who is in a constant and systematic interface with each pupil's learning over time. None of the other providers from outside agencies, good as they may be, are in this position. Your role is a privileged and necessary one. Yours, when you have qualified, is the role of the professional within this team, and you will be expected to make critical judgements and offer advice as to the appropriateness of what is being offered to the pupils.

Learning to learn

> The most effective process of learning is learning how to learn.
> (Nixon *et al.*, 1996, p. 128)

The last decade has seen an increasing interest in the learning society, learning organisations and reflective ability on one's own learning. It is in learning that the identity and dignity of each pupil can be valued. Your role in developing a positive approach to learning and the learning process within the PE curriculum is essential. It is here that the greatest and most significant distinction between the delivery of both PE and Sport is to be found.

Investigation into the learning process reveals that it embraces a number of assumptions. Consideration of how such assumptions might affect learning and teaching within PE open up some interesting debate and discussion. To enable you to ensure a coherent and systematic approach to learning, consider the following three assumptions about learning, which hopefully may become your working principles.

Assumption 1:

that 'how' children learn is essential and almost more important to address than 'what' they learn
This refers to the expressed need to equip young people to continue to be engaged in the learning process even after they have left school. If young people know what it means to learn, and how they individually prefer to learn (learning style), then they are more likely to be successful as they take on new learning situations. They need to be educated to

appreciate the process for themselves. See Chapter 9, for further information. You may also want to refer to Entwhistle (1988) and Ackerman, Sternberg and Glaser (1989) for further information about learning styles (see Further Reading at end of chapter).

Assumption 2:

that children understand what it means to engage in the learning process

This could be considered in the form of a learning contract between yourself and each pupil where both of you agree to commit to the completion of certain aspects of the shared process. This focuses learning on the motivation to learn which is so critical to involvement and success (see Chapter 7 for further information about motivation to learn). This approach to learning begins to lead the young person into a **deep** learning experience as opposed to a **surface** one, the former being potentially much more productive than the latter in terms of the quality and retention of the elements of the learning episode. Deep learning, where the learner is fully engaged in the contract to learn, does not occur naturally for all learners but must be encouraged by sensitive guidance, from you as the teacher, that takes account of each learner's preferred style of learning and equips them with the capacity to be critical about their own learning. Refer to Entwhistle (1988) in the Further Reading section for more information about the deep and surface approach to learning.

Assumption 3:

that children can self-assess the extent of their learning and estimate the possible barriers to better learning

This is compatible with personal profiles and self-assessment, both of which feature within the National Curriculum. So often (too often!) profiles are about end product achievements rather than about the grasp of an essential process which in the current climate of educational change will have a longer-term currency. Refer to Nisbet and Shucksmith (1986) in the Further Reading section for more information about self-awareness in learning, or metacognition.

These concepts and their understanding tend to be underplayed in the subsequent advice to you from within the National Curriculum for PE, which appears still to place too much emphasis on the outcome and

product of learning at the cost of the **process**. The process is not ignored but what is more subtle is that little has been written to help you to interpret this process into effective learning and teaching by giving concrete and practical advice. There is much encouragement to engage in the learning process, but you are then left with little real support. If we wish to retain an appropriate and significant distinction between PE and sport then it is essential that education focuses on process in relation to product while sport can afford to place more emphasis on the end product. PE loses this focus at its peril.

Process of learning within PE

What is the process of learning within PE, and why was the particular model for PE in the National Curriculum chosen?

The SWGPE debated this at some length and decided to propose the process of learning within PE as:

PLANNING: PERFORMING: EVALUATING

Together these form the single AT of the National Curriculum.

The source of the learning process model came from already established knowledge and good practice and can be seen as threefold.

1) Activities in PE have as their roots the motor ability, competence and skill of the participant that underpin and make possible effective and successful performance. You should remember from your work on skill acquisition and motor learning that the process which every performer employs within each skilled action is that of preparation and planning, performing, and evaluating – through feedback loops, both internal and external. These words are familiar and well documented in work by Schmidt (1991), Singer (1982), Kelso (1982) and others in the literature on skill acquisition and perceptual motor control. Writers such as Gallahue (1982) and Wickstrom (1977) have applied the model to the learning process in which we all engage as we refine performance skills. So the generalised learning process model is compatible with the specific holistic process employed in the learning of individual skills.

2) Performance in a physical activity engages the performer in a process of decision making as to tactics to be employed or the sequence to be composed **(planning)**, that leads to the actual execution

(performance) which is quickly followed by some appraisal or evaluation that acts as feedback for improvement **(evaluation)**.

The process of **planning** is concerned with identify: explore: select: formulate: carry out; that of **Performing** is concerned with establish: adapt: refine: vary: improvise; while that of **Evaluating** is concerned with observe: describe: analyse: compare: judge: evaluate.

During your teaching and the pupils' learning these processes should be systematically worked through within each new task as appropriate.

The two examples above emphasise that the model applies also to the total strategic and tactical process as well as the holistic process involved in skill learning. You could consider these as 'micro' and 'macro' versions of the same logical process.

3) The study of dance had for some time been structured around three aspects of dance: performance, choreography, criticism. The educational translation of this to focus on the individual as a learner easily became dancer, choreographer and critic or spectator as dance education sought to prepare the young learner to fulfil all roles. To reduce the particular specialist focus on dance the model then assumed a more generic structure of performer, planner or composer and evaluator or judge or critic, which allowed the model to be applied to all areas of activity within the PE curriculum. There was much debate about the terms used. Great pressure was exerted, especially by the Secretary of State himself, to strip the curriculum report of all jargon. You should appreciate that the terms finally proposed are not ideal, but you are asked to concentrate on the concepts underlying the terminology rather than on the words themselves. This example of the process is related to the adoption of, and the learning about, an external role of choreographer: dancer: critic or team manager: player: spectator.

This three-part learning process can be understood and conceptualised at three levels that could be described as intrinsic performance, process awareness and the adopting of external roles. These levels progress from the subconscious (as is seen in the process of motor control), through the conscious within a performance, to the deliberate (as in adopting specific roles). These co-exist and happen at least in some form at one level or more each time the pupil engages in a learning experience within PE. The fact that the learning process is capable of being understood at three different levels gives it an integrity that strengthens the uniqueness of the process to PE.

There is no doubt that these concepts are complex and will challenge you in coming to terms with them, but once you understand and appreciate the possible implications of them for pupils' learning, they open up to you the opportunity to question what might be happening within the learning process and at what level. Increased awareness in this way should form a very strong base from which you can make, with more confidence, better informed decisions about each pupil's learning. The most critical aspect of this for you is that being aware of the existence of these processes as you engage in setting up and supporting the pupils' learning should assist you to set appropriate learning tasks and adopt relevant and helpful language as you teach and give feedback (see Chapter 9 for further information about feedback). The following example may help to clarify how this may be achieved. The task is:

Gymnastics: A sequence that allows the performer to cross the vaulting box showing a controlled contrast between held balance and absorption of fast momentum.

If you are concentrating on the control and quality of the **performance** then you use phrases such as:

- how did that feel? (establish);
- can you repeat that exactly? (refine);
- where are you placing your hands and why? (adapt/vary);
- experiment with where your legs are in relation to your point of support? (vary);
- can you give an extra push with your arms about half a second sooner? (adapt), etc.

If you are concentrating on the composition or **planning** of the sequence then you use phrases such as:

- do you think you are approaching the box from the best angle? (explore);
- which was best? (select) . . .

See Chapter 5 for further information about communication, particularly language in PE.

TASK 17.5 PHRASES TO ASSIST PUPILS TO PLAN, PERFORM AND EVALUATE

Complete the phrases that might be helpful in *planning* and devise your own for *evaluation*. Focusing on the breakdown of the process as given acts as a check-list to ensure that you are exposing the learner to the complete process.

Try this with other activities and tasks you might be teaching and put these into practice in your lessons.

What is a physically educated person? What should be the hoped for outcome of taking part in PE within the curriculum and extra-curriculum during a pupil's school years?

In relation to what has been discussed above, the physically educated person would be one who would be able to:

- approach the majority of a range of physical tasks with confidence and success;
- have adaptable control over movement under all circumstances;
- be articulate about the learning process;
- describe and work within own personal learning style(s);
- appraise own performance and that of others;
- understand and participate in the process of tactical, compositional planning.

This is also discussed in Chapter 2.

The above does not preclude any person who has a disability, as confidence, success and control are still fully relevant in these situations. Where some interpretation and adaptation may need to be made is in those cases where the disabling condition is seen to be a significant handicap. See Chapter 10 for further information about working with pupils with different needs.

The description of a physically educated person given above is not arrived at by referring directly to the PoS in the National Curriculum for PE (i.e. the activities) and describing this person as a 'good' **games** player or an 'effective' **tennis** player or an 'inventive' **gymnast** (for example). However, what is proposed above does result in the description in terms of success in a specific activity also being possible while at the same time the more generic profile gives a very much better evaluation of someone who is well prepared to engage in lifelong **learning** rather than **specific performance**.

> ### TASK 17.6 LEARNING VERSUS PERFORMANCE IN PE
>
> Debate with another student teacher the issue 'Is it more important to focus on learning or on performance within the PE curriculum?'

Enjoy the debate . . . and enjoy your work with pupils as they learn to become physically educated people.

SUMMARY

This chapter has provided you with an overview of developments which led up to and influenced the National Curriculum for PE and factors influencing PE in schools since then. It has provided a great deal of background information to enable you to understand and put the following into context: what you learn on your ITE course; why PE teachers do what they do in schools today; and some of the environmental factors impacting on PE today. We hope that this chapter (together with Chapter 16) has made you aware of the need to be aware of the external environment in which you are working and to try to influence that environment rather than just responding to changes imposed on you.

FURTHER READING

We encourage you to refer to the various documents cited in this chapter so that you understand the background to current practice of PE in schools. This should put into context what you are doing in schools.

Ackerman, P.L., Sternberg, R.J. and Glaser, R. (eds) (1989) *Learning and Individual Differences: Advances in Theory and Research*, New York: W.H. Freeman and Company.
Chapter 4 focuses on learning styles

Entwhistle, N. (1988) *Styles of Learning and Teaching: An Integrated Outline of Educational Psychology for Students, Teachers and Lecturers*, London: David Fulton Publishers.
Chapter 4 focuses on deep and surface approaches to learning, and Chapter 5 focuses on learning styles.

Murdoch, E.B. (1990) 'Physical Education and Sport: The Interface', in N. Armstrong (ed.) *New Directions in Physical Education, Volume 1*, Champaign, Ill.: Human Kinetics, pp. 63–79.

This provides an overview of how PE and sport are different and how they complement one another.

Nisbet, J. and Shucksmith, J. (1986) *Learning Strategies*, London: Routledge. Chapter 1 and Chapter 8 focus on self-awareness in learning, or metacognition.

18 Professional development

INTRODUCTION

This chapter aims to focus your thinking on particular aspects of the work of the PE teacher for which you must take particular responsibility during your initial teacher education (ITE) and throughout your teaching career. By the time you take up your first appointment you should:

- be comfortable that your are developing into an effective teacher;
- be up to date and willing to extend your subject knowledge;
- understand that you have the opportunity for personal and career development.

By the end of your ITE course you will be assessed against the competences set out in *Circulars 9/92 and 35/92: Initial Teacher Training (Secondary Phase)* (DFE/WO, 1992). (Note that at the time of publication the Teacher Training Agency (TTA) is considering the introduction of standards rather than competences as the basis for assessment of student teachers in ITE in England and Wales.) *Teacher Competences: Guidelines for Teacher Training Courses* (Scottish Office Education Department, 1993) or *Arrangements for Initial Teacher Education in Northern Ireland from 1 September 1996* (Department of Education Northern Ireland, 1996). The competences in each of these documents are included as Appendices 2, 3 and 4 in Capel, Leask and Turner (1995).

You are also expected to arrive at your first teaching post with a Career Entry Profile (CEP). Your higher education institution (HEI) is responsible for providing you with your CEP. It is intended to help you, your tutors and the staff at your first appointment school to recognise your strengths and needs. This should allow the staff in charge of your induction the opportunity to provide a relevant and personal programme which acknowledges the abilities and competences which you bring with you.

OBJECTIVES

By the end of this chapter you should understand your responsibilities in:

- maintaining an accurate record of evidence of your professional development through use of your portfolio and profile of competences;
- ensuring that you share your progress and development with your school and HEI tutors during your ITE;
- preparing your CEP and Curriculum Vitae (CV)

You should also be able to:

- apply confidently for first posts and be well prepared for interview;
- recognise the need for further subject development and career development;
- understand the need to join a professional association.

DEVELOPING YOUR PORTFOLIO AND PROFILE OF COMPETENCES

Subject knowledge

You have arrived on your ITE course with very different experiences and understanding of PE from others on the course. An ITE course preparing you for teaching can assume a similar starting point in terms of working with pupils, but it cannot take into account the range of strengths and needs in terms of practical experience and subject knowledge in a subject as complex as PE.

It is important to recognise that subject knowledge is the basis for the development of most of your other abilities. Our starting point is to encourage you to assess your strengths and needs and plan how you will develop your strengths and redress gaps in your knowledge.

Subject knowledge is one of the key factors that employing schools are looking for in newly qualified teachers (NQTs) (Pachler and Watson, 1997). Further reference is made in this chapter to the factors you will need to take account of when applying for your first post.

You will need to review your subject knowledge during your ITE course. We suggest you review your development three times during the course; for example:

- at the beginning of your course (September);
- half way through your course (December);
- at the end of your course (May/June).

Figure 18.1 provides a method of recording evidence of your subject knowledge strengths and identifying the action you need to take to develop your competence further. This is not a complete chart with all your abilities, it only looks at aspects of the three subject knowledge competences required for NQTs in England and Wales as identified in *Circulars 9/92 and 35/92* (DFE/WO, 1992). You may wish to extend this to include all the competences identified in the circulars or the competences identified for your course.

TASK 18.1 REVIEWING YOUR SUBJECT KNOWLEDGE

Complete the grid shown in Figure 18.1 by identifying:

- the type of evidence that you can list to indicate ability at each of the three times during the course;
- the action you need to take to develop your subject knowledge.

You may have noted in your grid (Figure 18.1) that you can develop subject knowledge through, for example:

- observation in schools;
- sharing knowledge and understanding with other student teachers on your course;
- gaining governing body awards;
- peer teaching;
- teaching PE lessons;
- watching matches;
- officiating at school activities;
- reading;
- watching video recordings.

As a result of this exercise you should also recognise that PE is a vast subject for which you will need more than the time on your ITE course to develop sufficient knowledge and understanding in, for example, **all** the areas of activity in the National Curriculum for PE in England and Wales.

In recognising the breadth of PE you need to make some important decisions as to how you can best achieve a sound foundation across the National Curriculum areas of activity as well as specific depth and strength in one or two. If you arrived at your ITE course with a broad and a sound range of skills, knowledge and understanding in most of the

Subject Knowledge	September		December		May/June	
	Evidence you can offer to indicate ability	Action you need to take to develop ability	Evidence you can offer to indicate ability	Action you need to take to develop ability	Evidence you can offer to indicate ability	Action you need to take to develop ability
Safe Practice in all areas of activity	*AAA coach certificate Much experience in coaching all ages in most events. ASA swimming assistant coach certificate BCU inland certificate*	*Need to attend gymnastics course/observe and assist with gym clubs. Have yet to undertake any rugby training. Try to take an advanced course in canoeing over the next year.*				
Knowledge of rules List the games in which you have a **good** working knowledge of the rules	*tennis, hockey, netball, volleyball*	*Attend courses in rugby and basketball with a view to teaching them next term. Read the latest rule books.*				
Knowledge of: gymnastics, athletic activities, dance, swimming, O and A activities, games.	*Good knowledge of Athletics, some experience of O and A and swimming. I am quite reasonable at dance but limited in gymnastics*	*More experience in dance. Ask for some on timetable after half term. Much more gym needed.*				
Officiating awards. List governing bodies for which you have attained awards						

Figure 18.1 Review of subject knowledge

areas of activity this could be to your advantage as you can concentrate on one or two on which to develop a depth of understanding. However, it is just as likely that you arrived with a very superficial knowledge of several of the areas of activity and a depth of practical skill and knowledge in one or two. This means that you may have to forgo your particular strength(s) in order to learn more about the other areas of activity during your ITE.

To help you make decisions about your foci for development you should consult your school and HEI tutors. They should help you recognise the emphasis you need to place on certain Areas of Activity within PE. For instance, the National Curriculum places an emphasis on games in key stages 3 and 4. If you have limited knowledge and understanding of the major team games taught at your school, it will be to your advantage to select these as a focus for development. You will also need to keep a balance in your development. You must be able to teach gymnastic activities and/or dance at KS3. Athletic Activities feature as a major summer activity in many schools and therefore need to feature in your plan.

The key point is that over your ITE course you cannot be assessed on every possible activity in each area of activity, but there is an expectation that you will do all you can to develop a sound, safe and competent approach to most of the activities being taught in schools. As noted above, this is your responsibility but guidance is available from all who advise and support you.

After you have completed your ITE course and have achieved NQT status, it is fully recognised that your subject development will not be complete. It will still be your responsibility to extend your practical abilities and knowledge once you are qualified. You will, no doubt, want to take advantage of your induction programme and any other inservice education and training (INSET) made available to you through your school. Much of your subject-specific development will depend on the PE department in the school to which you are appointed and on the curriculum being presented to the pupils. You might have spent your ITE course learning about rugby and volleyball, but find that your new school does not have volleyball on the curriculum. It specialises in basketball instead and this is not a strength of yours. You will need to gain experience and confidence in the teaching of basketball. You might set about this by, for example, observing others teaching, undertaking an introductory course, shadowing an official during a match, asking for specific support and guidance from a knowledgeable teacher of basketball.

Other professional issues on becoming an NQT are explored later on in this chapter. These will include knowing the PE journals and publications that serve the teaching profession; reading research literature; joining professional organisations; and looking to extend your qualifications.

Prioritising your time during your ITE course

You will face conflicting demands on your time during your course of ITE as you will need to:

- develop your teaching skills further;
- collect evidence of your ability to add to your profile; and may also want to:
- play a greater part in the extra-curricular life of the school;
- continue your own personal fitness/training programme and commitment to your sport.

It will not be possible to leave decisions until you feel that you have the time to deal with them most effectively. You need to learn to cope with these tensions and recognise that you need to prioritise the demands on your time.

Your professional portfolio

As suggested by Capel, Leask and Turner (1995, unit 8.2) you should maintain a professional portfolio which provides as much **evidence** of your learning and development as possible. We cannot overemphasise how important your portfolio is to you at certain times in your career as a teacher; for instance when completing your CEP (see below), when applying for teaching posts, or preparing for an appraisal interview. The advantages of this are noted in Capel, Leask and Turner (1995), but it is important to emphasise the value that such a portfolio is to you throughout your ITE and teaching career. The completed chart from Task 18.1 is a good example of evidence that can be retained in your portfolio. This chart can also be used as a contribution to the assessment of your PE subject knowledge abilities. However, this is only one example. We encourage you to review your development with your tutor and update your portfolio during your course.

Your Career Entry Profile (CEP)

The TTA requires that you complete a CEP before the end of your ITE course. The CEP is intended to ease your transition from student teacher to NQT. It will provide the school where you obtain your first teaching post with important information about your strengths, development needs, targets and aspirations. The completion of your CEP will be a shared responsibility. The TTA requires you to complete a

---

TASK 18.2 IDENTIFYING YOUR STRENGTHS, NEEDS, TARGETS AT THE END OF YOUR ITE COURSE

This task should be undertaken towards the end of your ITE course.

Identify and note your **strengths**, **needs** and **targets** for your first year of teaching. You might write notes such as:

*strengths: organised, enthusiastic, experienced in the teaching of gymnastics and football and willing to become fully involved with school life; **needs**: greater confidence in teaching certain areas of activity, further experience in officiating, help with preparing appropriate pastoral sessions with a form tutor group; **targets**: attaining governing body awards, undertaking a pastoral role, introducing a new extra-curricular activity.*

Remember these can cover more than subject-specific aspects such as the pastoral role, or becoming a member of a school committee.

Identify and note your development needs and targets that you have for the next two to three years in teaching; for example, starting an MA, attending a middle management course. This may seem difficult, but you can ask practising teachers for advice on this type of target setting. A good starting point is to recognise your areas of strength or aspects you particularly enjoy in teaching. It is useful to recognise that this task will help focus your thoughts on your possible career development.

Identify and note your development needs and targets for the next five-plus years in teaching (for example, Head of Department, Head of Year). This is certainly more problematic; however, try to consider where you believe you may be able to get to (posts of responsibility) and what you might achieve. We strongly advise you to share your responses to this task with your tutor. She is in the best position to guide you in completing this aspect of your CEP. The key to any such task is to make your targets achievable and realistic.

section in conjunction with your HEI. The final section is left as an option for you to complete. Your tutors will not be able to complete this. As with all documentation which identifies your strengths and needs, it is strongly recommended that you complete this section. They allow you to recognise your strengths and identify your needs with a view to future development. Employing schools will be glad to see evidence of your ability to reflect upon your progress and needs. It indicates a clarity of thought and purpose if you, as an NQT, can provide your own targets for future development.

One of your major concerns is to obtain a first teaching post. The tasks identified above are designed to help you with that. Below, we consider how you approach obtaining a post. At this point you should refer to unit 8.1 in Capel, Leask and Turner (1995) for information about applying for your first teaching post, including examples of a letter of application and information to include in a CV.

BEGINNING THE SEARCH FOR A TEACHING POST

The more constrained you are in your choice of school for your first teaching post – in relation to its geographical location, the type of school you wish to work in and what you are willing to teach – the earlier in the year you should begin your search for your first teaching post. Independent schools often advertise in the autumn term for posts beginning the following September, whereas the vast majority of posts in maintained schools appear after Christmas. We would advise you to start your search for a post early and advise against leaving your search for a post until the summer term. There is significant evidence that those who begin the search early are more likely to secure a post as a PE teacher before the end of their ITE course.

You would be well advised to get into the habit of regularly consulting the educational press, particularly the *Times Educational Supplement*. Advertisements for teachers of PE are different from posts in other subjects as schools are permitted to specify whether the teacher is required to teach Girls' or Boys' PE. Write off for details of any post that interests you and that is suitable for someone seeking a first appointment. This will usually mean posts advertised on the Common Pay Spine (CPS) and without additional responsibilities.

A well constructed, informative and high quality CV is essential in your search for a teaching post. Drawing up your CV is a task which could be completed at an early point in your ITE course. Much of the information will be the same as that required for sections of the CEP. You could therefore complete the two tasks at the same time. Many schools will ask you to submit a CV as part of your application for a post. You may also wish to provide your referees with a copy of your CV to assist them in writing your reference.

When making an application for a teaching post, you need to give the names of at least two people who will provide you with a confidential reference about your suitability for teaching. Recent research (Pachler and Watson, 1997) indicates that what schools most require from references is an honest assessment of a candidate's teaching competence. You may therefore wish to nominate a school and a HEI tutor. You must seek their permission prior to using their name for this purpose.

Making the application

The majority of schools ask you to complete an application form and also to provide a letter of application. This is a time consuming business, as a new form has to be completed for every post applied for. The forms are usually standard forms and so not all sections of the form will necessarily be of relevance to you. You may find that the form does not provide a clear section where you can give details of governing body and coaching awards which you consider to be of particular importance to the post. However, these awards should be included in your CV. Unless the information from the school specifically states that a CV should not be included with your application (and few do) then it is perfectly acceptable to enclose a copy of your CV and to refer to it in your letter of application.

You may wish to photocopy the form and do a rough draft to ensure that you use the space provided effectively. The completed form provides the first impression of you as a person. Legibility and accuracy are therefore paramount. Whereas the application form provides information in a standard format enabling comparisons to be made between candidates, the letter of application provides the opportunity for you to make your case for being included in the short list of candidates. What is it that you alone have to offer **this** school? For instance, do you have strengths in some or all of the PE activities mentioned in the advertisement or job description? Can you offer to run some of the extra-curricular activities in the PE department's programme?

It is essential that each letter of application you write takes account of the particular needs of that school. Senior staff in schools are involved in making many appointments. They are looking for evidence that

TASK 18.3 WRITING A LETTER OF APPLICATION

Draft a letter of application for the post outlined below. We have underlined the sections which we would expect applicants to comment upon, indicating their experience in those areas, their educational philosophy and their aspirations. There may well be other experiences, strengths and interests that you wish to draw the school's attention to, but remember that the school will be looking for the **person who best meets their needs**. Before completing the letter, you may find it helpful to refer to your profile and portfolio of competence as well as to the example of a letter shown in unit 8.1 in Capel, Leask and Turner (1995).

Discuss your letter with your tutor, the professional mentor and other PE staff in school and your HEI, to obtain as much and as varied feedback as you can.

RIVERSHIRE EDUCATIONAL AUTHORITY
TROUTBROOK COMPREHENSIVE SCHOOL
FISHER LANE
ANGLERFORD
RIVERSHIRE

11–18 Co-educational Comprehensive. 1180 on role (Sixth Form 180)

TEACHER OF PE
Required for September, an enthusiastic and committed teacher of PE. The post offers an opportunity for someone to join a successful department with excellent facilities and an outstanding record in both curricular and extra-curricular work. In addition to the core PE programme, <u>GCSE courses are well established</u> and popular. <u>GNVQ Leisure and Tourism and A level PE are offered to the Sixth Form</u>. The PE department has 4 full-time staff, and is well resourced.

<u>Pupils are taught in both mixed and single sex groups. Outdoor pursuits is offered to all pupils. A large extra-curricular programme</u> includes <u>successful clubs and teams, with representation up to national level in a number of sports. PE staff contribute to the extensive Duke of Edinburgh Awards scheme.</u>

The post would suit either a new entrant or an experienced teacher and there will be ample <u>opportunity to develop interests and professional skills</u>. Relocation expenses are available.

candidates have the range of experience, the ideas and personal qualities that will enable them to work well in their school, with their pupils and their staff. The selection panel will easily identify the 'standard' letter of application which a candidate sends to all schools and the application will not progress beyond the first reading.

We suggest that you complete Task 18.3 to give you practice in writing a letter of application.

In writing your letter, we would expect you to provide an account of the experiences you have had to date that you feel equip you for the post. You may or may not have taught GCSE, and/or GCE A level or GNVQ courses. Even if you have not taught these courses, we would expect you to have familiarised yourself with the examination syllabuses and be able to comment on their value. You could then indicate that you would welcome the opportunity to be involved in the teaching of examination courses.

You would be expected to outline your philosophy of teaching PE. You will, for example, probably have experience of teaching and being taught in single sex and/or mixed groups and could discuss the merits of both. In discussing your experience of outdoor education, you could also indicate what you consider to be its particular contribution to the PE curriculum. Your letter should include any experience you have had in running or assisting in extra-curricular activities and you might well explain your beliefs about the value of teams and competition. See also Chapters 2, 16 and 17.

The job description invites you to indicate interests you would wish to develop and your professional aspirations. These need not necessarily be specific to the teaching of PE: they might involve work as a form tutor, with the community or with pupils with special educational needs. Staff in schools want to know that you like working with children, that you are enthusiastic about your subject and about teaching and that you can make an individual contribution to the life of their school.

Preparing for interview

There is evidence (Pachler and Watson, 1997) that interview procedures for first appointments are changing. Increasingly, candidates are required to teach a lesson as well as being interviewed. This practice is more common in certain subject areas and PE is one of these. You can expect to be informed in advance of the requirement to teach. If you are not told by the school of the activity you will have to teach and the age and experience of the pupils, then it is perfectly in order to ring the school to elicit this information.

You can expect that the interview process will include a tour of the school, led by staff or pupils. There is also likely to be time for informal discussions with members of the PE staff and other staff with whom the person appointed will work. These discussions may take place at any point: during the tour, over coffee or lunch, or as a separate part of the interview procedures. It is important that you use these times well to decide whether you would be happy to work in this school and with the other members of the PE department. You do need to remember that judgements about your suitability will be made throughout the time you are in the school.

Before you go for any interview it is important that you know which things are essential and which are desirable in a PE department in which you would be happy to work. For example, is it important to you that you will have the opportunity to coach teams, teach mixed ability groups? Task 18.4 is designed to help you identify your priorities.

TASK 18.4 DETERMINING YOUR PRIORITIES FOR A PE DEPARTMENT

1 Brainstorm a list of all those things that are important to you in a PE department. As a starting point you might consider the department(s) in your school experience school and list what you perceive to be their strengths and shortcomings, then add any others you can think of.
2 Go through your list and determine which of the items are essential for you and which are desirable.
3 For each of the items in the essential category, phrase a question you could ask the PE staff on the day of the interview to help you to assess whether the school would meet your needs. For example, is there ready access to a swimming pool? What are the length and number of lessons per day? What are the possibilities for holding clubs?

It is almost certain that the day will include a formal interview. This will usually be the last part of the proceedings. The interview panel can vary in size but very often includes the head teacher (and/or a deputy), the head of department or faculty and a member of the governing body. It is to be hoped that the chair of the interview panel will seek to put you at your ease. Interviews are, however, stressful for the candidates and for the panel. The best way to reduce the stress is to arrive at this stage of the interview process well prepared. To do this you will need to have:

- experienced a mock interview (with your tutor or another member of staff in your school experience school or in your HEI);
- read all the information provided by the school;
- reread your application form and letter of application (it is likely that the interview panel will refer to your letter in the interview);
- used the tour of the school and the opportunity to ask questions to become as well informed as possible about the school, its achievements, aims and plans for the future;
- assessed your strengths and needs and considered your targets as an NQT (completing your CEP before you attend for interview would be helpful);
- determined what contribution you feel you could make to the PE department and to the school.

The main purpose of the interview is to enable the panel to decide whether you will make the vital contribution to their school that they are seeking. They will want you to draw on your experience of working with pupils to illustrate a point rather than to rely on abstract generalities. You may actually be asked to describe a successful PE lesson or one that you were unhappy about. Take any opportunity to refer in your answers to anything from the literature sent by the school (for example, the wide range of clubs or its success in the regional athletics competition), or to draw upon in your answer anything you have seen or heard during your tour of the school (for example, the display of the school aims in the foyer). Remember to make eye contact with the person asking the question and to smile.

It is important to see the interview process as one of matching the person to the post rather than as one of 'passing' or 'failing'. If you are not selected for a post, it means that another candidate has been judged to have more closely matched the school's requirements in terms of experience, potential to contribute to the life of the school, and ability to work with the staff and pupils there – not necessarily that you have interviewed badly or failed to come up to scratch in any other respect. You will usually be offered a debriefing at which any shortcomings in the interview will be discussed so that you can take account of this in the future. We would strongly advise you to take advantage of this opportunity to learn about your performance at interview. Interviews are always valuable learning experiences.

When you are offered a post and accept it verbally your acceptance is a binding contract. Schools will rarely give you time to think about the offer. In fact, you will usually be asked either at the start or at the end of the interview whether or not you are still a firm candidate for the post. If you have doubts, this is the point at which they should be raised. You may, of course, decide to withdraw at any stage during the interview proceedings.

INDUCTION

Securing a teaching post and successfully completing your course of ITE is just the start of your development as a teacher. The importance of continued support and professional development for NQTs and subsequently throughout your teaching careers is now fully recognised. You can expect help in the following ways.

Visit(s) to the school prior to taking up the teaching post

There is an expectation that you will want to visit the school before you formally take up the post. Some schools arrange a programme which may extend over several days for all new appointees. The purpose of such a programme is to familiarise new staff with the school's procedures and with the curriculum. It is more usual that you will be invited to visit the school towards the end of the summer term to collect useful documentation (for example, your timetable, copies of schemes of work and examination syllabuses, dates of fixtures, the staff handbook) and to spend more time getting to know the teachers with whom you will be working. In addition, you may be invited to visit the school when pupils meet their form teachers for the following year. If you are taking on the duties of a form teacher, this is a valuable opportunity to meet your form/tutor group informally. You may also be invited to assist with the sports day or a similar school event run by the PE department.

These preliminary visits can be a very valuable boost to your confidence by providing an opportunity to ask those questions which only occurred to you after the interview. You can also ensure that you have the resources necessary to guide your thinking and preparation for the term ahead. If you are to make best use of this time, it is well worth doing some preparation for the visit by making a check-list of all the questions you wish to ask, resources you need to collect, people you need to meet. Task 18.5 encourages you to do this.

TASK 18.5 PREPARING FOR YOUR PRELIMINARY VISIT

Prepare as comprehensive a check-list as you can in preparation for your visit. The following headings may be of help:

Induction programme:	School? Local Education Authority (LEA)? Will you be given a mentor?
Curriculum:	What exactly will you be teaching?
Pupils:	Numbers in classes? Names of classes? Basis for organisation of groups? etc.
Procedures:	For changing rooms?, registers?, marking?, rewards and sanctions?, etc.
Resources:	What facilities does the school have? Where is the equipment stored? How do you access it? What resources are there for theory lessons?
Extra-curricular activities	When do these take place? What part will you be expected to play? What is the schedule of matches for the year?
Dates:	Of terms? Any special events? INSET days?
Clothing:	Are there any special requirements?
Accommodation:	You may need somewhere to live. Can anyone help? Where will you be doing your teaching? Are there any travel implications, for example, if you are timetabled to teach in the town's recreation centre?
Expenses:	What expenses will you face? Will they be reimbursed? If so, how?
Social events:	Are there any events for staff links with parents or other parts of the community?
Useful contacts:	Names and telephone numbers
Any others?	

Your induction into the teaching profession

One of the people you will probably meet either on your preliminary visit or at the very start of your first term is the school's professional tutor. The professional tutor will probably be a senior member of staff, often one of the deputy heads. Many secondary schools organise an induction programme specifically for the NQTs on the staff. This programme will often consist of information-giving sessions where NQTs are introduced to the school's procedures, key personnel including union representatives, and are prepared for important events on the calendar (for example, parents' evenings). There will usually be opportunities to raise issues and discuss any problems as they arise. Unit 8.2 in Capel, Leask and Turner (1995) includes a more detailed discussion of schools' induction programmes.

If your school is an LEA school, you may find that the LEA also provides an induction programme for all the NQTs in its schools. The sessions may take place during the school day, but it is rather more likely that some, if not all, of the sessions occur after school. You may find, therefore, that you have to decide between attending the sessions and your normal extra-curricular commitments. It is unlikely that there will be more than one NQT teaching PE in your school. The LEA induction programme will provide you with the opportunity to meet other NQTs who teach PE, and a chance to share experiences and solutions to problems. Some sessions may be focused specifically on PE issues and may be run by an adviser or inspector, another useful person to get to know. We would strongly advise you to attend at least some of the sessions provided by the LEA.

You should seek an early opportunity to discuss your CEP with your school's professional tutor and/or your mentor. The purpose of the CEP is to smooth your transition between student teacher and NQT. It is intended that the completed profile should provide the focus for discussions of your strengths and needs, identify any aspects of teaching in which you have had little or no experience and take account of your own personal targets and aspirations. On the basis of these discussions an individual development programme should be agreed which will complement and extend the general induction programme provided for all NQTs. This process will help to ensure your continued professional development and assist you in meeting the expectations of the school.

CONTINUING PROFESSIONAL DEVELOPMENT (CPD)

Much of your time during your NQT year is directly focused on your teaching, taking extra-curricular activities and on carrying out pastoral responsibilities. However, we hope that you will continue to keep up to date, both with your subject knowledge and with general educational issues. You will probably be recommended certain reading within your induction programme and by colleagues. The *Times Educational Supplement* is a useful guide to further reading. It always contains reviews of recent publications. But additionally there are biannual inserts on each subject in the school curriculum.

It is equally helpful to maintain, and if possible develop, your specialist interest(s). It will be to your advantage if you subscribe to the appropriate specialist journals (for example, the National Association for Outdoor Education's quarterly journal entitled *Adventure Education*), keep up to date with the governing body awards and renew existing certification such as the life saving and first aid awards.

We hope that you will make time to read recent and relevant research in PE and teaching. Some suggestions are listed in the Further Reading section at the end of the chapter. This is by no means an exhaustive list, just a few examples of journals which will help you keep up to date with subject knowledge to continue your professional development from the start of your career.

There are several routes you might follow to further your professional development once you have settled into your first teaching post, depending on your interests and strengths. They could be in subject knowledge, academic development, management development, pastoral development, and as subject mentor.

Subject knowledge

You might be interested in taking your subject knowledge development further by undertaking higher coaching awards in your specialist sport/activity. This could lead you onto working at county, regional and national levels in this sport.

You may wish to expand your range of subject knowledge through undertaking introductory local courses provided by the LEA or the sport governing bodies in your area.

You might become involved with PE curriculum development projects, or develop a particular strength in the teaching and examining of PE at GCSE, GNVQ or GCE A level. These could allow you to become a marker or moderator for examination boards.

You could also write for publication, including journal articles, coaching manuals and books.

Academic development

Your interests may be in the extension of your academic qualifications. Today many teachers study for higher degrees. You can obtain a Master's qualification by research or by following a taught course. Opportunities to do this full time on a seconded basis are now very rare indeed; however, there is a wide range of opportunities for advanced study through part-time or distance learning.

Management development

A common career development for PE teachers is one which utilises their skills of management and organisation. You may wish to become head of a PE department. To do this you would normally be expected to have gained at least three years of experience and have a proven record of good teaching, organisation and interpersonal skills. These are just a few examples of expectations head teachers have when looking for a head of PE. It is expected that you will have undertaken additional award and non-award bearing courses covering a range of aspects including subject development and middle management skills. These courses could be provided by your LEA or school. There are also many management courses advertised in the educational press.

Pastoral development

You may wish to extend the time you spend on this aspect of the curriculum by undertaking the teaching of pastoral programmes in the school, attending conferences and courses for teachers interested in pastoral issues. These experiences could lead you to become assistant year/house tutor and then head of year/house.

Subject mentor

There is also the option in many schools for mentoring student teachers. After gaining some teaching experience you may be able to become a subject mentor and, with further experience as a mentor, look at the broader role of mentorship with a view to becoming a professional tutor.

No matter which route you may wish to follow it is your responsibility to remain up to date in your area(s) of interest. You can do this through attending local, regional and national conferences. These conferences also allow you to develop useful contacts and networks in your area of interest.

We have mentioned just a few career development possibilities. You may find that you wish to follow a combination of options, but there is always a need to 'take stock' of your career and make judgements based on your experience and interests.

JOINING AN ASSOCIATION

It is crucial that you are aware of the importance of joining a professional association. This may be any one of the teachers' unions. As a PE teacher you have particular need and responsibility to ensure that you have adequate insurance cover and ready access to professional advice. You will be aware of recent highly publicised incidents where tragedy has befallen pupils involved in PE or physical activities. In these instances LEAs, schools and individual teachers have, on occasion, been taken to court. See Chapter 8 for information about legal aspects of your teaching. The Physical Education Association of the United Kingdom (PEAUK) is an association for PE teachers in the United Kingdom and also provides personal insurance for PE teachers should you wish to take out their additional premium which provides extra cover against personal liability for PE teachers. Their address is in the addresses at the end of the book.

SUMMARY

Figure 18.2 shows how the different elements of your development as a teacher interrelate throughout your career. We hope that you now appreciate the need to take every opportunity to develop both your subject knowledge and your professional competence if you are to gain a teaching post and go on to become a successful teacher. At some later stage in your career you may wish to give a greater emphasis to either developing your subject expertise or to taking on responsibilities in school that are not specifically related to PE. However, as long as you work within the education profession it is unlikely that you will entirely lose contact with your own subject specialism or the professional skills you have gained through working with pupils.

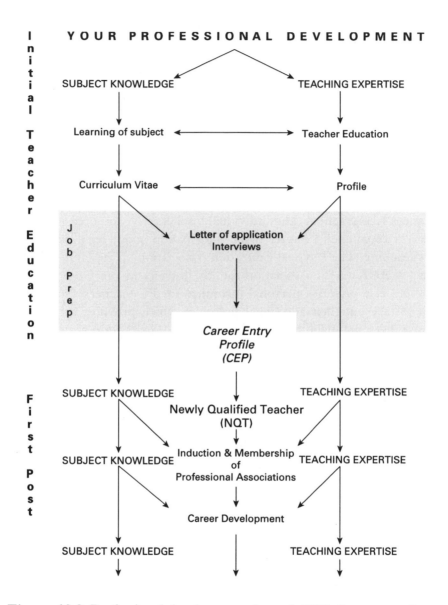

Figure 18.2 Professional development through ITE, first post and beyond

FURTHER READING

Hoyle, E. and Johns, P. (1995) *Professional Knowledge and Professional Practice*, London: Cassell.
A concise text which provides an opportunity to reflect upon the issues surrounding professional knowledge and practice.

Useful publications

Times Educational Supplement: First appointment supplements.

Journals

British Journal of Physical Education, British Journal of Sociology, Bulletin of Physical Education, Cambridge Journal of Education, Education Review, European Physical Education Review, International Journal of Physical Education, Journal of Education for Teaching, Journal of Physical Education, Recreation and Dance, Journal of Teaching in Physical Education, Pastoral Care in Education, Sport, Education and Society.

Activity specific journals, such as Journal of Adventure Education and Outdoor Leadership.

Appendix 1

GATHERING INFORMATION: EXAMPLES OF QUESTIONS AND OBSERVATION SCHEDULES

(P. Breckon and De Montfort University Bedford)

1 Gathering information about the school and the PE department.
2 Gathering information about the PE facilities and resources.
3 Use of voice.
4 Questioning.
5 Teacher positioning.
6 Self-presentation.
7 Motivation.
8 Academic Learning Time–Physical Education (ALT–PE) (Siedentop, Tousignant and Parker, 1982).

These examples have been selected to show observation schedules for a number of different teaching skills and also a range of methods of recording observations. For example:

- ticking boxes;
- selecting from alternatives (for example, yes/no; good/adequate/poor);
- counting the number of times an activity or behaviour occurs;
- recording the length of time spent on a task;
- providing brief descriptions of a situation, activity or behaviour;
- visual recording (for example, of teacher movement or positioning).

You can use these examples of observation schedules to help devise your own for a specific purpose.

GATHERING INFORMATION ABOUT THE SCHOOL AND THE PE DEPARTMENT

Some questions that you need to ask on your preliminary visit to a school on each school experience to gather information about the work of the PE department. Work through the check-list of questions and tick each item to confirm that it has been attended to. As you work through these questions some school and/or department documents are identified. Obtain a copy of these documents to help you to answer the questions, but make sure you make a note of any documents you have borrowed. Add any comments you feel appropriate.

Question	Tick/Comment
Who are the members of staff in the PE department and what are their duties and responsibilities?	
What expectations are there regarding staff dress and conduct?	
What is the safety policy of the department? Where are the first aid kits? What procedure is adopted in the event of an accident?	
What do pupils learn and when? What are the schemes and units of work?	
What examinations take place in PE? What examination syllabuses are used at GCSE, GCE A level, GNVQ? Any other?	
What extra-curricular activities take place? Which ones will you be asked to help with?	
Is there a 'special events' programme for the year (for example, dates of swimming galas, sports day, activities week)?	
How does the department communicate with parents and in what circumstances?	
What liaison is there with the local community (for example, links with local clubs, help from parents or coaches)?	

GATHERING INFORMATION ABOUT THE PE FACILITIES AND RESOURCES

Below are some questions that you need to ask on your preliminary visit to a school on each school experience to help you to gather more specific information about the facilities and resources of the department. Much of the information should be documented but some comes from discussion with teachers as well as observation of rules and routines in operation in lessons.

Question	Description/Tick/Comment
What facilities does the PE department have at its disposal, both on-site and off-site (number of pitches/courts, indoor spaces)?	
What is available in terms of line markings, wall markings, grid markings, other field markings?	
What fixed equipment is available (for example, basketball rings and backboards, fixed gym apparatus)?	
What equipment does the department possess, and in particular what is available for the lessons you are helping with (for example, number of balls, markers, cones, mats, benches, bibs, rackets, shuttles)?	
Are there any safety restrictions on the use of these facilities and equipment (for example, slippery floor, holes on court)?	
How does the department normally adapt facilities for a large group (for example, teaching volleyball in a small gym)?	
What arrangements are used in the case of bad weather?	
What teaching resources does the department have (for example, videotapes, curriculum guidelines, textbooks for examined courses, dance music, posters, rule books)?	

USE OF VOICE

Name of Teacher/   **Date:** ....
Student Teacher Observed: ....

Name of Observer: ....

1. Note ONE occasion when the teacher uses each of the following tactics. Describe the context briefly.

(a) spoke LOUDER than usual	
(b) spoke SOFTER than usual	
(c) spoke HIGHER than usual	
(d) spoke LOWER than usual	
(e) spoke FASTER than usual	
(f) spoke SLOWER than usual	

(g) used emotional content of voice
     (i) to encourage
     (ii) to control	

2. Answer these questions at the END of the teaching episode (tick one box).

   (a)   Was the teacher's voice: always audible
                                 sometimes inaudible
                                    often inaudible

   If some teacher's speech was inaudible, suggests reasons for this below.

   (b)   Was the teacher's voice: always interesting
                                  sometimes boring
                                     often boring

   If some teacher's speech sounded boring, suggest reasons for this below.

3. Note any word used habitually (you can record the number of times each word is used)

QUESTIONING

Name of Teacher/   **Date:** ....
Student Teacher Observed: ....

Name of Observer: ....

Note as many questions as you can. Try to reproduce exactly what is said.

	Question	Who answers?				Comment here if question is extensive or unexpected
		Teacher	No Answer	Pupils	Many pupils	
1						
2						
3						
4						
5						
6						
7						
8						
9						
10						
11						
12						

At end of observation fill in:

Number of **open** questions .... Number of **recall** questions ....

Number of **pupil** questions .... Number of questions **requiring thinking** ....

Number of **question sequences** (guided discovery) ....

TEACHER POSITIONING

Name of Teacher/   **Date:** ....
Student Teacher Observed: ....

Name of Observer: ....

Teacher positioning:
Giving instructions: able to see all
Monitoring work: circumference patrol
Helping individuals: keep eye on all, never turn your back on whole class

Brief description of teacher moves and comments	Good	Adequate	Needs Attention
1			
2			
3			
4			

Teacher **positioning** – when giving instructions to **whole** class/group

(Put an X each time instruction given)	Comments:

Teacher **movement and positioning** as **monitors** work and **helps individuals**

(Draw a pathway)	Comments:

SELF-PRESENTATION

Name of Teacher/   **Date:** ....
Student Teacher Observed: ....

Name of Observer: ....

✓ each time you notice these

1   Teacher CONFIDENCE

      poised, calm   _____
      positive approach   _____
      smart   _____
      brisk transitions   _____

2   Teacher INVOLVEMENT

      own demonstration   _____
      assisting individuals   _____
      assisting groups   _____
      developing material   _____

3   Teacher INTERACTION

      using names   _____
      giving feedback   _____
      using pupil demonstration   _____

4   Teacher ENTHUSIASM

   (a) non–verbal
      smiling   _____
      other facial expressions   _____
      positive gestures   _____
      lively, brisk movement   _____

   (b) verbal
      expressive voice   _____
      praise   _____
      encouragement   _____

On the other side of this sheet, give:
5   Other evidence of an enthusiastic teacher.
6   Other comments at the end of the teaching episode (e.g. which
    areas need improvement)

MOTIVATION

Name of Teacher/   **Date:** ....
Student Teacher Observed: ....

Name of Observer: ....

Concentrate on ONE pupil throughout the teacher episode and complete the record for that one pupil only. The teacher should not know which pupil you have chosen.

Record of Praise and Criticism: Name of Pupil ....

	Instances of:		Given to:			Comments (e.g. for good work or effort or improvement or behaviour or other reason)
	PRAISE	**CRITICISM**	**Indi-vidual**	**Group**	**Class**	
1						
2						
3						
4						
5						
6						
7						
8						
9						
10						

Task appropriateness for this SAME pupil

	Task	Too Easy	Reasonable Challenge	Too Difficult	Comments
1					
2					
3					
4					
5					
6					
7					

Other Comments:

ACADEMIC LEARNING TIME–PHYSICAL EDUCATION (ALT–PE)
(Siedentop, Tousignant and Parker, 1982)

Purpose

This instrument is often used to judge teaching effectiveness in PE. Specifically, its purpose is to describe the amount of time pupils are engaged in motor activity at an appropriate level of difficulty. This is based on the assumption that the longer pupils are engaged in motor activity at an appropriate level of difficulty, the more they learn.

Definitions of categories

Four categories of activity are identified:

Motor appropriate (MA). The pupil is engaged in a motor activity related to the subject matter in such a way as to produce a high degree of success.

Motor inappropriate (MI). The pupil is engaged in a motor activity related to the subject matter, but the task or activity is either too difficult or too easy for the pupil's capabilities, therefore practising it does not contribute to the achievement of lesson objectives.

Motor supporting (MS). The pupil is engaged in a motor activity related to the subject matter with the purpose of helping others to learn or perform the activity (for example, holding equipment, sending balls to others or spotting the trampoline).

Not motor engaged (NM). The pupil is not involved in a motor activity related to the subject matter.

Recording Procedures

There are four different methods of observation available to collect ALT–PE data about the categories above. These methods use:

- **Interval recording**. This involves alternating observing and recording at short intervals. One pupil or an alternating sample of pupils is used. The observer watches one pupil during the **observing interval**. During the **recording interval**, the observer records the observation as **MA, MI, MS** or **NM**. Data can be presented as a percentage of each category. This is the most common observation method used.

- **Group time sampling**. This involves the observer scanning the group for 15 seconds every 2 minutes, and counting the number of pupils engaged at an appropriate level of motor activity (**MA**). Data can be presented as an average for the class.
- **Duration recording**. This involves the observer using a time line to categorise into one of the four categories (**MA, MI, MS** or **NM**), what one pupil is doing the entire period. Alternatively, the observer can measure **MA** time only. A stopwatch is started when the pupil is appropriately engaged and stopped when the engagement stops. Total **MA** time for the lesson can be presented as a percentage of total lesson time.
- **Event recording**. This involves the observer counting the number of **MA** practice trials at an appropriate level of difficulty (the practice must include discrete trials). Trials are measured (and data presented) per minute or over longer units of time.

Example of ALT–PE using the interval recording method

To use this method of recording the coding format is divided into **intervals**. In each interval box there are **two levels**: a top level and a lower level.

The **top** level of the interval box is used to describe the **context of the interval (C)**. There are ten choices of context from three categories: general content, subject matter knowledge and subject matter motor (see below). This decision is made on the basis of what the class as a whole is doing, for example, are they involved in warm-up, a lecture on strategy, or skill practice?

The **lower** level of the interval box is used to describe the **involvement of one pupil (LI)**. Choices are from the categories described as not motor engaged and motor engaged (see below).

The **letter code** for the appropriate category is placed in the appropriate part of the interval box.

Typically, it is suggested that **three pupils** of differing skill levels are observed, **alternating observation** of them at every interval.

This system provides a total picture of what the class does throughout the lesson and a finely graded picture of the involvement of several pupils.

Those interval boxes marked as motor appropriate (**MA**) are **ALT–PE** intervals. Total ALT–PE is the total for the pupil during the lesson.

P_____   C [grid 1–24]
         LI

P_____   C [grid 1–24]
         LI

P_____   C [grid 1–24]
         LI

P_____   C [grid 1–24]
         LI

P_____   C [grid 1–24]
         LI

P_____   C [grid 1–24]
         LI

P = Pupil
C = Context of the interval
LI = Level of involvement of pupil

Context level (C)

General content	Subject matter knowledge	Subject matter motor
Transition (T)	Technique (TN)	Skill practice (P)
Management (M)	Strategy (ST)	Scrimmage/routine (S)
Break (B)	Rules (R)	Game (G)
Warm-up (WU)	Social behaviour (SB)	Fitness (F)
	Background (BK)	

Learner involvement level (LI)

Not motor engaged	Motor engaged
Interim (I)	Motor appropriate (MA)
Waiting (W)	Motor inappropriate (MI)
Off-task (OF)	Supporting (MS)
On-task (ON)	
Cognitive (C)	

Appendix 2

SAMPLE APPARATUS PLANS FOR GYMNASTICS
(K. Morgan, De Montfort University Bedford)

APPARATUS KEY

Long mat (7) -

Roll mat (15) -

Bench (3) -

Ropes -

Small mat (17) -

Low beam (5) -

Spring board (13) -

High table (10) -

Bars/beams -

Safety mattress/ -
Crash mat (25)

Pommel horse -

Box -

Blue bar box (1) -

Trampette (3, 2)

SAMPLE APPARATUS PLAN: LOCOMOTION

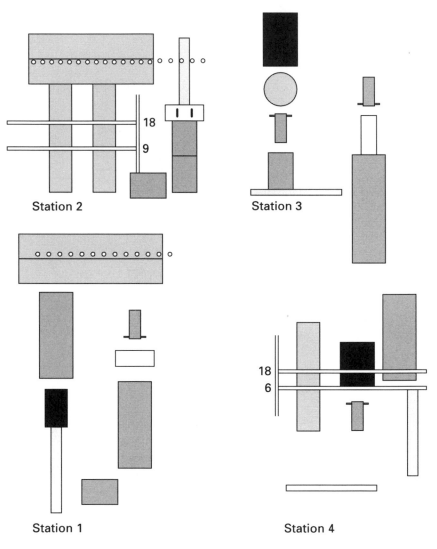

Station 2

Station 3

Station 1

Station 4

SAMPLE APPARATUS PLAN: BALANCE

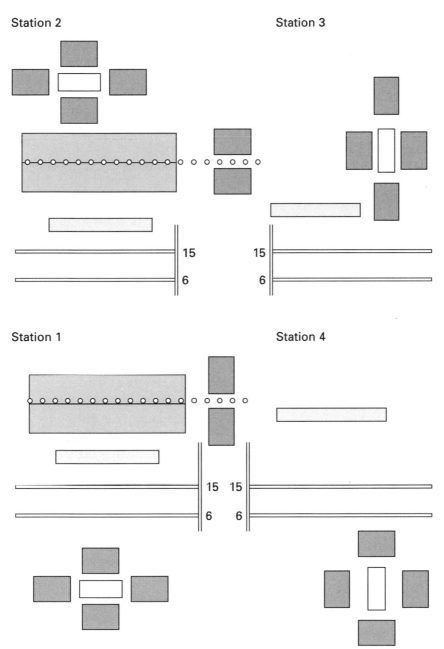

Glossary

This glossary includes terms and abbreviations used in this book and applicable to PE. Capel, Leask and Turner (1995) include a glossary of general education terms. You may also want to refer to that glossary.

All terms used below with * are taken from OFSTED (1993) *Handbook for the Inspection of Schools, Part 6: The Statutory Basis for Education*, London: HMSO, August, 1993; those with ** are taken from Department for Education (1994) *Code of Practice on the Identification and Assessment of Special Educational Needs*, London: DFE; those with *** are taken from *The Education Year Book* (1995) London: Longman; and those with **** are taken from Dearing, R. (1994) *The National Curriculum and its Assessment: Final Report*, London: SCAA.

AAA	Amateur Athletic Association.
AEB	Associated Examining Board.
Areas of Activity	The grouping of activities within the National Curriculum for PE to provide breadth in PE. There are six areas of activity: athletic activities, dance, games, gymnastic activities, outdoor and adventurous activities and swimming. The activities to be taught at each key stage (q.v.) vary. Refer to DFE (1995) for details.
Attainment Target	The knowledge, skills and understanding to be acquired within the Programme of Study (q.v.) for each subject, i.e. the sum total of all the end of Key Stage Statements. In PE there is one Attainment Target which includes the processes of planning,

	performing and evaluating physical activities and aspects of health-related exercise.
BAALPE	British Association of Advisers and Lecturers in Physical Education.
BCU	British Canoe Union.
BGA	British Gymnastics Association.
BTEC	Business and Technician Education Council.
C & G	City and Guilds.
CAL	Computer Assisted Learning.
CCPR	Central Council for Physical Recreation.
CEP	Career Entry Profile.
Closure days *	Days on which the school is closed to pupils so that staff can participate in in-service training (INSET), usually school-based.
Core Subjects (of the National Curriculum) Coursework	The Foundation subjects (q.v.) of English, Mathematics, Science, and, in Wales, Welsh. Work carried out by pupils during a course of study marked by teachers and contributing to the final examination mark. Usually externally moderated.
Curriculum ***	A course of study followed by a pupil.
Curriculum guidelines *	Written school guidance for organising and teaching a particular subject or area of the curriculum.
Dearing Report	A review of the 'National Curriculum and its Assessment' 1994. This recommended a review of subject orders and a five-year moratorium on further change.
Department *	Section of the curriculum/ administrative structure of a (secondary) school, usually based on a subject.
DFEE	Department for Education and Employment (formerly DES (Department of Education and Science) and DFE (Department for Education)).

DFEE Circular ***	Advice issued by the Department for Education and Employment to LEAs (q.v.). They do not have the status of law.
Differentiation *	The matching of work to the differing capabilities of individuals or groups of pupils in order to extend their learning.
e-mail	Electronic mail services (e-mail) are usually provided for subscribers of the internet (q.v.) through the electronic linking (networking) of computers.
End of Key Stage Descriptions (EKSD)	The types and range of performance the majority of pupils should characteristically demonstrate by the end of the key stage (q.v.), having been taught the relevant Programme of Study (q.v.).
End of Key Stage Statements (EKSS) ****	These summarise what a pupil should know, understand and be able to do by the end of the key stage (q.v.) for Art, Music and Physical Education.
ERA	Education Reform Act (1988).
Faculty *	Grouping of subjects for administrative and curricular purposes.
Foundation Subjects ****	Ten subjects in England (eleven in Wales) which state-maintained schools are required by law to teach. The foundation subjects of English, Mathematics, Science, and, in Wales, Welsh – are designated as core subjects (q.v.). The other foundation subjects are Art, Geography, History, Modern Foreign Language (from age 11), Music, Physical Education, Technology and, in Wales, Welsh second language. After the age of 14, some options are available: pupils may drop Art and Music; either History or Geography or follow a short course in each; and may opt to follow short courses in a modern foreign language and technology.

Further Education ***	All post-school education outside the university sector. Sometimes the term is restricted to apply only to vocational education.
GCE	General Certificate of Education.
GCSE *	General Certificate of Secondary Education. National external qualification usually taken at age 16 after a two-year course. Introduced in 1988 to replace GCE O-level and Certificate of Secondary Education CSE examinations.
GNVQ	General National Vocational Qualification.
HEI	Higher Education Institution.
Higher Education ***	Education which is received in a university, or college of higher education and which usually leads to the award of a degree or diploma.
HMCI	Her Majesty's Chief Inspector (of schools).
HMI	Her Majesty's Inspectors (of schools).
Information Superhighway	This is a term that encompasses all forms of information technologies including computer mediated communication and telecommunication based technologies (e.g. Internet, CD-Is and CD-ROMs, interactive TV, videoconferencing, electronic mail) which can be transmitted over the Internet (the superhighway).
Information Technologies	A term which includes both computer-based systems (see Information Technology) and telecommunications-based systems such as satellite and cable communication systems and telephone, radio and TV broadcasting systems. There is now a wide range of electronically-based information and communication systems, e.g. the database and electronic mail facilities

available through the Internet, interactive TV, videoconferencing and associated developments, CD-Is and CD-ROMs (which are similar to music CDs but they carry pictures as well as sound).

Information Technology (IT) **

Covers a range of microcomputers, both portable and desktop; generic or integrated software packages, such as word processors, spreadsheets, databases and communication programs; input devices such as keyboards, overlay keyboards, specialised access switches and touch screen, output devices such as monitors, printers and plotters; storage devices such as CD-ROM, and microelectronics controlled devices such as a floor turtle.

INSET

In-service education and training.

Internet

(The superhighway). The Internet is formed through the electronic linking (networking) of various computers around the world so that the material held on their hard disks can be accessed freely or for a charge from any linked point. The linked computers (known as servers) are usually owned by private companies or large public organisations (schools, universities). Electronic mail services (e-mail) are usually provided for subscribers. No one owns the Internet as a whole and no one is in overall control of the information available on the Internet.

JANET

Joint Academic Network.

Key Stages (KS)

The periods in each pupil's education to which the elements of the National Curriculum (q.v.) apply. There are four key stages (KS), related to the age of the majority of the pupils in a teaching group. They are: KS1, pupils aged 5 to age 7 (year groups reception, 1 and 2); KS2, pupils aged 7 to 11 (year groups 3 to 6); KS3, pupils aged 11 to 14 (year groups 7 to 9); KS4, pupils aged 14 to 16 (year groups 10 and 11).

Lesson Plan
The detailed planning of work to be undertaken in a lesson. This follows a particular structure, appropriate to the demands of a particular lesson. An individual lesson plan is usually part of a series of lessons within a unit of work (q.v.).

Local Education Authorities (LEAs)
Each Local Education Authority (LEA) has a statutory duty to provide education in its area.

Local Management of Schools (LMS) *
The arrangements by which LEAs (q.v.) delegate to individual schools responsibility for financial and other aspects of management.

MEG
Midlands Examining Group.

Moderator ***
An examiner who monitors marking and examining to ensure that standards are consistent in a number of colleges and schools.

Multimedia
This is defined by the National Council for Educational Technology (1995) as 'the mixing of words, pictures, motion video, sound, animation and photographic images on a computer'. Multimedia packages are commonly available on CD-Is and CD-ROMs. Videodiscs are an older version of this technology. Sites on the Internet may provide multimedia packages that can be downloaded, i.e. taken from the Internet to your own computer. In some schools, pupils produce their own multimedia compositions, including sound and motion pictures as well as texts and still pictures.

National Curriculum (NC)	The core and foundation subjects (q.v.) and their associated Attainment Targets (q.v.), Programmes of Study (q.v.) and assessment arrangements. Note Religious Studies is not part of the National Curriculum but all schools are required by law to teach it. Sex Education is a statutory requirement at key stages (q.v.) 3 and 4.
NCC	National Curriculum Council. This merged with SEAC (q.v.) in 1993 to form SCAA (q.v.).
NCVQ	National Council for Vocational Qualifications.
NEAB	Northern Examining and Assessment Board.
Network	Computers linked by cable and able to exchange information.
Networking	The electronic linking of various computers around the world so that the material held on their hard disks can be accessed freely or for a charge from any linked point.
NSG	Non-statutory guidance (for National Curriculum (q.v.)). Additional subject guidance for the National Curriculum but which is not mandatory. NSG is found attached to National Curriculum subject orders.
NVQ	National Vocational Qualifications.
OFSTED	Office for Standards in Education. Non-Ministerial government department established under the Education (schools) Act (1992) to take responsibility for the inspection of schools in England. Her Majesty's Inspectors (HMI) (q.v.) form the professional arm of OFSTED. See also OHMCI.
OHMCI	Office of Her Majesty's Chief Inspector (Wales). Non-Ministerial government

	department established under the Education (schools) Act (1992) to take responsibility for the inspection of schools in Wales. Her Majesty's Inspectors (HMI) form the professional arm of OHMCI. See also OFSTED.
PoS	Programmes of Study (of National Curriculum) (q.v.).
Pre-vocational Courses *	Courses specifically designed and taught to help pupils to prepare for the world of work.
Programme of Study (PoS) *	The subject matter, skills and processes which must be taught to pupils during each key stage (q.v.) of the National Curriculum (q.v.).
QTS *	Qualified teacher status. A formal period of probation for new teachers is no longer required in England and Wales.
RSA	Royal Society of Arts.
SCAA	School Curriculum and Assessment Authority. This body is responsible to the Secretary of State for all curriculum and assessment matters in state schools in England. Formed in 1993 from a merger of NCC (q.v.) and SEAC (q.v.).
Scheme of Work	This represents long-term planning as it describes what is planned for pupils over a period of time (for example a key stage (q.v.) or a year). It is derived from the Programme of Study (q.v.) and End of Key Stage Statements (q.v.) and should contain the knowledge, skills and processes required for each area of activity (q.v.).
SEAC	School Examinations and Assessment Council. This merged with NCC (q.v.) in 1993 to form SCAA (q.v.).
SEG	Southern Examining Group.
SEN *	Special Educational Needs. Referring to pupils who for a variety of

intellectual, physical, social, sensory, psychological or emotional reasons experience learning difficulties which are significantly greater than those experienced by the majority of pupils of the same age.

Standard Assessment Tasks (SATS) * — Externally prescribed National Curriculum assessments which incorporate a variety of assessment methods depending on the subject and key stage. This term is not now widely used, having been replaced by 'standard national tests'.

Statement of Attainment ****** — These seek to define what a pupil should know, understand and be able to do at each level.

Super JANET — Super Joint Academic Network.

Surfing — Surfing the Internet, i.e., interrogating the databases available on line.

TTA — Teacher Training Agency. Established in 1994 to take over the work of the Council for the Accreditation of Teacher Education (CATE). The TTA is responsible for teacher education and educational research in England.

UCLES — University of Cambridge Local Examinations Syndicate.

ULEAC — University of London Examinations and Assessment Council.

Unit of Work — This represents medium-term planning as it describes what is planned for pupils over half a term or a number of weeks. The number of lessons in a unit of work may vary according to each school's organisation. A unit of work usually introduces a new aspect of learning. Units of work derive from the scheme of work (q.v.). The number of units in each area of activity (q.v.) varies from school to school.

WJEC — Welsh Joint Examination Committee.

Useful addresses

British Association of Advisers and Lecturers in Physical Education (BAALPE)
c/o Geoff Edmondson
Nelson House
6 The Beacon
Exmouth
Devon EX8 2AG

The Central Council of Physical Recreation
Francis House
Francis Street
London SW1P 1DE
Tel. (0171) 828 3163

European Education Consultants
Gate House Lodge
Station Road
Chapeltown
Bolton BL7 0HA
Tel./Fax (01204) 853554

The National Coaching Foundation
114 Cardigan Road
Headingley
Leeds LS6 3BJ
Tel. (01532) 744802

The Physical Education Association of the United Kingdom (PEAUK)
Suite 5
10 Churchill Square
Kings Hill
West Malling
Kent ME19 4DU
Tel. (01732) 875888

Sports Fair UK
Phyl Edwards,
Sports Fair Manager
Liverpool John Moores University
IM Marsh Centre for PE, Sport & Dance
Barkhill Road
Liverpool L17 6BD
Tel. (0151) 231 5319

The Youth Sport Trust
Rutland Building
University of Loughborough
Leicester LE11 3TU
Tel. (01509) 228293

United Kingdom Sports Council
Walkden House
3-10 Melton Street
London NW1 2EB
Tel. (0171) 383 5543

The English Sports Council
16 Upper Woburn Place
London WC1H OQP
Tel. (0171) 273 1500

Sports Council for Northern Ireland
House of Sport
Upper Malone Road
Belfast BT9 5LA
Tel. (01232) 381222

Scottish Sports Council
Caledonia House
South Gyle
Edinburgh
Lothian EH12 9DQ
Tel. (0131) 317 7200

Sports Council for Wales
Sophia Gardens
Cardiff CF1 9SW
Tel. (01222) 397571

There are nine regional Sports Councils in England

Bibliography

Ackerman, P.L., Sternberg, R.J. and Glaser, R. (eds.) (1989) *Learning and Individual Differences: Advances in Theory and Research*, New York: W.H. Freeman and Company.

Adams, N. (1983) *Law and the Teacher Today*, London: Hutchinson.

Ahlberg, A. (1983) *Please Mrs Butler*, Kestrel Books, Harmondsworth: Penguin Books Ltd.

All England Netball Association (AENA) (1991) *Official Netball Rules*, Hitchin, Herts: AENA.

Almond, L. (1991) 'Summary of the Response to the National Curriculum Physical Education Working Group Interim Report', The Health Education Authority in conjunction with the Physical Education Association of Great Britain and Northern Ireland, *Health and Physical Education Project, Newsletter Number 27*, March, pp. 2–5.

Argyle, M. (1988) *Bodily Communication* (2nd edn), London: Methuen.

Barrell, G.R. and Partington, J.A. (1985) *Teachers and the Law*, Cambridge: Cambridge University Press.

Bell, J. (1993) *Doing your Research Project: A Guide for First-Time Researchers in Education and Social Science*, Milton Keynes: Open University Press.

Bennett, N. (1976) *Teaching Styles and Pupil Progress*, London: Open Books.

British Association of Advisers and Lecturers in Physical Education (BAALPE) (1989) *Physical Education for Children with Special Educational Needs in Mainstream Education*, Leeds: White Line Publishing Services.

British Association of Advisers and Lecturers in Physical Education Areas 3 and 4 (BAALPE) (1992) 'The Development of Effective Partnerships between Schools and Outside Agencies', *The Bulletin of Physical Education*, 28, 1, Spring, pp. 29–31.

British Association of Advisers and Lecturers in Physical Education (BAALPE) (1995) *Safe Practice in Physical Education*, West Midlands: Dudley LEA.

British Council of Physical Education (BCPE) (1990) 'The National Curriculum in Physical Education', BCPE unpublished paper.

British Council of Physical Education (BCPE)/Sports Council (1994) *Why Physical Education?*, London: Sports Council.

British Vocational Qualifications (1995) *A Directory of Vocational Qualifications Available from all Awarding Bodies in Britain*, London: Kogan Page.

Bruner, J.S. (1960) *The Process of Education*, New York: Vantage.

Campbell, S. (1995) 'Coordination of Effective Partnerships for the Benefit of School Aged Pupils', *British Journal of Physical Education* 26, 2, pp. 10–12.

Capel, S., Leask, M. and Turner, T. (1995) *Learning to Teach in the Secondary School: A Companion to School Experience*, London: Routledge.

Capel, S., Leask, M. and Turner, T. (1997) *Starting to Teach in the Secondary School: A Companion for the Newly Qualified Teacher*, London: Routledge.

Carroll, B. (1994) *Assessment in Physical Education: A Teacher's Guide to the Issues*, London: The Falmer Press.

Cheffers, J., Amidon, E. and Rogers, K. (1974) *Interaction Analysis: An Application to Nonverbal Activity*, Minnesota: Association for Productive Teaching.

Cohen, L. and Manion, L. (1989) *A Guide to Teaching Practice* (3rd edn), London: Routledge.

Cooper, P. and McIntyre, D. (1996) *Effective Teaching and Learning: Teachers' and Students' Perspectives*, Buckingham: Open University Press.

Crouch, H. (1984) *Netball Coaching Manual*, Kingston upon Thames: Croner Publications.

Cruickshank, D.R., Bainer, D.L. and Metcalf, K. (1995) *The Act of Teaching*, New York: McGraw-Hill.

Darst, P., Zakrajsek, D. and Mancini, V. (eds) (1989) *Analyzing Physical Education and Sport Instruction*, Champaign, Ill.: Human Kinetics.

Dearing, R. (1994) *The National Curriculum and its Assessment. Final Report* (The Dearing Report), London: SCAA Publications.

Dearing, R. (1996) *Review of Qualifications for 16–19 Year Olds: Summary Report*, London: SCAA Publications.

Department for Education (DFE) (1994) *Code of Practice on the Identification and Assessment of Special Educational Needs*, London: DFE.

Department for Education (DFE) (1995) *Physical Education in the National Curriculum*, London: HMSO.

Department for Education and the Welsh Office (DFE/WO) (1992) *Circulars 9/92 and 35/92: Initial Teacher Training (Secondary Phase)*, London: HMSO.

Department for Education and Employment (DFEE) (1995) *Our School – Your School*, London: DFEE.

Department for Education and Employment (DFEE) (1996) *Sports Colleges – A Guide for Schools*, London: DFEE.

Department of Education and Science (DES) (1985) *The Curriculum from 5 to 16: Curriculum Matters 2. An HMI Series*, London: HMSO.

Department of Education and Science and the Welsh Office (DES/WO) (1989) *Discipline in Schools. Report of the Committee of Enquiry Chaired by Lord Elton (The Elton Report)*, London: HMSO.

Department of Education and Science and the Welsh Office (DES/WO) (1990) *Physical Education National Curriculum Working Group: Interim Report*, London: HMSO.

Department of Education and Science and the Welsh Office (DES/WO) (1991a) *National Curriculum for Ages 5–16*, London: HMSO.

Department of Education and Science and the Welsh Office (DES/WO) (1991b) *Physical Education for ages 5 to 16. Final Report of the National Curriculum Physical Education Working Group*, London: HMSO.

Department of Education and Science and the Welsh Office (DES/WO) (1992) *Physical Education in the National Curriculum*, London: HMSO.

Department of Education Northern Ireland (1996) *Arrangements for Initial Teacher Education in Northern Ireland from 1 September 1996*, Bangor: Department of Education Northern Ireland.

Department of National Heritage (DNH) (1995) *Sport: Raising the Game*, London: DNH.

Department of National Heritage (DNH) (1996) *Setting the Scene*, London: DNH.

Department of the Environment (1989) *Building on Ability: Sport for People with Disabilities (Report of the Minister for Sport Review Group 1988–1989)*, London: HMSO.

Eassom, S. (1996) 'Legal Liability Case Studies', in *So . . ., you think you're a safe PE teacher?* Bedford: De Montfort University.

Education Reform Act (ERA) (1988) *Education Reform Act, 29 July 1988; Sections 1, 2, Aims of the School Curriculum*, London: HMSO.

Edwards, P. (1996) 'Getting Active – Sports Fair', *Magazine of Youth Clubs UK*, Summer, pp. 20–1.

Elliott, J. and Adelman, C. (1975) *The Language and Logic of Informal Teaching*, Cambridge: Cambridge Institute of Education.

English Sports Council (1996) *National Junior Sport Programme*, London: Sports Council.

Entwhistle, N. (1988) *Styles of Learning and Teaching: An Integrated Outline of Educational Psychology for Students, Teachers and Lecturers*, London: David Fulton Publishers.

European Education Consultants (1997) *Whole School Management of Health and Safety: Risk Assessment Database*, Bolton: European Education Consultants.

Evans, J. (ed.) (1993) *Equality, Education and Physical Education*, London: The Falmer Press.

Evans, J. and Williams, T. (1989) 'Moving Up and Getting Out: The Classed and Gendered Career Opportunities of Physical Education Teachers', in T.J. Templin and P.G. Schempp (eds) *Socialization into Physical Education: Learning to Teach*, Indianapolis, Ind.: Benchmark Press, pp. 235–48.

Fitts, P. and Posner, M. (1967) *Human Performance*, Belmont, Calif.: Brooks/ Cole.

Flanders, N. (1960) *Interaction Analysis in the Classroom: A Manual for Observers*, Minneapolis, Minn.: University of Minnesota Press.

Francis, J. and Merrick, I. (1994) 'The Future for Advanced Level GCE Physical Education and Sport Studies', *British Journal of Physical Education* 25, 3, pp. 13–16.

Gallahue, D.L. (1982) *Understanding Motor Development in Children*, New York: John Wiley and Sons.

Galton, M., Simon, B. and Croll, P. (1980) *Inside the Primary Classroom*, London: Routledge and Kegan Paul.

Gipps, C.V. (1995) *Beyond Testing: Towards a Theory of Educational Assessment*, London: The Falmer Press.

Godefroy, H. and Barrat, S. (1993) *Confident Speaking*, London: Judy Piatkus.

Guillaume, A.M. and Rudney, G.C. (1993) 'Student Teachers' Growth Toward Independence: An Analysis of Their Changing Concerns', *Teaching and Teacher Education* 9,1, pp. 65–80.

Haskins, D. (1997) 'From School to Community: The Next Step with Top Play and BT Top Sport', *Primary Focus, The British Journal of Physical Education* 28, 1, Spring, pp. 11–14.

Health and Safety at Work Regulations (1992) Kingston upon Thames: Croner Publications.

Hellison, D.R. and Templin, T.J. (1991) *A Reflective Approach to Teaching Physical Education*, Champaign, Ill.: Human Kinetics.

Higham, J., Sharp, P. and Yeomans, D. (1996) *The Emerging 16–19 Curriculum*, London: David Fulton Publishers.

Hodgson, B. (1996) 'Which Exam?', *British Journal of Physical Education* 27, 2, pp. 23–6.

Home Office (1975) *Sex Discrimination Act*, London: HMSO.

Home Office (1976) *The Race Relations Act 1976*, London: HMSO.

Home Office (1986) *The Public Order Act 1986*, London: HMSO.

Hopkins, D. (1993) *A Teacher's Guide to Classroom Research* (2nd edn), Buckingham: Open University Press.

Hoyle, E. and Johns, P. (1995) *Professional Knowledge and Professional Practice*, London: Cassell Education.

Hunt, J. and Hitchin, P. (1988) *The Residential Course Planner*, Kendal: Groundwork Group Development.

Kelso, J.A.S. (1982) *Human Motor Behavior: An Introduction*, Hillsdale, N. J.: Lawrence Erlbaum Associates.

Kyriacou, C. (1991) *Essential Teaching Skills*, Oxford: Basil Blackwell.

Laventure, B. (1992) 'School to Community: Progress and Partnership', in N. Armstrong (ed.) *New Directions in Physical Education, Volume 2: Towards a National Curriculum*, Champaign, Ill.: Human Kinetics, pp. 169–97.

Lawrence, D. (1988) *Enhancing Self-esteem in the Classroom*, London: Paul Chapman.

Lloyd, J. and Fox, K. (1992) 'Achievement Goals and Motivation to Exercise in Adolescent Girls: A Preliminary Intervention Study', *British Journal of Physical Education Research Supplement* 11: pp. 12–16.

McConachie-Smith, J. (1996) 'PE at Key Stage 4', in N. Armstrong (ed.) *New Directions in Physical Education: Changes and Innovation*, London: Cassell Education, pp. 82–93.

McNiff, J. (1993) *Teaching as Learning: An Action Research Approach*, London: Routledge.

Marland, M. (1993) *The Craft of the Classroom*, London: Heinemann Educational.

Mawer, M. (1995) *The Effective Teaching of Physical Education*, London: Longman.

Mawer, M.A. and Brown, G.A. (1983) 'Analysing Teaching in Physical Education', in M.A. Mawer (ed.) *Trends in Physical Education*, Aspects of Education, Journal of the Institute of Education, University of Hull, pp. 71–95.

Maynard, T. and Furlong, G.J. (1993) 'Learning to Teach and Models of Mentoring', in D. McIntyre, H. Hagger and M. Wilkin (eds) *Mentoring: Perspectives on School-Based Teacher Education*, London: Kogan Page, pp. 69–85.

Metzler, M.W. (1989) 'A Review of Research on Time in Sport Pedagogy', *Journal of Teaching in Physical Education* 8, 2, pp. 87–103.

Metzler, M.W. (1990) *Instructional Supervision for Physical Education*, Champaign, Ill.: Human Kinetics.

Morrison, A. and McIntyre, D. (1973) *Teachers and Teaching* (2nd edn), Harmondsworth: Penguin.

Mosston, M. and Ashworth, S. (1986) *Teaching Physical Education* (3rd edn), Columbus, O.: Merrill Publishing.

Murdoch, E.B. (1987) *The Desk Study: Sport in Schools*, London: Sports Council.

Murdoch, E.B. (1990) 'Physical Education and Sport: The Interface', in N. Armstrong (ed.) *New Directions in Physical Education, Volume 1*, Champaign, Ill.: Human Kinetics, pp. 63–79.

National Coaching Foundation (NCF) (1993) *Champion Coaching: The Power of Partnership*, Leeds: White Line Publishing Services.

National Coaching Foundation (NCF) (1994) *Planning and Practice Study: Pack 6*, Leeds: NCF.

National Council for Educational Technology (NCET) (1993) *Defining Differentiation in Differentiating the School Curriculum*, Wiltshire: Wiltshire Local Education Authority.

National Council for Educational Technology (NCET) (1995) *Highways for Learning*, Coventry: NCET.

National Curriculum Council (NCC) (1990a) *Curriculum Guidance 3: The Whole Curriculum*, York: NCC.

National Curriculum Council (NCC) (1990b) *Curriculum Guidance 4: Education for Economic and Industrial Understanding*, York: NCC.

National Curriculum Council (NCC) (1990c) *Curriculum Guidance 5: Health Education*, York: NCC.

National Curriculum Council (NCC) (1990d) *Curriculum Guidance 6: Careers Education and Guidance*, York: NCC.

National Curriculum Council (NCC) (1990e) *Curriculum Guidance 7: Environmental Education*, York: NCC.

National Curriculum Council (NCC) (1990f) *Curriculum Guidance 8: Education for Citizenship*, York: NCC.

National Curriculum Council (NCC) (1992) *Physical Education Non-Statutory Guidance*, York: NCC.

Nisbet, J. and Shucksmith, J. (1986) *Learning Strategies*, London: Routledge.

Nixon, J., Martin, J., McKeown, P. and Ranson, S. (1996) *Encouraging Learning: Towards a Theory of the Learning School*, Buckingham: Open University Press.

North West Sports Council (1993) *Going for Gold: A Regional Strategy Study on Performance and Excellence in the North West*, Manchester: North West Sports Council.

Oeser, O.A. (1965) *Teacher, Pupil and Task*, London: Harper and Row.

Office of HM Chief Inspector of Schools (1995) *Physical Education and Sport in Schools: A Survey of Good Practice*, London: HMSO.

Open University (1991), eds H.G. Mackintosh, D. Nuttall and P. Clift, p. 234: *Curriculum in Action: An Approach to Evaluation. Block 6: Measuring Learning Outcomes*, Milton Keynes: Open University Press.

Pachler, N. and Watson, G. (1997) 'Student References and Interview Practices for CPS Posts (Secondary)', Unpublished conference paper.

Parry, J. (1988) 'Physical Education: justification and the National Curriculum', *Physical Education Review* 11, 2: pp. 106–18.

Perrott, E. (1982) *Effective Teaching: A Practical Guide to Improving Your Teaching*, London: Longman.

Piaget, J. (1962) *Judgement and Reasoning in the Child*, London: Routledge and Kegan Paul.

Randall, L.E. (1992) *The Students Teacher's Handbook for PE*, Champaign, Ill.: Human Kinetics.

Rink, J.E. (1985) *Teaching Physical Education for Learning*, St. Louis, Mo.: Times Mirror/Mosby College Publishing.

Schmidt, R.A. (1991) *Motor Control and Learning: A Behavioral Emphasis* (2nd edn), Champaign, Ill.: Human Kinetics.

School Curriculum and Assessment Authority (SCAA) (1996) *Consistency in Teacher Assessment: Exemplification of Standards in Key Stage 3*, London: SCAA Publications.

School Curriculum and Assessment Authority (SCAA) (1997) *Physical Edu-*

cation at Key Stages 3 and 4. Assessment Recording and Reporting: Guidance for Teachers, London: SCAA Publications.

School Curriculum and Assessment Authority/The Curriculum and Assessment Authority for Wales (SCAA/ACAC) (1995) *GCSE Regulations and Criteria*, London: SCAA/ACAC Publications.

School Sport Forum (1988) *Sport and Young People: Partnership in Action*, London: Sports Council.

Scottish Office Education Department (1993) *Teacher Competences: Guidelines for Teacher Training Courses*, Edinburgh: Scottish Office Education Department.

Shenton, P. A. (1994) 'Education and Training through Partnership: A Possible Way Forward', *British Journal of Physical Education* 25, 4, pp. 17–20.

Shenton, P. (1996) 'Physical Education and Sport in Partnership! Is the Youth Sport Trust Realising a National Vision Through a Local Recipe of Good Practice?', *British Journal of Physical Education* 27, 2, pp. 17–19.

Shenton, P.A. (1997) 'Resource document for PE teachers', unpublished manuscript, Liverpool: John Moores University.

Siedentop, D. (1991) *Developing Teaching Skills in Physical Education* (3rd edn), Mountain View, Calif.: Mayfield Publishing Co.

Siedentop, D., Tousignant, M. and Parker, M. (1982) *Academic Learning Time–Physical Education Coaching Manual*, Columbus, O.: School of Health, Physical Education and Recreation.

Singer, R.N. (1982) *The Learning of Motor Skills*, New York: Macmillan Publishing Company.

Smart, J. and Wilton, G. (1995) *Educational Visits*, Leamington Spa: Campion Communications Ltd.

Smith, C.J. and Laslett, R. (1993) *Effective Classroom Management: A Teacher's Guide*, London: Routledge.

Sports Council (1988b) *Sport and Young People: Partnership in Action*, London: Sports Council.

Sports Council (1991) *Conference Report: Active Lifestyles: From School to Community – Theory into Practice*, Coventry: Sports Council.

Sports Council (1993) *Young People and Sport: Policy and Frameworks for Action*, London: Sports Council.

Stock, B. (1993) *Health and Safety in Schools*, Kingston upon Thames: Croner Publications Ltd.

The Education Year Book (1995) London: Longman.

Thorpe, R., Bunker, D. and Almond, L. (eds) (1986) *Rethinking Games Teaching*, Loughborough, Leics.: University of Loughborough, Department of Physical Education and Sports Science.

Underwood, G.L. (1988) *Teaching and Learning in Physical Education: A Social Psychological Perspective*, London: The Falmer Press.

Underwood, J. and Underwood, G. (1990) *Computers and Learning: Helping Children Acquire Thinking Skills*, Oxford: Basil Blackwell.

Vygotsky, L.S. (1962) *Thought and Language*, Cambridge, Mass.: MIT Press.

Wheldall, K. and Merrett, F. (1989) *Positive Teaching in the Secondary School*, London: Paul Chapman Publishing.

White, M. (1992) *Self Esteem: Its Meaning and Value in School*, Cambridge: Daniels Publishing.

Whitehead, M.E. (1990) 'Teacher/Pupil Interaction in Physical Education – The Key to Success', *The Bulletin of Physical Education* 26, 2, pp. 27–30.

Wickstrom, R.L. (1977) *Fundamental Motor Patterns*, Philadelphia: Lea and Febiger.

Williams, A. (1987) *Curriculum Gymnastics*, London: Hodder and Stoughton.

Williams, A. (1993) 'Aspects of Teaching and Learning in Gymnastics', *British Journal of Physical Education* 24, 1, pp. 29–32.

Wragg, E.C. (ed.) (1984) *Classroom Teaching Skills*, London: Croom Helm.

Wragg, E.C. (1994) *An Introduction to Classroom Observation*, London: Routledge.

Young, R. (1992) *Critical Theory and Classroom Talk*, Clevedon: Multilingual Matters Ltd.

Youth Sport Trust (1996a) *Annual Report 1995/96*, Loughborough: Youth Sport Trust.

Youth Sport Trust (1996b) *Curriculum Training Pack. Top Play and Top Sport*, Loughborough: Youth Sport Trust/Sports Council.

Author index

Subject index